Storey's ✳ Gardening Skills
ILLUSTRATED

Paul White
Windswept Hill Rd
P.O. Box 909
Campton, NH 03223-0909

P9-ELR-210

Pruning Made Easy

A Gardener's Visual Guide to When and How to Prune Everything, from Flowers to Trees

LEWIS HILL

STOREY
BOOKS

*The mission of Storey Publishing is to serve our customers
by publishing practical information that encourages personal independence
in harmony with the environment.*

Edited by Terri Dunn and Gwen W. Steege
Cover and text design by Mark Tomasi
Cover photograph courtesy of Collins & Brown
Cover photograph by Geoff Dann
Production assistance by Susan Bernier and Eileen Clawson
Illustrated by Elayne Sears, except page 11 by Judy Eliason
Indexed by Susan Olason, Indexes and Knowledge Maps

Copyright © 1997 by Lewis Hill

All rights reserved. No part of this book may be reproduced without written permission from the publisher, except by a reviewer who may quote brief passages or reproduce illustrations in a review with appropriate credits; nor may any part of this book be reproduced, stored in a retrieval system, or transmitted in any form or by any means — electronic, mechanical, photocopying, recording, or other — without written permission from the publisher.

The information in this book is true and complete to the best of our knowledge. All recommendations are made without guarantee on the part of the author or Storey Publishing. The author and publisher disclaim any liability in connection with the use of this information. For additional information please contact Storey Books, 210 MASS MoCA Way, North Adams, MA 01247.

Storey books are available for special premium and promotional uses and for customized editions. For further information, please call the Custom Publishing Department at 1-800-793-9396.

Printed in Canada by Transcontinental Printing
10 9 8

Library of Congress Cataloging-in-Publication Data

Hill, Lewis, 1924–
    Pruning made easy / Lewis Hill.
        p.   cm. — (Storey's gardening skills illustrated)
    Includes index.
    ISBN 1-58017-007-2 (alk. paper). — ISBN 1-58017-006-4 (pbk. : alk. paper)
    1. Pruning.   I. Title.   II. Series.
SB125.H475   1998
635.9'542—dc21   97-32223
                                                           CIP

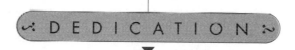

DEDICATION

*To Gwen Steege, my outstanding editor and
friend at Storey for many years, with great appreciation
for her skill, understanding, and help. Sincere thanks also
to editors Nancy Ringer and Teri Dunn,
and to artist Elayne Sears, for transforming words
into artistic and helpful images.*

Contents

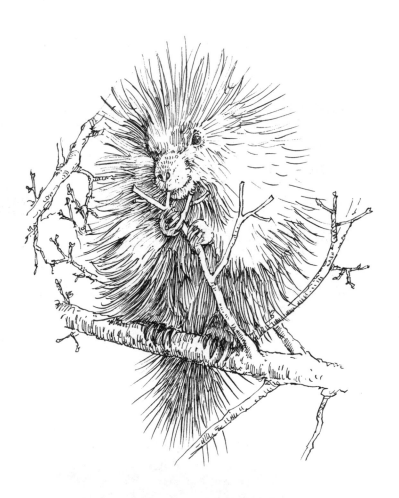

Reasons to Prune

One fall day when I was working in the woods, I heard a noise high above me. A porcupine was sitting in the crotch of a large elm tree, skillfully cutting off large limbs and dropping them to the ground for easier nibbling. And in our back field last winter I came upon a flock of pine grosbeaks carefully nipping the buds off the Scotch pine trees.

Rabbits, mice, deer, elk, moose, and beavers also prune — just not in a way that you and I would consider a horticultural achievement. They're simply eating out at their favorite restaurants, but in doing so they fit into the forest's scheme of life quite well.

Nature's Pruning

Long before man ever thought of smithing his spear into a pruning hook, Nature was at work pruning, and she still is. High winds, snow, and ice storms help to keep trees healthy by snapping off old and weak branches. Occasionally an old tree loses an entire limb or top, then grows an abundance of new branches, thus getting a new lease on life. In forests, spreading tops and crowding shade the lower limbs of tall trees, causing them to die and fall off. Blights, hurricanes, floods, and fires set by lightning frequently thin out old trees and allow new ones to take their place.

Nature has even set up a system whereby fruit trees prune themselves by thinning their crops. We've all seen the hundreds of little apples or peaches that fall from trees in early summer if the fruit set is unusually heavy. A tree drops extras when it lacks the resources to develop them to full maturity.

From the beginning of recorded time, our early ancestors observed Nature's pruning methods and tried to improve on them. They developed the art so successfully that long before the great cities of Babylon,

In This Chapter

- Pruning with a Purpose
- Pruning When Planting or Transplanting
- Pruning to Train
- Pruning to Control Size
- Pruning for Appearance
- Pruning for Health
- Pruning for Production
- Pruning for Rejuvenation
- Pruning to Create a Barrier

Jerusalem, or Athens had a stone in place, pruning was an accepted practice. It is mentioned frequently in the Bible and other ancient literature. As a matter of fact, pruning was so well developed back then that it has changed amazingly little since. Although no one is likely to use a pruning hook now, we still prune for the same reasons and in much the same way.

Why Should We Intervene?

In spite of the long history of pruning, however, some people still question the wisdom of it. Should we interfere with the natural scheme of things? How can we improve on Nature? A walk in the woods shows that trees grow to magnificent beauty all by themselves.

The answer to these questions, I feel, is that we don't live in the wilderness anymore. We aren't able to spend all our days foraging for food. Instead we're more likely to live on tiny lots where our trees and shrubs must provide beauty, protection, food, and companionship, yet still not crowd us off our claim. We can no longer abandon our berry patch or orchard when it gets overgrown and cross the ridge to look for another homesteading plot. We can't move on just because the spruces we planted as a windbreak have begun to shut out the sun and view.

In other words, Nature is too leisurely and wasteful for our modern way of life. Although its function is to provide a healthy balance of plant and animal life, the reality is that humans upset the balance long ago. These days we can't let our trees grow to full size, die, and rot peacefully for decades on the ground. We must, instead, give our plantings careful attention so that we can get the best possible use from them. We have to fertilize, prune, and protect them, and sometimes, when they have outlived their usefulness, remove them before they become a hazard. When we do these jobs we are not interfering but rather working closely with Nature.

I've met many gardeners who don't feel completely comfortable about pruning and never take off quite enough wood, because they are nervous about hurting the plant. They know that plants look nicer and that fruit trees bear much better when they have been pruned, but they fear that each cut may be painful to the tree and that the whole idea is a bit sinful. The thought of keeping a tree sheared to a runty 4 feet when it might otherwise grow to 80 feet makes them feel guilty and uneasy. The fact is that pruning, when properly done, strengthens rather than weakens the tree.

Do I Really Have to Prune?

A little knowledge can be a dangerous thing. One day a friend invited me into his backyard to point out a badly mutilated viburnum. "I read somewhere that all shrubs should be pruned occasionally, but I really didn't know how," he said apologetically. Probably his plant would survive and look fine after a few more growing seasons, but his cuts could have killed a less sturdy plant.

Don't prune just for the sake of pruning. Pick up the clippers only to correct a faulty growing condition, to prevent a future problem, or to stimulate or redirect new growth. My friend's bush likely didn't need pruning at all, since viburnums grow quite well on their own. If you're growing raspberries, however, pruning is absolutely mandatory or the patch deteriorates and eventually disappears. Understand the growing habits of each of your plants, and decide exactly what you want them to do for you.

Pruning by the Rules

As in all skills, certain rules must be followed, however, or pruning can be harmful. Some diseases can be spread by pruning tools, for instance. Pruning certain trees in late winter can result in a harmfully large sap loss. Cuts should be made so that the plant will grow attractively. Large cuts must be done skillfully, so there is no danger that the limb might accidentally split when it is only half cut off and tear back into the tree. In short, your shearing and cutting should be done for the right reason, in the right way, and at the proper time.

Pruning with a Purpose

Some plants can be pruned in a variety of ways, depending on your needs. If you are raising a crab apple primarily for jellies and juice, for instance, prune as carefully as you would any other fruit tree. On the other hand, a crab apple grown for the beauty of its flowers and fruit may need minimal pruning. Many varieties, such as the popular 'Dolgo', grow into beautiful specimens with almost no training. Crab apples can also be pruned into dense hedges that are almost impenetrable to animals and people by shearing them tightly several times during the summer, when they are growing, just as you would an evergreen hedge. They can even be grown as miniature trees in tubs or as espaliers against walls or fences.

The Best for Your Plants

You can prune with a clear conscience, because it is one of the best things you can do for your plants. Liberty Hyde Bailey, the famous horticulturist, said it best many years ago: "Of all the operations connected with horticulture, pruning, shaping, and training bring the person into closest contact and sympathy with his plant."

To Create a Holiday Shrub

Suppose you want to grow a little blue spruce near the front steps of your one-story house and plan to put lights on it at Christmas. Shear it close every summer to keep it in a neat, tight, 6-foot size almost forever.

To Create a Barrier

To grow a dense barrier of blue spruce between you and your noisy neighbors, prune the trees quite differently, lopping off the tops and allowing the side branches to grow thick.

To Assure a Plentiful Harvest

You'll get a better harvest if you prune your crab apple annually. While it's still dormant (in late winter or early spring), thin the branches to let in sunlight.

To Create a Beautiful Shape

Prune sparingly, removing only damaged or weak wood and branches that are crossing or rubbing others. Many varieties become beautiful specimens with very little intervention from you.

To Create a Hedge or Screen

Shear tightly several times during the summer, when the plants are growing lustily and will rebound quickly from such treatment.

To Train an Espalier

This special technique is not as difficult as you may think, but it does require diligence. For best results, start while the crab apple is still quite young.

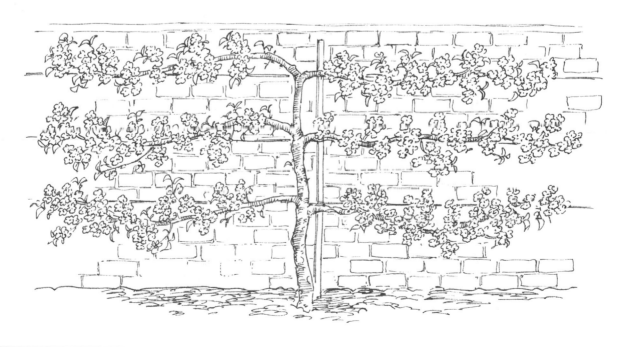

Pruning When Planting or Transplanting

When you purchase a dormant bare-root tree or bush — or dig and move one yourself — there is a chance that the roots will be damaged. In general, the small, "feeder" hair roots are completely lost, and there are not enough large roots left to support all the branches. As a plant leafs out, therefore, the diminished root system may be unable to meet the increasingly heavy demands of the top for nourishment.

The traditional method of remedying this undesirable situation is to cut back the top directly after planting. This helps delay early new growth until the plant has developed enough of a root system to support it. With plenty of water and perhaps a little protection from dehydrating breezes, the youngster should survive and develop roots enough to support the growth that will start after a few weeks. (*Note:* This type of pruning does not apply to potted or balled-and-burlapped trees. Those root systems tend to be in better shape.)

....
HINT FOR SUCCESS
....

Sometimes a nursery will have done the trimming for you. This is especially true of mail-order plants. If in doubt, ask. You don't want to chop back the plant twice!

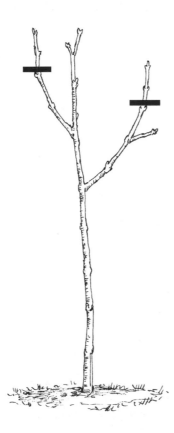

Pruning a young maple tree at planting time. Cut back the slender side branches by about a third, to just above a bud. Leave the central leader.

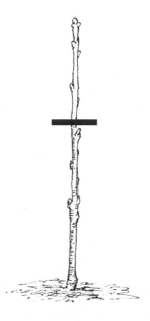

Pruning a one-year-old, unbranched fruit tree (called a whip) at planting time. Cut back by about one-third, to just above a bud.

Pruning to Train

In their maturity, most plants reap the benefits of some early training — just as do animals and humans — so don't neglect them in their formative years. Getting your newly planted tree off to a good start is one of the most important reasons for pruning. It's better to snip off undesirable branches when they are small than to saw them off later. You'll do a good job of training if you keep in mind the future use of the tree.

- **A white pine** that is to be kept dwarfed and bushy should have its sides and top sheared each year starting in its infancy. If instead you prefer that the pine grow into a large shade tree, gradually snip off the lower limbs as the tree matures, thereby forcing its growth upward.

- **Fruit trees** should be pruned sparingly for their first few years, so that their bearing won't be delayed. However, you should still prune a young tree to correct any bad crotches, to rectify any tendency the tree might have to grow lopsided, and to keep it from growing branches too close to the ground.

- **Most low-growing flowering shrubs** can and should be pruned when they are quite small. Snip back any skinny, tall-growing limbs; this encourages bushiness.

- **Encourage young shade trees** to grow tall and straight by correcting crotches and gradually removing lower limbs.

MASTER GARDENING TIPS

An Alternative to Pruning

If you hesitate to prune off the recommended third of an expensive bare-root tree, even though you know it is beneficial, there is another way to ensure that top growth doesn't outdistance new root growth. In fact, this method often leads to better growth. The drawback is that it demands your daily attention.

1. For the first month, water generously every day that it doesn't rain hard.

2. For the first month, fertilize once a week. Use a liquid fertilizer such as a manure-water mixture, fish emulsion, or a liquid chemical plant food like Miracle Gro — in the amounts recommended on the label.

3. Allow the plant to leaf out normally, but prevent any new growth from starting by pinching back all fresh sprouts as soon as they appear.

4. Keep pinching for about a month after the first leaves develop. At the end of the month you can stop and let new branches grow.

5. During dry periods, water about twice a week and reduce liquid feeding to once every two weeks until the first of August.

6. Except in frost-free regions, cease fertilizing in late summer so the plant's new growth can harden before the first frost.

Pruning to Control Size

If you're a gardener who works with a limited amount of land, you'd probably prefer to grow as many small plants as possible on your lot, rather than only one or two large specimens. By pruning, you can enjoy a wider variety than would be possible if you let the plants develop as they would in their natural state. Even large trees can be kept small by severe pruning. A standard-size apple tree that might naturally reach 35 feet high and 30 feet in spread can be kept to a fraction of that size. And with very little trouble, hemlock or arborvitae trees that might otherwise grow to 80 feet tall can be sheared into a hedge 2 feet tall by 1 foot wide.

Pruning is sometimes necessary for large trees and bushes that have begun to crowd power lines, driveways, sidewalks, or buildings. By snipping back the offending branches, you can keep the plants useful, yet under control, for many years.

MASTER GARDENING TIPS

Alternatives to Pruning

▶ You can make life easier for yourself by selecting fruits, evergreens, and shrubs that are labeled dwarf; bear in mind, though, that these will still require some control or they'll eventually outgrow their bounds.

▶ Maximize limited space by espaliering small fruit trees against a sunny wall.

▶ Plant fruits or ornamentals in large tubs placed on a patio, terrace, or sunporch, where confined roots and judicious trimming on your part will lead to smaller plants.

A good planting connects the house to the land, provides an attractive setting, and gives the yard a finished look.

Pruning for Appearance

Sometimes we're too close to our plants to see them objectively. One way to view them more clearly is to analyze your property with a fresh eye when you return home from a trip, or to compare old and new photos of your land. Even careful gardeners who take great pride in their homes sometimes let their plantings get away from them. Often the problem can be traced back to a yard's original landscaping. It's unfortunate that many landscapers like their work to look finished the day they put it in. To accomplish this they often use far more plants than necessary, which means that after a few years everything is too crowded. When this occurs, the extra plants should be removed, not just cut back.

Pruning for appearance involves much more than just controlling plant size. It also means keeping evergreens and flowering shrubs well proportioned, removing sucker growth from the bottoms of the trees, and taking off limbs or blooms that detract from a plant's appearance. The entire area should be taken into consideration when you're deciding how to prune. Just as each tree and shrub should be chosen carefully and planted in the right spot, it should also be pruned so that it relates well to the rest of the planting, the house, other buildings, walks, and walls. A well-cared-for landscape provides an attractive background for a house, just as a proper setting enhances a fine jewel. Trees and shrubs should never be so showy that they detract from the house or hide it. And, when possible, plantings should look nice viewed from either inside or outside the house.

MASTER GARDENING TIPS

Pruner's Evaluation

New plants grow so slowly that they usually need little pruning the first few years. Suddenly, though, they begin to grow rapidly, and soon they have become too large. Ask yourself:

▶ Are the proportions right?

▶ Do the shapes attractively complement each other?

▶ Am I being severe enough, or am I too permissive?

Some common landscape mistakes include: (**1**) improper placement of shrubs; (**2**) unpruned spreading evergreens that crowd paths; (**3**) doorway plantings that have grown too large; (**4**) foundation plants that crowd each other; (**5**) foundation plantings that hide windows; (**6**) shade tree in front of and too close to house; and (**7**) flowering shrub that hides rather than frames the house.

Pruning for Health

Sometimes cuts are made as preventative medicine or to eliminate a disease. Even young trees and bushes occasionally have problems that pruning can solve, and aging trees — like aging people — often have numerous ones.

In spite of strict quarantine and inspections, some plants are already infected with diseases or insects when you buy them. Others, if they are newly dug, are in a weakened condition, or have just changed locales, may easily acquire them, because plants that are foreign to an area often do not have a built-in resistance to local troubles. Cultivated plants are usually subject to more diseases and insect infestations than are wild, native specimens.

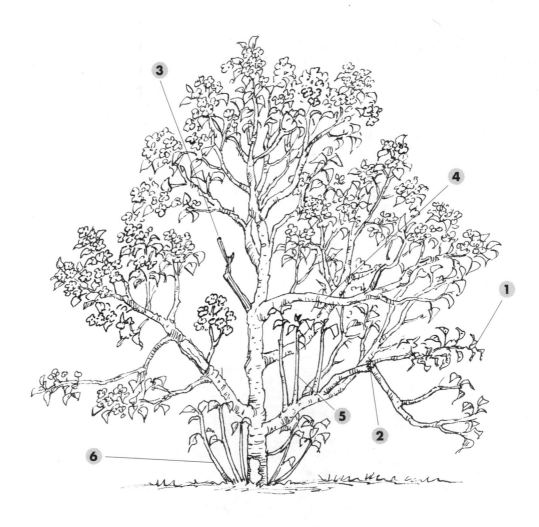

Your plantings will be healthier if you prune out all (**1**) diseased growth; (**2**) branches too close to ground; (**3**) dead branches; (**4**) crossing branches; (**5**) water sprouts; (**6**) suckers.

Pruning for Production

People frequently choose to prune their plants so that they will produce larger or more attractive crops. A florist growing cut flowers for the market prunes differently from someone working in a front-yard perennial border. A fruit grower prunes his apple trees differently from someone growing a decorative apple tree in the backyard for sentimental reasons. A berry grower wants his bushes to look nice, but his main concern is that the plants produce large crops of attractive fruit each year for as many years as possible. A forester prunes all the lower limbs off his timber trees so that the first sawlog will be completely free of knots and make fine lumber.

Commercial growers seldom have time to putter around their plants, and to a home gardener they sometimes seem careless and rather ruthless about their pruning. Actually, they are sensible. They have learned how to prune for the greatest yield from their plants, and the vast amount of pruning they have to do makes them very efficient. Amateur gardeners can learn much from commercial pruning techniques.

Anyone growing boughs for the Christmas market cares for the plants quite differently from a home gardener with a prize bush.

MASTER GARDENING TIPS

Steps to a Healthier Tree

If you can see, or suspect, that a plant is struggling, step in to help.

▶ Getting rid of obvious problems is the first order of business. Clip off stems, twigs, and branches that are mildewed or infested with borers, scale, or other insects.

▶ Burn or bury debris deeply so that the problem won't spread.

▶ Cut off dead, broken branches smoothly to the main trunk or a limb to prevent dead stubs and jagged edges that provide an ideal situation for insect and disease invasion. Dead stubs will rot eventually, and the rot may spread into the rest of the tree.

▶ Clip off all the suckers or little trees that sprout up from either the trunk or the roots. These sap a tree's energy, and if you allow them to grow, they will spoil its appearance, turning it into a large bush. Furthermore, unchecked suckers growing from the wild rootstock of a grafted fruit, shade tree, or rosebush can crowd out the desirable part of the plant and make it useless.

▶ Trees, especially deciduous ones, are also damaged when branches rub against buildings and other branches. Remedy these situations by snipping off the offending limbs as soon as you notice them. If you do nothing, they'll usually suffer bark damage, which invites infection.

▶ Remove water sprouts (the clusters of branches that grow straight upward, often from an old pruning wound) as soon as they form. These weaken a tree and cause unattractive growth that will be hard to deal with later.

▶ Prune for air circulation and sunlight. Many fruit trees are especially susceptible to insects and disease, and should be pruned to prevent these. Trouble is encouraged by too-warm or too-cool temperatures and high humidity; by thinning out superfluous branches, you can admit beneficial moving air and more light into a tree's interior.

Pruning for Rejuvenation

Pruning often restores vitality to a shrub or tree that is beginning to show symptoms of age but is not quite ready to retire. Although you may be tempted to chop back every elderly planting to stimulate new growth, this doesn't always work. Some trees and shrubs seem to enjoy being rejuvenated by severe pruning, and some do not. It is usually a risky procedure on old shade trees. And broadleaf evergreens and conifers are unlikely to benefit greatly from severe dehorning (beheading) measures. Unless a tree is young and vigorous, a drastic slashing may prove fatal.

But there are many kinds of plants that respond well. Many roses, even old ones, do their best only if you cut them back nearly to the ground each spring. And clematis, potentilla, hydrangea, lilac, and honeysuckle all seem to benefit from occasional drastic pruning. A young, forked tree can often be shaped into a strong, straight specimen by cutting off one of the forks and staking the other. In time, the crook in the stem should straighten.

Most berry-producing shrubs, on the other hand, such as cotoneaster and viburnum, need little or no pruning. Older trees and bushes prefer rejuvenation by light and frequent pruning. In general, regular pruning that begins early in a plant's life is not only less of a shock, but also always looks better than a full-scale attack with shears and saw. For instance, orchardists prefer to renew the bearing wood on their fruit trees gradually by removing part of the older branches annually. This is also the best way to prune bush fruits such as blueberries, currants, and gooseberries. The bearing is uninterrupted, regrowth is moderate, and the bush or tree suffers no serious setbacks.

MASTER GARDENING TIP

Different Approaches for Different Climates

In warmer parts of the country and in tropical and semitropical climates, severe pruning is practiced more widely than in cooler areas. Fast regrowth almost always follows a major pruning job, and in the North the soft, new growth often doesn't completely harden before autumn frosts begin. Winter injury results, and the tree, already weakened by abnormal pruning and regrowth, may be permanently weakened or killed outright.

MASTER GARDENING TIPS

Coping with Animal Damage

Animals can be a menace to the health of a tree, and seem to do their greatest damage during winter, when they are foraging for food.

▶ *Mice, voles, and rabbits* chew bark off branches that are near the ground. Snip off low branches. Any limb that has had its bark removed completely around it will not live long, no matter how narrow the girdle. It may leaf out and appear to be healthy for a while, but eventually it will die. Protect the trunks of fruit trees and other tasty plants that are susceptible to rodent nibbling with wire screening

or plastic guards. Make sure the barriers extend to the height of the expected snow cover.

▶ *Porcupines* may damage trees higher up. Trim off upper limbs on large trees that have been damaged by these creatures. If the chewing does not go completely around the limb, paint the wounded areas with a good tree paint such as Treekote.

▶ *Elk, deer, and other large animals* sometimes chew off smaller branches and may even snap off whole limbs. Cut back ragged, chewed ends to the next undamaged limb.

Pruning to Create a Barrier

Tall shrubs and trees are often planted for shade, windbreaks, and sound barriers. If you live in an exposed area, a strategically placed planting of a few trees may help you save on your heating or air-conditioning bills, or provide protection for a swimming pool, picnic spot, play area, or terrace. A tight-growing windbreak can also shield from cold winds plantings of roses, berries, or fruit trees that may not be completely hardy in your area. A hedge allows the soil in a vegetable or flower garden to warm up more quickly in the spring by shielding it from the wind. Evergreen hedges stop snow from drifting onto roads and paths, help to block out annoying traffic noises and fumes, and hide undesirable vistas. And in crowded neighborhoods, a hedge can provide privacy.

Many plants make desirable wind-breaking hedges, especially those that grow densely. Here a buddleia offers some protection to the smaller annuals and perennials at its feet.

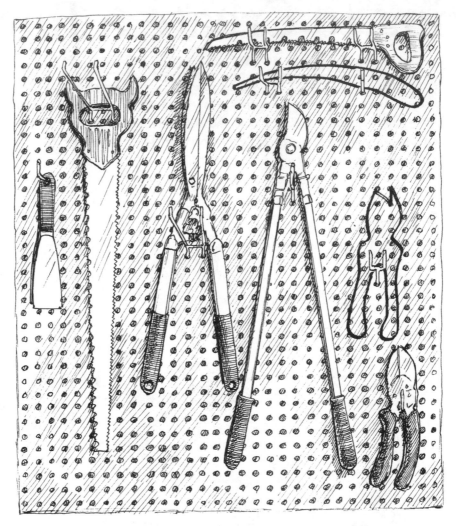

A few basic tools, well organized and conscientiously maintained, will help you stay on top of your pruning chores.

MASTER GARDENING TIPS

Smart Shopping

▶ *Price.* Tool quality varies widely. Hand pruners, for instance, range from cheap ones for less than $10 to deluxe models that cost more than $60. For most home gardening you won't need the heavy-duty, expensive tools that commercial growers prefer, but the very lightweight, cheaply made ones are no bargain.

▶ *Feel.* If possible, look over the different models available and try out how they feel in your hand before buying. Ask yourself: Is it too heavy? too light? too large or too small? Give it a few squeezes and try to decide whether the effort required is comfortable for your hand, wrist, and arm.

▶ *Hand or power tool?* Whether you use power tools is a matter of personal preference. If you have lots of shearing and heavy pruning to do, you will find electric hedge shears and power saws useful. Naturally, those people who love motors and expensive gadgets will buy power equipment; those who prefer the economy and quiet of hand tools will shy away from it.

▶ *Advice.* Ask your gardening friends what they use, for what, and why.

Tools and Equipment

When shopping for pruning tools, you might be a bit overwhelmed by the assortment available. The home gardening boom has caused manufacturers and importers to offer as wide a range as possible. On my desk there's a mail-order catalog that features forestry and horticultural supplies. It lists 24 kinds of hand-pruning shears, 14 long-handled pruners, and 19 hedge shears, as well as dozens of handsaws, pole pruners, power tools, plus a large assortment of tools for sharpening, tree paints, and other supplies. Most hardware stores, garden centers, and department stores sell pruning equipment, though their offerings may be more modest than are those in mail-order catalogs.

You don't need a large variety of tools to do competent pruning. I have seen garden sheds filled with more equipment than most stores contain, but there's really no need to have a different tool for each plant. A few basic tools will handle most home pruning needs.

When you go shopping, you'll notice that there have been some improvements in design and quality. Pruning tools were made in much the same way for many years, but recently manufacturers have succeeded in designing equipment that fits the hand better, causes less effort or wrist strain, is more comfortable to use, and has more or improved safety features.

Good news for left-handers: Many pruning tools are offered "backward" for your grip. You may have to do some hunting to find them, though, or you can order from a catalog.

In This Chapter

- Clippers and Loppers
- Sharpening Pruning Shears
- Saws
- Shearing Equipment
- Tree Paints and Sealers
- Tool Storage

Clippers and Loppers

Hand Clippers

Hand clippers, shears, pruners, or snips, as they are variously called, are the main tool for home use and a real necessity. Choose a quality product. The cheap ones don't hold up well under repeated use, and don't make a smooth cut. There are two kinds of hand pruners: anvil-style and scissors-type pruners. Obviously some people prefer one and some the other, or both kinds wouldn't be manufactured, but I prefer the snap or anvil type for most jobs. It is less likely to need adjusting, and the blade can be easily sharpened or replaced.

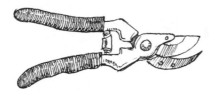

Scissors-type pruners allow a sharp blade to move past an edged blade.

Anvil-style pruners employ a snap-cut method in which a sharp blade hits squarely against an anvil. Most are about 6 inches long and can be used for everything from clipping houseplants to pruning small twigs in an orchard.

Loppers

If you have high shrubbery or fruit trees, you'll also need pruners with long handles. Choose a well-made tool that won't break on the heavier jobs. Some have compound levers for extra-heavy work, and you'll find these especially useful for cutting brush or thinning out excessive growth, such as when taming an overgrown lilac.

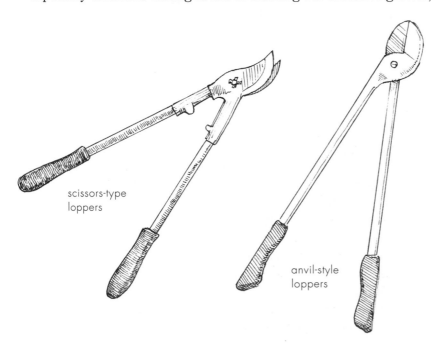

scissors-type loppers

anvil-style loppers

Long-handled loppers provide more leverage than hand clippers.

The hand pruner has been developed into a pole pruner, incorporating a set of extensions that allow you to reach farther up into a tree. The blade is activated by pulling on a rope that, when released, allows the blade to return to its normal position by the action of a strong spring. Pole pruners are handy for a lot of high work, especially in places where the use of a ladder would be difficult or dangerous.

Sharpening Pruning Shears

Sharp tools make clean cuts that heal quickly. Keeping them in good condition is easy and well worth the time and effort.

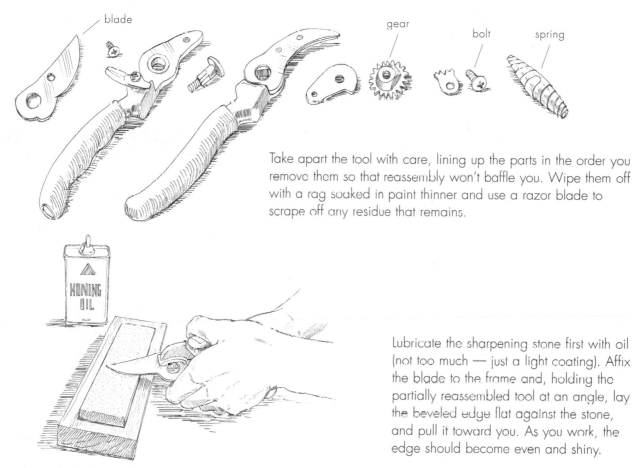

blade   gear   bolt   spring

Take apart the tool with care, lining up the parts in the order you remove them so that reassembly won't baffle you. Wipe them off with a rag soaked in paint thinner and use a razor blade to scrape off any residue that remains.

HONING OIL

Lubricate the sharpening stone first with oil (not too much — just a light coating). Affix the blade to the frame and, holding the partially reassembled tool at an angle, lay the beveled edge flat against the stone, and pull it toward you. As you work, the edge should become even and shiny.

MASTER GARDENING TIPS

Tool Care

▶ If you're removing diseased branches, dip the tool's cutting blades in a bleach solution when you move from one plant to another to prevent spreading problems to healthy tissue.

▶ If you use your tools on evergreens, clean off the pitch deposits regularly. A solvent will do the trick; I use kerosene.

▶ Apply an occasional drop of light motor oil or 3-in-1 oil to the moving parts of pruners, loppers, hedge shears, and electric clippers to keep them operating well.

▶ After pruning, clean sticky sap and bits of bark or wood from the blades.

▶ To keep metal blades rust-free, wipe them with a soft cloth dipped in light oil before you put them away. Do this little chore without fail before you store the tools each winter.

▶ Sharpen your pruner's blades with a grindstone, carborundum stone, whetstone, or steel file. Periodically take apart clippers and hedge shears to clean, sharpen, and oil.

Saws

For all heavy work, use a pruning saw. Heavy-duty, long-handled pruners, even those with compound levers, tend to squeeze the limb being cut, straining the tool and damaging the bark. It is usually best to saw any limb measuring over ¾ inch in diameter. I prefer a lightweight bow saw because it is fast, easy to use, and a handy tool in the woodlot.

Pole saws give you extra reach to let you do heavy cutting while standing securely on terra firma, but I find them slow and rather laborious to use.

Use fine-toothed saws for smooth work and coarse-toothed saws for large limbs. You may want one of each if you do a lot of pruning. Or choose a saw with two edges, one with coarse teeth and the other with fine.

A curved-blade, fine-toothed saw is versatile for gardeners with light to average amounts of pruning.

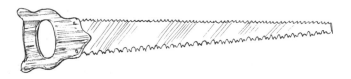

Chain saws are useful for removing and cutting up entire trees and for sawing off large limbs, but most are designed more for cutting wood or lumber than for pruning. They tend to make rough cuts, and the machine is difficult to control for precision work. Even if your chain saw is small, it is extremely easy to slash into the wrong limb, scar the trunk, or do other damage when you're pruning a tree with limbs that are close together.

gas-powered

electric-powered

HINT FOR SUCCESS

Carpenter's saws are not effective on live wood, as they tend to gum up and stick too much.

MASTER GARDENING TIPS

Chainsaw Safety

Remember that chain saws are the most dangerous pruning equipment. I know many expert woodsmen who have had serious accidents while using them.

► Wear plastic safety goggles to protect your eyes from sawdust and bits of debris.

► Avoid making the type of cuts that will pinch the saw or cause it to kick back.

► Keep the saw a safe distance from your body at all times.

► Be particularly careful when you're working on a ladder.

► Never use a chain saw when you're overtired.

► Always keep your chain saw sharpened — a dull saw is dangerous. But unless you have been trained in sharpening these tools, leave the job to an expert. You can usually find a local sharpener by looking in area newspapers or the Yellow Pages. Hardware stores sometimes offer this service.

Shearing Equipment

Shearing, a form of pruning, involves removing soft new growth in order to get the tree to grow into a certain shape. Shearing is done primarily to dwarf trees, to shape hedges, or to develop formal or topiary shrubbery. Because shearing does not involve any cutting of heavy wood, you'll need different equipment from what you use for regular pruning.

Machetes and Knives

Instead of hedge shears or electric clippers, some gardeners prefer to use a light, fast, thin-bladed machete called a shearing knife. It's popular with Christmas-tree growers and foresters because of its light weight and the fact that it is so easy and fast to use. A shearing knife also has the advantage of being low priced, durable, and easy to keep sharpened. Because the blade is long, this is not the best tool to use in close work such as shearing miniature evergreens, but it is very useful on hedges, windbreaks, and overgrown thickets.

A major drawback is that machetes and other knives are dangerous. You must be extremely careful not to slice yourself. Professionals wear heavy gloves and leg guards or very thick pants. For safety's sake, I also keep a pair of hand clippers or a sharpening stone in my left hand as I shear with my right, avoiding the dangerous temptation to hold up a limb in front of the knife. It sounds something like preventing a smashed thumb by holding the hammer in both hands while driving nails, but it works.

MASTER GARDENING TIPS

Shearing-Tool Safety

▶ Make sure that electrical tools have the Underwriters Laboratory Seal of Approval.

▶ Be careful to keep blades away from your arms and legs when the tool is in operation.

▶ Don't let the cord get in the way while you're working. Several times I have accidentally snipped off the cord along with the shrubbery.

▶ To prevent accidentally cutting the electrical cord, I enclose the 2 feet nearest to the clippers in a piece of ½-inch plastic pipe, taping it in place so it won't slip.

▶ Keep your shears well oiled at all times so that they run smoothly and don't overheat.

▶ Consider buying a cordless model. These come with rechargeable batteries that eliminate the nuisance of a long electrical cord.

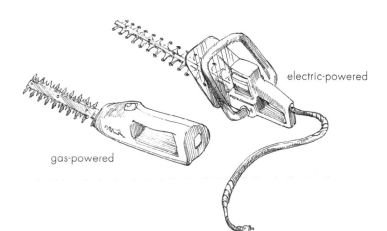

gas-powered

electric-powered

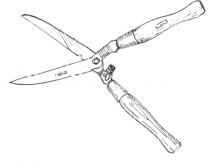

For extensive hedge shearing, electric shears are well worth the price. These shears, or clippers, vary from small, light, inexpensive models to the heavy-duty kind necessary for rugged work. Base your choice on what type of hedge you have. Small, lightweight models are suitable for most deciduous plants; coarse-twigged evergreens need shears that open wide enough to make clean cuts.

Long-handled hedge shears are safe, durable, easy to control, and inexpensive. They are adequate for most shearing jobs, are easily sharpened, and require little muscle power. Some are available with extra-long handles, making them especially good for high work such as reaching to the top of a hedge.

Tree Paints and Sealers

It has long been the custom to paint over pruning cuts or seal them with a tree dressing. Various shellacs, varnishes, and all types of paints, including special tree paints and sealers, are used. (An easy-to-spread tree paint has even been developed for use in the cold winter months.)

Recently, however, these practices have been questioned by some expert horticulturists and foresters, who believe that a tree quickly seals off any wounded areas and starts the healing process itself, and that untreated wounds heal better than those sealed by a paint or dressing. Other experts disagree. They say that sealants keep out weather, insects, and disease, all of which attack wood and delay healing. Most agree that young evergreens readily produce the necessary pitch and resins for satisfactory self-healing, but they remain unconvinced that deciduous trees and all older trees are able to set up enough of a natural defense before deterioration sets in. My own compromise is to paint over all large cuts on older trees. I also seal up open wounds with a tree dressing.

MASTER GARDENING TIPS

Applying Paints and Sealers

▶ Is tree paint any better than ordinary house paint? The question is debatable. Many people feel that paint merely seals up the wood and keeps out the weather, and therefore nearly any outdoor paint will protect the tree. But paints formulated specifically for trees often contain an antiseptic that is supposed to help prevent future infections.

▶ Apply paints with a paint-brush, or use an aerosol spray for small jobs.

▶ Large tree wounds often take many years to heal properly, and since no paint is permanent, you should repaint or reseal every year or two until new growth completely covers the wound.

Tree dressings are thicker than paints, and are good for filling cracks in bark and other small wounds. Some also can be used as a substitute for wax when grafting fruit trees. Apply dressing with a small paddle or putty knife.

Tool Storage

Before winter it is important to store your tools properly so they will be in good shape for the spring. Clean, sharpen, and oil all metal parts. Hang everything possible on nails or pegs on a wall. Never leave tools or equipment outdoors overnight or exposed to rain.

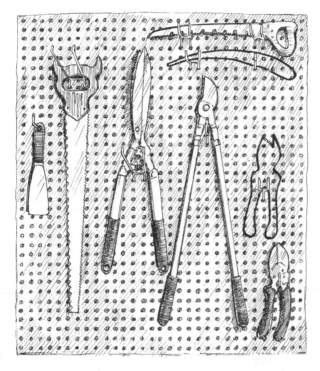

Some gardeners like to hang all their tools on a pegboard or plywood sheet with a drawing or sign to indicate which goes where. This organized system makes it easy to identify missing tools and helps ensure that they won't be left outside overnight or during a rain shower.

MASTER GARDENING TIPS

General Pruning-Tool Safety

Although most pruning is not hazardous, it would be embarrassing to shift from performing surgery on a tree to having some performed on yourself. Keep the following safety pointers in mind.

▶ Wear gloves to prevent blisters and to protect your hands. Gloves are also useful when you need to move heavy or thorny limbs or evergreen brush.

▶ Wear plastic safety goggles to protect your eyes from sharp twigs, snapped-back branches, and flying debris.

▶ When you use a ladder, make sure it is solidly placed at the correct angle against a strong limb or the trunk of a tree. Resist the temptation to climb that extra rung or to reach out too far. And even if

it's handy, a chair is never a safe substitute for a ladder. If you work on a ladder while using electrical equipment, a wooden one is safer than one made of metal.

▶ Wear a hard hat or motorcycle, snowmobile, or bike helmet for added protection when you're using pole pruners and when sawing off limbs over your head.

▶ Avoid using electrical tools during or directly after rain. Wear rubber boots for insulation when the ground is at all wet.

▶ You'd probably never think of using metal pole pruners or aluminum ladders anywhere near overhead power lines, but if we're to judge from the obituary column, some people do.

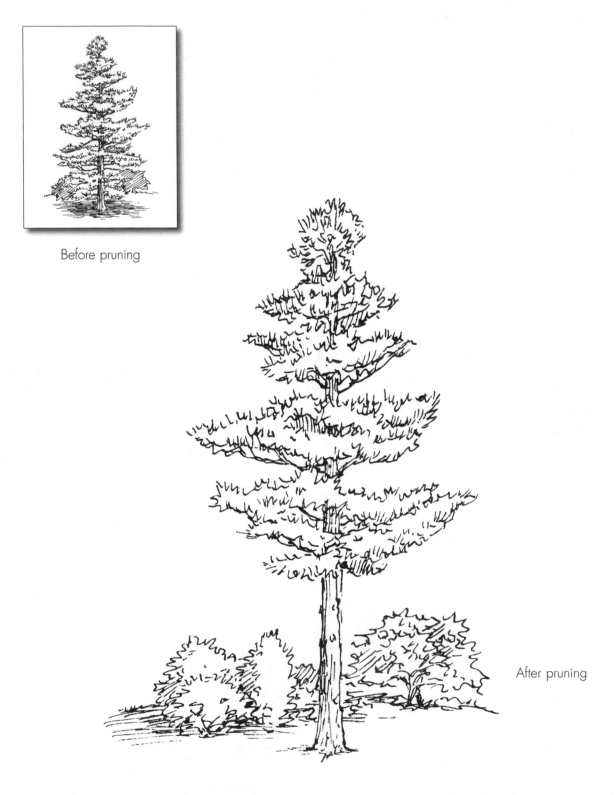

Before pruning

After pruning

Gardeners prune to achieve a variety of goals, from improving the health and productivity of plantings to manipulating an entire view. Pruning the lower limbs from the tree at the upper left is an example of the latter.

Pruning Methods

Just as an artist develops an individual style of painting, each pruner develops a personalized method. However, there are certain basic rules and methods to follow that make the job neater, easier, and more beneficial to the plant.

Before you begin to prune, it helps to understand how woody shrubs and trees grow. Most of them make their spring and summer growth from buds that were set during the previous season. Although I occasionally meet someone who thinks that a tree grows by slowly pushing itself up out of the ground like a snake coming out of a hole, most people know better. You only have to find a tree where lovers carved their initials a half century ago to see that this isn't so! Trees and shrubs grow from the top and from the tips of their side branches. The trunk itself grows larger by the expansion of the cambium layer just under the bark, adding a new layer of wood to the outside of the trunk each year (hence, the rings on a cut log that enable you to determine a tree's age).

In This Chapter

- A Proper Pruning Cut
- Pruning at Different Life Stages
- When to Prune
- Training
- Shearing
- Pinching
- Removing Large Limbs
- Beheading
- Disbudding
- Thinning Fruit
- Basal Pruning
- Root Pruning

2 lateral bud

1 terminal buds

3 dormant bud

Bud vocabulary. Terminal buds (**1**) are found at the top of a plant and ends of its branches. Lateral buds (**2**) form along the limbs. Dormant or internodal buds (**3**) are less obvious, tiny buds along the branches and sometimes under the bark. These are reserve buds, the plant's insurance policy. They will grow only if something happens to the regular buds. Most garden and forest plants and trees have them, some more than others.

A Proper Pruning Cut

New buds may start under the stem of a leaf or form anywhere along a branch. If undisturbed, they grow into new tops, leaves, and branches during the following season. Much of the skill in pruning involves knowing how to make good use of buds in order to redirect growth or rejuvenate the plant. The drawings below show, first, three incorrect ways to prune in relation to a bud, followed by illustrations of the correct pruning method.

MASTER GARDENING TIPS

Places Where Pruning Cuts Can Be Made Safely

▶ Above a promising bud

▶ Above a promising side branch

▶ To a main branch

▶ At the ground

Incorrect Cuts

Too close to the bud. The tender part of the bud will be too near the cut, may not receive enough sap, and will dry out — or it may be damaged by freezing temperatures.

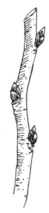

Too far from the bud. The dead stub will rot and look ugly, and the rot can spread easily to the rest of the tree. Likewise, when you're cutting off dead branches, always cut back to a live bud or branch so that no deadwood will be left on the plant.

A flat-topped cut. This cut is not only stubby and unattractive, but it is also slow to dry out after a rain, inviting rot and disease.

Correct Method

A slanting cut, about ¼ inch above a bud. In addition to being the best spot to inspire new growth in the bud below, it leaves less stub and the slant dries out faster after a rain.

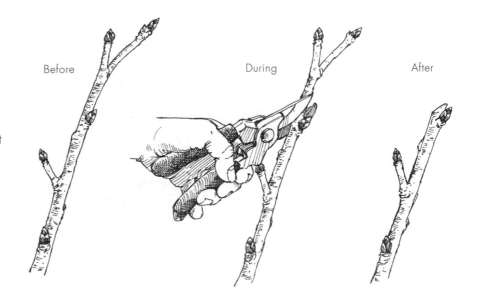

Before   During   After

Pruning at Different Life Stages

Pruning should be done in different ways depending on the age of various plants. We sometimes forget that they, like animals and humans, go through various life stages, from infancy to old age.

- **When a tree or shrub is small,** much of the pruning you need to do is corrective, such as pinching buds and redirecting branches to persuade the plant to grow in a strong, attractive shape.

- **During the prime of its life,** the plant may benefit if you give it some additional help, including more corrective pruning, and pruning for rejuvenation, production, beauty, or usefulness.

- **In a tree's old age,** prune mainly to keep it healthy and prolong its useful life. The life expectancy of the individual tree must be taken into account. No amount of pruning will prolong the life of a Lombardy poplar much beyond its anticipated 20 or 30 years, but a bristlecone pine may live for thousands of years without ever having a branch removed. Find out the approximate life span of each of your plants in order to prune properly.

The vitality of a tree or shrub is a factor as well. Extremely vigorous trees can be pruned more severely than those with tired sap. Vitality not only varies with each species, but it can also vary from year to year, depending on soil and weather, and can change considerably as the plant grows older. You should adjust your pruning to the plant's present state of vitality. Just because a flowering crab throve from a severe cutback when it was 6 years old doesn't mean that it could stand the same treatment at age 40.

Sooner or later, each tree will reach a stage when it is impractical to spend vast amounts of time and money on it, and you must consider replacing it. Often it's difficult to make the decision to recycle an old tree as firewood and mulch, but this process is also a part of good gardening and conservation. Old, derelict trees are not only unsightly, but they are also dangerous and harbor insects and disease.

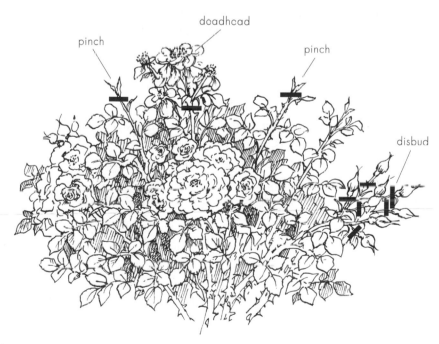

This rosebush will benefit from pinching, deadheading, and disbudding, each a pruning technique with a specific purpose and an optimal time.

When to Prune

If you were to ask the question "When should I prune?" at a gathering of gardeners, whether professional nurserymen or weekend green thumb gardeners, you'd be assured a stimulating conversation. Each person has a definite idea on the subject. Some even maintain that the best time to prune is whenever you feel like it.

The best time, in my opinion, depends on several variables, including the condition of the plant, the length of its growing season, when it blooms, and whether its buds form on new growth or only on older wood. On the following pages you will learn about various pruning techniques, such as pinching, training, removing large limbs, shearing, beheading, disbudding, thinning, basal pruning, and root pruning. Each technique is appropriate for a specific purpose and/or a specific plant, and in each case I also give you some advice about when to prune using that particular technique.

It Depends on Where You Live

Because of the tremendous difference in weather conditions throughout the continent, it is difficult to give good, precise directions on how much or when to prune everywhere. However, you can follow two basic principles:

1. If you live where summers are humid, good air ventilation is necessary to prevent disease, so prune sufficiently to let in sun and air. On the other hand, where summers are hot and dry, trees — as well as their owners — benefit if the leaves and branches are thick. The limbs can grow close together with no harm to the tree and should not be pruned heavily.

2. If you live in an area of harsh winters, where snows drift deeply and icy crusts form, prune deciduous trees so that they will branch above the snow line and thus avoid breakage of the lower branches. Also, in snow regions, evergreens should be pruned into a pointed or rounded shape so that heavy ice and snow loads won't collect on top and crush them.

MASTER GARDENING TIP

Are You a Relocated Gardener?

Southerners who move to the North and northerners who move to the South both usually realize that a large part of all necessary pruning should be done when a plant is dormant. The problem is that, in their new location, they aren't always sure when dormancy takes place and how long it lasts.

Newcomers to the South often prune too early in the autumn, before the tree or plant has become completely dormant. Southerners who move north often prune tender plants such as roses, grapes, peaches, and cherries heavily in late fall or early winter.

In both cases severe winter injury is likely. If you are gardening in unfamiliar territory, check with your extension service or a local garden expert before you begin any major pruning.

Seasonal Notes

Late-winter pruning. Most gardeners like to prune many of their trees and shrubs in late winter while the plants are still dormant. Fruit trees are often pruned then, as are roses, broadleaf evergreens, vines, and some flowering trees. Since "late winter" means a different time in each locale, take it to mean whenever the days have begun to lengthen and warm up noticeably, but with no sign of swelling buds or new growth. The gardener and orchardist aren't so busy at this time of year, and the first breaths of spring stimulate the feeling of wanting to get busy in the garden. Branches are bare then, too, so it's easier to see what you're doing.

Although most pruning is done in later winter, this can encourage a fast regrowth of wood, often at the expense of fruit and flowers. It's true that if you prune annually, the pruning is usually moderate and regrowth therefore is seldom excessive. However, if you're a year or two behind with your pruning and must do a heavy amount at once, winter may not be the best time.

Most experts don't like to prune when the wood is frozen. Not only is a warm, sunny day more comfortable for working, but cutting on cold days also damages the cells in the frozen wood, and cut areas don't heal properly.

Spring pruning. This is the time for repair work. Inspect your plants each spring, and remove any branches damaged by ice, snow, or wind. Repair any wounds that may have been inflicted by roving animals or winter sportsmen.

Spring is also the time to pinch off buds that may be starting branches or tops in the wrong places, and to remove new suckers, water sprouts, or any other branches that are beginning to grow in the wrong direction.

Early-summer pruning. This is the season when every plant is making its greatest growth. For this reason it is a good time to shear evergreens and hedges. It is also the best season for pruning shrubs that bloomed in the spring, such as lilac, bridal wreath,

honeysuckle, and spring-blossoming spirea. These plants should be pruned just after they finish blooming so that they will have time to start developing a new set of buds that will bloom the following spring.

Early summer is also the best time to do corrective pruning on young trees, such as pinching or cutting off any limbs that might form extra tops, bad crotches, or suckers.

Late-summer pruning. Late summer, when all growth has stopped but the leaves have not yet fallen, is a good time to prune certain trees. The birches and maples that bleed so badly when pruned in late winter and spring can be safely trimmed in late summer, as can most other shade trees.

This is a good time to do basal pruning on evergreens. The small amount of pitch that oozes out of cut limbs is sufficient to seal the wound, but not enough to distress the tree.

Many people like to prune their fruit trees at this time. The trees will be stimulated to set more flower and fruit buds and fewer branch and leaf buds the following year. By removing branches in late summer, you will cause far less regrowth than you would in late winter.

Fall pruning. Some growers prefer to do all their pruning just before winter sets in. The leaves having fallen off, they can see what they are doing; also, there's no sap running, and the weather is still pleasant.

It sounds like the perfect time to prune, but the feeling isn't unanimous. There is the argument that fall pruning encourages winter injury that must be corrected with additional spring pruning, which in turn encourages more regrowth.

In all but the most northern areas, autumn is an excellent time to cut back roses, especially hybrid teas. It's also a good time to cut back clematis, hydrangea, buddleia, crape myrtle, potentilla, small-flowered tamarisk, hibiscus, and many other shrubs. Woody vines should be pruned at this time, as well as small fruits and grapevines.

Training

When you're aiming to have an increasingly spreading and upward-growing tree and want to avoid any crossed or inward-heading branches, to which bud should you cut? Trees have buds at various places on their limbs. Look for an outside bud and cut just above it. A limb or twig growing from an outside bud tends to grow outward and upward; a branch from an inside bud tends to grow inward.

Most deciduous trees and shrubs have alternate buds: When you see a bud on one side of the branch, usually you will find one farther along on the other side. A few trees, however, including maples and ashes, grow their buds and leaves directly opposite each other. When you're pruning a branch with opposite buds, cut just above one of these double buds and snip or rub off the inside bud, leaving only the outside one intact.

MASTER GARDENING TIP

When Should You Train Plants?

Early spring is a good time; this way you can see the buds easily before foliage hides them. Don't prune too early, though, as late frosts can damage a freshly cut plant.

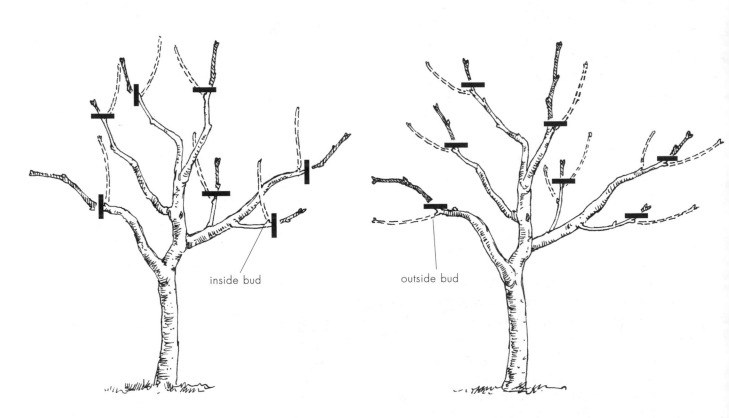

inside bud

outside bud

Pruning branches to inside buds will lead to ingrown limbs (left). Cutting above outside buds produces a more spreading tree (right). *(Future growth is shown by dotted lines.)*

Shearing

Ordinarily you don't want to remove lots of new growth from actively growing plants, but sometimes a rampant plant requires shaping. In such cases, you don't need to give any special consideration to where you make your cuts, and you'll find that the softness of the growth makes the work comparatively easy. When you're finished, the newly cut ends will heal over, form a bud at the end, and be ready to grow the following spring.

Shearing involves redirecting growth as well as removing unwanted greenery. By shearing a plant that would normally head upward and outward, you stimulate the dormant buds among the inner branches to wake up and grow. This results in a thick, bushy appearance.

A common mistake in shearing evergreens and hedges is to wait until the end of the growing season. If a plant has its new growth neatly chopped off late each year, few buds will have a chance to get started and it will never get bushier. Plus, no new growth will appear to cover the clipped ends, so they'll remain exposed throughout the year.

Shear to shape and control.

MASTER GARDENING TIP

When Should You Shear?

Shear a few days after plant growth starts in late spring. This way, redirecting will begin early enough to be effective. The growth of the end buds will be curtailed immediately, and new buds will eventually form where the cuts were made. But even before that the dormant buds will be stimulated to grow, resulting in a bushier plant or a tighter hedge.

Pinching

Most good gardeners like to do a great deal of their pruning by pinching off any new growth that is heading in the wrong direction. By removing a terminal bud or a wayward lateral bud with your thumb and forefinger, you'll temporarily stop all growth in that area. Some gardeners like to carry a pair of pruners on their belt, ready to draw them out at the first sign of unwanted growth. I know one grower who prefers a sharp jackknife for minor pruning of new growth that is too advanced for hand pinching. In any event, with dedicated, frequent pinching throughout the growing season, you can efficiently remove suckers, shorten branch growth, take off extra tops, and redirect growth with the least possible shock to the plant. It is also a useful way to disbud flowers and thin out fruit.

MASTER GARDENING TIP

When Should You Pinch Plants?

Spring and summer, when plants are actively growing.

Strolling frequently through your yard and orchard during the growing season, pinching as you go, is an excellent, low-tech way to avoid future trouble.

Removing Large Limbs

When you're pruning fruit trees and older shade trees, it may be necessary to cut off large limbs. Just as you'd cut to a live bud on small trees and shrubs, be sure to cut a large limb back to a live branch or to the main trunk of the tree so that no stub is left to rot away. (The new bark cannot grow over and cover even a short stub.)

When you cut off a larger, heavier limb, make the cut so that its weight doesn't cause the partially sawed-off branch to break and split back into the next branch or the trunk of the tree. Avoid this problem by cutting in stages, as illustrated below.

MASTER GARDENING TIP

When Should You Remove a Large Limb?

Anytime is fine, though spring and summer are easier for you and less stressful for the tree.

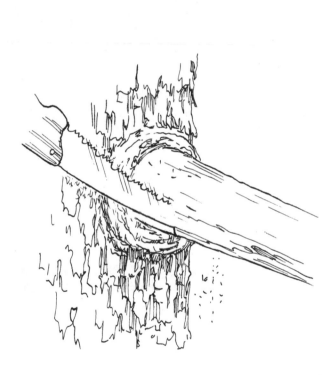

1 Make an undercut with the saw about 6 inches out from the trunk.

2 About 1 inch beyond the first cut, saw off the limb. Don't bear down on the saw — let the sharp teeth do the cutting.

MASTER GARDENING TIP

Gently Does It

Most people are likely to be gentler with their small trees and bushes, and to forget that large trees need protection as well. If you use a ladder, don't let it slide along the branches and scar the bark. It may be best to use a rope to carefully lower pruned limbs and thus avoid letting them crash into other limbs.

3 Cut off the remaining stub. Cut close to the trunk (left) or to the enlarged collar that some trees develop where a large limb joins the trunk (right). The result is a smooth cut with no damage to the tree.

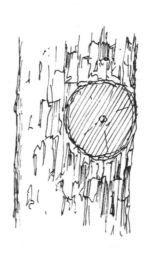

MASTER GARDENING TIP

A Note about Shoes

Choose the shoes you wear with your tree in mind. Climbing in rubber or plastic soles is less harmful to the tree — and you — than climbing in leather ones that might slip. And, of course, never wear lineman's spikes or hobnailed shoes while climbing in a valuable tree.

Beheading

Trees have the wonderful habit of growing each year, whether or not we pay much attention to them. Suddenly we notice that they have reached up into utility lines or are beginning to block a choice view. Since most of us hate to cut down a good, healthy tree unless we really must, we are faced with deciding if we can safely solve the problem by cutting off the top of the tree.

Beheading — also known as tree topping or dehorning — is often done successfully. Power companies frequently top large trees that are menacing their wires. Country dwellers sometimes behead trees that are hiding lake or mountain views, and city dwellers (where ordinances don't prohibit it) lop off trees that are obscuring a good view of the skyline or the water. Fruit trees that have grown too tall for pest control, pruning, and harvesting may be pruned drastically to make them more accessible.

A benefit of this practice is that the beheaded shrub or tree ought to spread and grow more bushlike. Still, I don't generally recommend tree topping, especially in cooler climates, where the shorter summer means less time for recovery from the wounds. At best, beheading spoils the appearance of a tree; at worst, it ruins its health. Do it if you must, but only if the tree is in good health and you're careful not to remove more than a quarter to a third of the limb area.

MASTER GARDENING TIP

When Should You Behead a Plant?

Late summer or fall is best, when the tree is dormant, to avoid excessive bleeding.

Disbudding

We have several large old peony plants that produce hundreds of buds each year. If left to their own devices, they would bring forth lots of small and medium-size blooms. But peonies are such a magnificent flower that it's a shame to let them miss their full potential. So when the buds are still small, we pinch off most of them, leaving only one to a stem. We don't get nearly as many flowers, but each one is a gorgeous giant and so heavy that the plant has to be carefully staked to support them.

Disbudding can also be done later, when flowers are about to go in a bouquet. Florists commonly disbud plants because sometimes one large blossom is more desirable than a lot of smaller ones in an arrangement.

MASTER GARDENING TIP

When Should You Disbud a Plant?

Intervene anytime you see swelling flower buds; the timing will vary depending on the plant.

Remove the extra little buds on a peony plant to force it to produce fewer but larger blooms. The sooner you do this, the faster the plant's strength will become concentrated on the remaining ones — with magnificent results.

MASTER GARDENING TIP

Plants to Disbud

Professional exhibitors of plants often disbud for show-quality specimens. While this technique is fun to try, especially if you like to pick flowers for bouquets, don't get carried away in your own yard; too many king-size blooms can look unnatural. The following plants benefit from disbudding:

- ▶ Asters
- ▶ Begonias
- ▶ Carnations
- ▶ Dahlias
- ▶ Hibiscus
- ▶ Large-flowering mums (not pom-poms)
- ▶ Peonies
- ▶ Roses
- ▶ Zinnias

Thinning Fruit

Thinning does for fruit what disbudding does for flowers. Indeed, it is done in about the same way and for the same reason. Many fruit trees have a tendency to set a large crop every other year, and some produce well only every third year. There's no doubt that thinning, together with proper pruning, helps your tree not only to produce larger fruit, but to produce annually as well. Most commercial growers thin their fruit in order to get the perfect-looking specimens you see in stores.

You, too, can grow fruit resembling the beauties you see in catalogs. The best time to thin is after the natural drop in early summer. Keep an eye on your trees, and whenever you see a lot of little fruits on the ground, give nature a helping hand by thinning the fruit still on the tree. Thinning is worth the trouble, because two nice things happen:

1. Because the remaining fruits grow much larger and in such good condition, you'll end up with more bushels of usable fruit than if you hadn't thinned at all. It will be the kind of fruit you'll be happy to use and proud to give away.

2. The tree will be producing only a small fraction of the seeds that would grow otherwise. Since it takes far more of a tree's strength to mature seeds than to produce fruit flesh, the tree is more likely to bear a good crop every year — its energy hasn't been sapped by bearing a big crop of seeds.

MASTER GARDENING TIP

When Should You Thin Fruit?

Don't wait too long! Go out and remove excess fruits early in the season while they are still tiny, so the tree doesn't invest any more energy in them.

MASTER GARDENING TIP

Best Candidates for Thinning

Thinning is good for the plant and good for you because it improves the size and quality of the remaining fruit. Remember that each variety of fruit has a built-in size limit, however, and no amount of disbudding or thinning will produce a fruit larger than that limit.

These fruits will benefit from thinning:

- Apples
- Apricots
- Blackberries
- Blueberries
- Gooseberries
- Grapes
- Nectarines
- Peaches
- Pears
- Plums
- Strawberries

Note: Thinning is usually less practical on crab apples, cherries, and quinces; these benefit more from pruning.

If there are two or more fruits in a cluster, leave the biggest and best one and pick off all the rest. Make sure that there is a space of about 6 inches between each fruit you leave on the tree. Since this involves picking off 80 to 90 percent of the fruits, it's a big job.

Basal Pruning

Basal pruning involves cutting off limbs at the base of the tree. Sometimes this is performed for purely aesthetic reasons. You can create interesting effects with evergreens and flowering trees. There are practical reasons for basal pruning as well, though. You can open up living areas under large trees, keep a tree at the proper size for its function, or make it easier to control trunk-boring insects. Highway departments and power companies sometimes practice basal pruning on shade trees to force the growth away from highway traffic or power lines. Woodsmen basal-prune to grow long, straight logs that are knot-free. Christmas-tree-plantation owners do it to produce better-shaped Christmas trees, as do orchardists to aid in mechanical harvesting of fruits and nuts.

before pruning   after pruning

By basal pruning this spreading evergreen (left), the area under the tree (right) is opened up to provide a view and access to the lower-growing plantings beyond.

To create a mushroom or umbrella tree:

1. Prune over a period of years rather than in one drastic session, so the process is gradual and the tree can adjust.

2. Remove basal limbs to keep the base open and bare.

3. At the same time, remove top limbs to encourage wide growth.

MASTER GARDENING TIPS

Tips for Successful Basal Pruning

▶ *Cut off only a few limbs during any one year,* so that you don't shock the tree too much. Usually a fifth of the height of a branched part of a tree can be basal-pruned at one time with no severe setback to the tree. Thus, a tree 30 feet tall with 25 feet of limb growth could be basal-pruned up to about 5 feet in any one year without endangering the tree. If you're working with an older tree that has lower limbs that are quite large, only a few should be removed in any one three-year period.

▶ *Wait two or three years* before you attempt the next basal pruning.

▶ *Remove dried-out limbs at any time.* The lower limbs of evergreens are often dead or nearly so, especially if the trees are growing close together. All of these can be cut off, in any season, without damage to the tree.

▶ *Always cut a large limb back to living wood,* either a branch or the main trunk of the tree, so that no stub is left to rot away.

Root Pruning

Root pruning probably is understood less, and therefore less practiced, than any other type of pruning. Many dedicated gardeners will have no part of it. They don't mind pruning trees and shearing hedges, but they consider the roots of a plant sacred or mysterious and not to be disturbed.

Sometimes root pruning involves digging up a plant and cutting back its exposed roots. Root pruning also is practiced without moving the plant from its spot in the ground; you don't see the roots in this process, but simply cut all around the tree with a spade that has a long, sharp blade. There's no need to feel guilty or nervous about either practice. As with regular top pruning, the plant doesn't seem to mind, and usually thrives afterward.

When your wisteria produces plenty of lush foliage but none of those lovely chains of flowers, and lack of sunlight or water is not the problem, it's time to consider root pruning. The process is easier and less risky than you think, and ought to inspire your plant to burst into glorious bloom.

MASTER GARDENING TIPS

Good Reasons for Root Pruning

We could all take a lesson from the skilled Asian and European gardeners who know how to use root pruning as proficiently as any other garden practice. Use this valuable skill to:

▶ Control plant size

▶ Move large trees easily and with less trauma

▶ Get young trees and shrubs off to a good start

▶ Keep houseplants at a manageable size

▶ Persuade slow-to-start fruit trees to begin bearing

▶ Force reluctant flowering trees and shrubs to bloom

MASTER GARDENING TIP

When Should You Root-Prune?

You can root-prune any time of year when the ground isn't frozen, but early spring is best. Trees need a large root system to supply their required moisture during the winter, and by pruning them in the spring you allow maximum time for additional roots to grow.

Root Pruning before Transplanting

Nurseries often cut a small circle around each growing tree or shrub every year or two to encourage a compact yet full root system so that the plant can be transplanted with little shock or setback. If you wish to move trees or shrubs in your own yard or to dig up wild specimens, you can use the same method. Simply root-prune them at least one growing season before you move them. The process is easy and practically ensures planting success. The method described here is appropriate for a medium-size tree or shrub. The operation is spread over two years to avoid shock to the plant.

MASTER GARDENING TIPS

▶ For a small tree or shrub, cut the entire circle at once.

▶ Leave the pruning and moving of large trees to professionals.

2 In the spring, cut off the ends of the remaining roots in the same fashion.

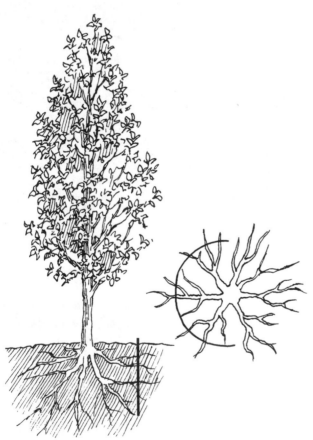

1 In early spring, using a sharp, long-bladed spade, make a downward cut halfway around the plant about 2 feet from the trunk. Some of the larger roots may be tough, and a firm thrust will be necessary to sever them. When digging an evergreen, cut the circle just at the outer spread of the branches. New roots will then grow within the circle, resulting in a tight rootball that will be safe to move without excess stress to the plant. Mark the side you have cut so you can identify it the following year.

3 That same year in late fall, or the following spring, dig a hole where you want to set the tree or shrub. Then cut another circle completely around the tree that is slightly outside the one where you had previously pruned the roots. This will ensure that you include all the new roots in the rootball. Then dig and transplant it to the new location, keeping the rootball intact. Follow the usual directions for planting, including watering and fertilizing.

Root Pruning to Check Top Growth

An established tree is sometimes root-pruned, even if it will never be transplanted, in order to slow down its growth. Although you might think it more logical to check tree growth by cutting back the branches, this isn't always the best way. Pruned trees usually try to grow back branches to replace those they've lost as soon as possible, so the tree may grow faster than ever. Root pruning, on the other hand, cuts off part of the supply of nutrients and thus slows down growth.

In addition to controlling tree size, you may want to slow down top growth for other reasons. Fruit trees in rich soil often do so well that they go right on growing for many years without producing any fruit. Sometimes flowering trees will also make lush growth for a long time but won't bloom. Root pruning can slow down a tree's growth activity and force it to bloom and bear.

Root pruning is also useful to control houseplant growth. Most houses don't have room enough for indoor gardeners to keep repotting their plants indefinitely into larger containers. If you have a plant that is becoming unwieldy, you can carefully remove it from its pot, cut back all the outside roots, and replant it with some new soil in the same pot. Bonsai growers rely heavily on root pruning to keep their plants small yet ancient looking (see chapter 13).

Root Pruning at Planting Time

Many gardeners ignore the nursery's directions for root pruning their newly purchased stock. Cutting back the tops is understandable, but why would anyone want to cut off roots? Don't new plants need all the roots they can get?

Sometimes it isn't necessary to trim the roots, but more often than not, a newly dug, bare-root plant has received some ugly wounds caused by the digging. Broken, ragged ends should be cut off cleanly so that they will heal over quickly and begin to send out the hair roots that supply food to the plant.

Roots need to be shortened occasionally to make the plant more convenient to handle. Strawberry plants, for example, should have their long, stringy roots clipped back a few inches at planting time, both to make them easier to plant and to stimulate fast, new root growth.

The Oklahoma Air-Root Pruning Method

An interesting method of making trees grow faster and inspiring fruit and nut trees to produce sooner was developed in the '70s by horticulturist Carl Whitcomb at Oklahoma State University.

Whitcomb noted that a great deal of a tree's first growing season is spent developing a long taproot that will be capable of reaching moisture even in dry weather. Only after this growth has been accomplished does the tree produce fibrous lateral roots (those that pick up the soil nutrients) and start to grow. He decided to find a way to cut short the lengthy taproot development and speed up desirable root growth. His method is as follows:

MASTER GARDENING TIP

When Should You Air-Root Prune?

Start in early spring with seedlings, trees, or shrubs.

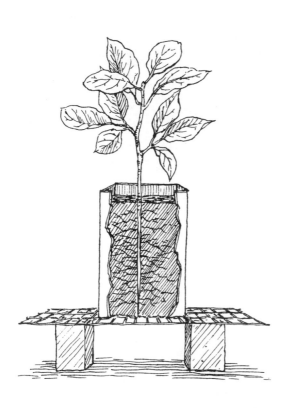

1 Cut off the tops and bottoms of some milk cartons and fill them with a mixture of peat, perlite, and slow-release fertilizer, then plant your seed or seedling.

2 Rather than placing the cartons on the ground or on benches, set them on a wire screen that is slightly elevated off the ground, leaving air space beneath.

3 Water well, and soon the young plants will begin to grow.

4 When the taproot reaches the bottom of the carton and hits the wire screen with the air beneath, you'll observe that the root tip promptly dies and feeder side roots begin to grow instead, soon filling the carton. This signals that it's time to transplant into a nursery bed or the garden proper, where it can continue its speedy lateral-root development.

Whitcomb noted that not only was the growth rate of the air-pruned trees greatly increased, but also their survival rate, when transplanted into the field, was a surprising 100 percent — even when planted out in the heat of summer. He even succeeded in transplanting trees that are usually so difficult to move that nurseries seldom carry them — black gum and Kentucky coffee tree, for instance.

This technique can also speed up the growth rate of all seedling plants, even those that produce short taproots. It is of less value to rooted cuttings, because most plants grown from cuttings naturally develop a heavy fibrous root system.

Prune According to Growth Habit. Each plant has its own natural growth habit. A Lombardy poplar grows straight up; it would be difficult to prune it into a low hedge or spreading shade tree. An American elm is slender, tall, and spreading at the top, and a spruce grows into a cone shape. Even individual varieties have distinctive growth patterns. Within the apple family 'McIntosh' is a broad, spreading tree, but 'Yellow Transparent' grows upward, forming lots of tops and crotches that need corrective pruning so that the tree won't split when loaded with fruit. Certain varieties of birch and willow "weep" and should be pruned to emphasize that pattern of growth. Creeping hemlocks, junipers, and globular or pyramidal arborvitae also have distinctive shapes that can be nurtured with pruning. Pruning can alter a plant's natural habits to some degree, but you should try to work with them as much as possible. All species look best when they are pruned to conform to their natural growth habits.

Beware of Overpruning. With pruning, just as with fertilizer and medicine, more is not necessarily better, and sometimes it is disastrous. So keep your pruning urge under control. Plants live and grow because of photosynthesis. Whenever too much growth is removed, the plant can no longer manufacture enough food (that is, the organic compounds that maintain living tissue), and if it doesn't die, it will at least end up struggling to develop flowers and seeds.

Always Have a Good Reason for Making Each Cut. All pruning should be done with an eye toward preventing future problems. When you prune skillfully, it is not obvious. But like weeding your garden, it becomes quite noticeable when you haven't done it.

Well-pruned trees, like this flowering crab apple, are not only more attractive, but also much healthier and thus longer lived.

· CHAPTER · 4 ·

Ornamental Trees and Shrubs

A popular song of the '60s, "Little Boxes," protested the thousands of little suburban modern houses that all looked alike: ". . . little boxes on the hillside, little boxes all the same." The song didn't mention that much of the landscaping was similarly dull, consisting of a tall ever-green in each corner, groups of spreading evergreens around the house, one green shade tree, and a green lawn.

Fortunately, during the last decades that picture has been changing. Flowering trees and shrubs have become popular in the United States. Each spring we see more and more beautiful flowering crab apples, dogwoods, azaleas, hawthorns, redbuds, and lilacs. Throughout the summer, roses and other colorful flowering shrubs compete with peren-nial borders, and in the fall there are more blooms, berries, fruits, and colored foliage than ever before. Some shrubs and trees are planted just because their colored bark brightens a barren landscape during the winter.

Pruning at Planting Time

When you buy a tree, perhaps its roots are bare, wrapped only in peat moss or some other material to keep them moist: Such a tree is called bare-root. Or you may buy a shrub that is growing in a large pot, or has its roots enclosed in a ball of soil wrapped in burlap or plastic. These trees are termed container-grown or balled-and-burlapped. In either case, the new plant will benefit from some attention from you and your clippers before you place it in your garden.

In This Chapter

- Pruning a Bare-Root Shrub
- Pruning Container-Grown or Balled-and-Burlapped Plants
- Pruning Flowering Trees
- Pruning Flowering Shrubs
- Pruning a Viburnum
- Pruning a Lilac
- Restoring an Old Flowering Tree or Shrub
- Turning a Shrub into a Tree
- Pruning Shrubs That Produce Fruits or Berries
- Plants with Colored Bark
- Shrubs and Trees That Need Special Care in Pruning
- Pruning Roses
- General Rose Maintenance
- Pruning a Hybrid Tea Rose
- Pruning Shrub and Species Roses
- Pruning Climbers and Ramblers
- Pruning Tree Roses
- Choosing a Tree or Shrub

41

Pruning a Bare-Root Shrub

The drawings below show a young shrub, just home from the nursery. The care you take now will ensure it a great start and a promising future in your garden. Begin by inspecting the roots to determine how badly they were damaged when the plant was dug up. Be sure to keep the roots in a tub of water when you inspect them, because they will suffer badly if they are exposed to the air for more than a few minutes. (Newly acquired, bare-root nursery stock should always be soaked for five or six hours after you get it home.)

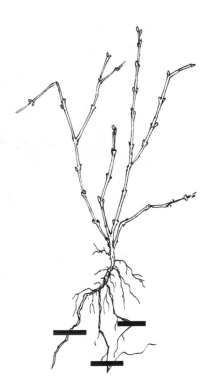

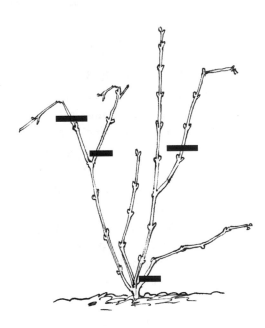

1 If any roots are broken, use hand pruners to cut them so there will be a minimum amount of wound to heal over. Leave all other roots intact.

2 Remove any dead or damaged branches.

Pruning Tall Flowering Shrubs

Shrubs that will eventually grow 6 feet tall or more, such as lilacs and viburnums, should be treated as trees when you plant them. Prune them back from a third to a half, cutting out any weak branches. Leave a few of the tall, stronger branches intact to encourage upward growth and earlier blooming.

Pruning Short Flowering Shrubs

Smaller-growing flowering shrubs, including most roses, potentillas, spireas, and weigelas, should have all of their branches cut back by half when they are planted, to encourage bushy growth.

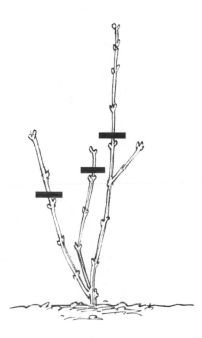

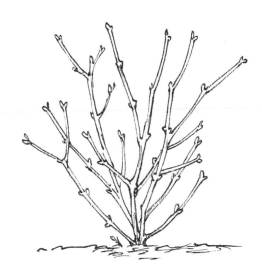

3 Prune back one-third to one-half of the plant. The top can be pruned either before or after planting, although it is easier to do it after, since the plant is then held firmly upright by the soil. The amount depends on how much of the root system is left. If it looks small and was damaged, you should take off half of the top to compensate for the loss, but never more, because the plant will need enough leaves to sustain the roots that are left. If the roots are in good shape, cut back the top and the limbs to two-thirds of their former length. Many gardeners prefer to cut off some limbs entirely, leaving others undisturbed. Either way seems to work well. Always remember to cut on a slant above an outside bud. (See page 24.)

4 If you've pruned your new shrub correctly, it will reward your efforts with strong new growth on a sturdy framework.

Pruning Container-Grown or Balled-and-Burlapped Plants

You've just brought home a young rhododendron. It may not need any pruning now, particularly if you can determine that the roots have been undisturbed and are in good condition. Still, it's a good idea to check and do whatever may be needed.

1 Tip the rootball out of the pot. Check the outside roots. Some trees that have been growing for several years in a large container before being sold will develop a circular habit of root growth. If this pattern continues after the tree is planted, the increasing size of the encircling roots can strangle the tree in later years.

2 Slice through the encircling roots with a sharp, stout knife. Don't worry about harming the plant; you are actually doing it a favor by helping it to grow more freely.

3 Untangle the rootball. Now gently comb the remaining tangle of roots with your fingers. This will encourage quick growth of new, outward-reaching roots. Then plant in a good mixture of soil and compost.

Common Name	Scientific Name	Remarks
American smoke tree	*Cotinus obovatus*	Prune to grow as bush or small tree; cut off fading flowers.
Bayberry	*Myrica pensylvanica*	Prune to remove suckers, winter injury.
Buckthorn	*Rhamnus davurica*	Prune to shape in late winter.
Burning bush	*Euonymus atropurpurea*	Prune in late winter, only if necessary.
Cranberry bush, nannyberry, black haw	*Viburnum*	Prune in late winter, only as necessary.
European hornbeam	*Carpinus betulus*	Prune to tree form.
Flowering almond, apricot, cherry, peach, plum	*Prunus*	Prune to shape in late winter.
Flowering crab apple	*Malus*	Prune to shape; renew old wood, if necessary.
Flowering dogwood	*Cornus florida*	Prune as little as possible; heals slowly.
Franklin tree	*Franklinia alatamaha*	Prune to tree form.
Golden-chain	*Laburnum anagyroides*	Prune after blooming.
Golden rain tree	*Koelreuteria paniculata*	Prune to shape when young.
Golden-shower, senna	*Cassia fistula*	Cut back season's growth to short spurs after blooming.
Grandiflora hydrangea 'Peegee'	*Hydrangea paniculata*	Prune in late winter; for large flower panicles, thin the plant to 5 to 10 primary shoots.
Hawthorn	*Crataegus*	Prune to shape in late winter; renew branches, if necessary.
Japanese tree lilac	*Syringa reticulata*	Prune right after blooming, if necessary.
Kousa dogwood	*Cornus kousa*	Prune as little as possible; heals slowly.
Magnolia	*Magnolia*	Prune just after blooming.
Mountain ash	*Sorbus*	Prune to tree form in late winter.
Oriental hornbeam	*Carpinus orientalis*	Prune to tree form.
Redbud	*Cercis*	Prune after blooming, if necessary.
Russian olive	*Elaeagnus*	Prune only to control size, if necessary, in late winter.
Shadbush	*Amelanchier*	Prune only to shape, as either bush or tree.
Silver-bell	*Halesia monticola*	Needs pruning rarely.
Sourwood	*Oxydendrum arboreum*	Needs pruning rarely.
Sweetleaf	*Symplocos paniculata*	Prune to shape; renew old branches.
Wax myrtle	*Myrica cerifera*	Prune to remove winter injury, or to shape, in late winter.

Pruning Flowering Trees

A properly pruned flowering tree will be strong and less likely to break in wind- and ice storms. It will also be longer lived. Flowering crabs can live for over a century and tree lilacs for even longer. The key is to train the tree to grow with a central leader for the first 10 feet at least. In other words, train a flowering tree as a tree rather than as a large bush.

Some plants, such as tree lilac and mountain ash, form a lot of lower limbs, so prune frequently for a tree-like effect, especially until the specimen is mature. As a rule, the branches on most ornamental flowering trees are not heavy, and their berries and fruit seldom add much weight, so careful training of the limb structure is not as necessary as it is on fruit trees.

Water sprouts should be removed whenever they appear.

MASTER GARDENING TIPS

Pruning Guidelines

▶ Be strict about keeping the tree trunk as a single stem. Don't allow groups of heavy branches to grow from the lower part of the tree.

▶ Cut off all suckers that sprout from the roots. Grafted trees in particular, such as flowering crabs and hawthorns, tend to send up a lot of suckers. Cut them off immediately, because they grow so fast that they can quickly overtake and crowd out the good part of the tree.

▶ Prune off the branches that upset the symmetry and appearance of the tree.

▶ Remove all branches that are growing close to the ground. They interfere with lawn mowing and don't look attractive.

▶ Thin. As the tree gets older, take out branches that are growing too densely or that cross others, so the remaining ones will continue to bloom well. Thinning will also help prevent the tree from aging too fast.

MASTER GARDENING TIPS

When to Prune Flowering Trees

▶ Prune flowering trees just after the blooms fade.

▶ Prune in late winter any trees that produce berries or fruit, so you won't interfere with production.

suckers

1 This untrained flowering crab apple has many suckers.

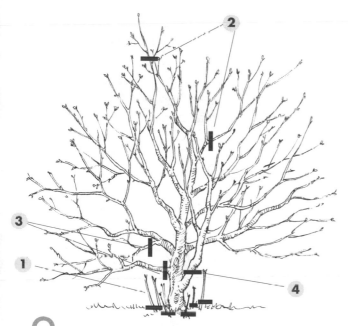

2 Cut off all suckers (**1**). Prune branches that upset the tree's symmetry (**2**). Remove low-growing branches (**3**). Thin out crossed and densely growing branches (**4**).

3 The result is a graceful, airy tree, which is not only more attractive but also healthier.

Pruning Flowering Shrubs

Like flowering trees, most deciduous flowering shrubs rarely need pruning, although sometimes you must remove old wood to rejuvenate them, thin out wood that is growing too thickly, or keep them from growing all over the place. Some shrubs, such as honeysuckles, viburnums, and lilacs, may grow too tall and will need to be cut back.

• **When to prune dormant shrubs.** Shrubs that form flowers on wood grown the same season should be pruned before the buds show green (in late fall or late winter), not when they are actively growing.

• **When to prune after blooming.** The best time to prune a shrub that blooms on year-old wood is just after the blossoms have faded. You should then allow it to grow new branches and form the buds that will bloom the next year.

MASTER GARDENING TIPS

When to Prune Flowering Shrubs

▶ Check to see whether your shrub blooms on wood produced the same year or on wood that grew during the previous season, then refer to chart.

▶ Late winter is the best time to prune the shrubs that are grown mostly for their fall foliage (Amur maple and euonymus) or those grown primarily for the beauty of their winter bark (bright, red-twigged dogwood).

▶ Remove broken, dead, or diseased branches whenever you notice them.

Shrubs to Be Pruned When Dormant

Abelia (*Abelia* x *grandiflora*)
Abelia (*Abelia schumannii*)
Alder buckthorn (*Rhamnus frangula*)
American elder (*Sambucus canadensis*)
Beautyberry (*Callicarpa japonica*)
Bluebeard (*Caryopteris*)
Broom (*Cytisus nigricans*)
Bush clover (*Lespedeza*)
Bush honeysuckle (*Diervilla sessilifolia*)
Butterfly bush (*Buddleia*; exception: *Buddleia alternifolia*)
Buttonbush (*Cephalanthus occidentalis*)
Chaste tree (*Vitex agnus-castus*)
Cinquefoil (*Potentilla*)
Coralberry, snowberry (*Symphoricarpos*)
Crape myrtle (*Lagerstroemia indica*)
False spirea (*Sorbaria*)
Flowering raspberry (*Rubus odoratus*)
Franklin tree (*Franklinia alatamaha*)
Heather (*Calluna vulgaris*)
Hills-of-snow (*Hydrangea arborescens* 'Grandiflora')

Indigo (*Indigofera incarnata*)
Japanese angelica (*Aralia elata*)
Japanese fatsia (*Fatsia japonica*)
Oak leaf hydrangea (*Hydrangea quercifolia*)
Ocean-spray (*Holodiscus discolor*)
Peegee hydrangea (*Hydrangea paniculata* 'Grandiflora')
Rose of Sharon (*Hibiscus syriacus*)
Sacred bamboo (*Nandina domestica*)
Saint-John's-wort (*Hypericum*)
Silk-tassel (*Garrya*)
Spirea: all species that bloom in summer, including Billiard, Japanese, and hardhack (*Spiraea* spp.)
Spreading euonymus (*Euonymus kiautschovica*)
Tamarisk (*Tamarix odessana*)
Viburnum (*Viburnum*)
Witch hazel (*Hamamelis virginiana*)

Shrubs to Be Pruned After Blooming

Barberry (*Berberis*)
Beautybush (*Kolkwitzia*)
Butterfly bush (*Buddleia alternifolia*)
Daphne (*Daphne*)
Deutzia (*Deutzia*)
Forsythia (*Forsythia*)
Honeysuckle (*Lonicera*)
Japanese rose (*Kerria japonica*)
Jasmine (*Jasminum*)
Lilac (*Syringa*)
Mock orange (*Philadelphus*)
Ninebark (*Physocarpus*)
Pieris (*Pieris*)
Smoke tree (*Cotinus coggygria*)
Spirea, including bridal wreath, 'Thunberg', and 'Veitch' (spring-blooming varieties) (*Spiraea*)
Weigela (*Weigela*)

Pruning a Viburnum:
Example of Pruning When Dormant

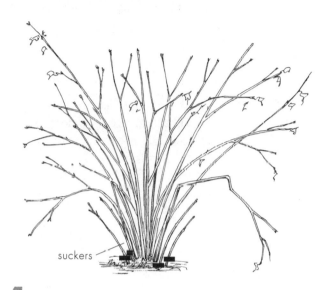

1 Remove all suckers.

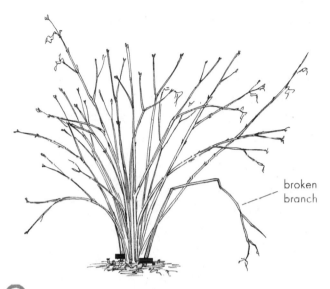

broken branch

2 Remove all dead, broken, and weak wood.

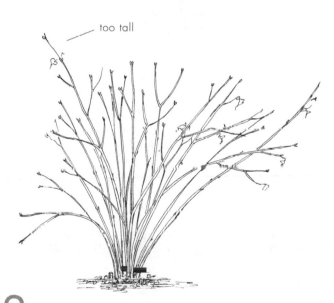

too tall

3 Remove a few of the older, taller branches.

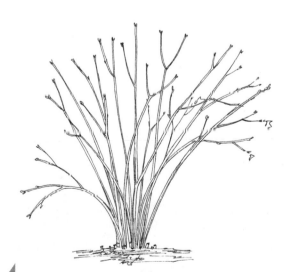

4 The finished product — a neater, healthier shrub.

Pruning a Lilac:
Example of Pruning after Blooming

Lilac *(Syringa)* is one of the most widely planted and most beloved flowering shrubs in the country. Because they were introduced into the colonies so long ago and are such long-lived plants, many of the bushes now growing in American yards are more than 200 years old. Obviously, some of them are long overdue for a bit of attention.

MASTER GARDENING TIP

Restrain Yourself

Resist the urge to hack away randomly at the thicket. Neglected, elderly bushes require careful pruning, using both clippers and a saw. You'll have to do pruning this major only once a decade or so.

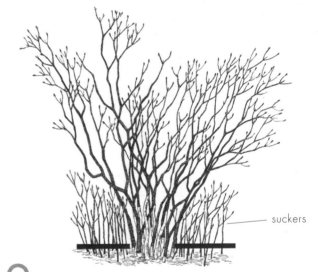

suckers

1 Select several of the strong, younger trunks to remain. These will become your new bush. Cut off all the rest (those shaded in drawing), especially old and decrepit ones — these have lost most of their vitality anyway. Make all cuts close to the ground, and cut carefully so that you don't slash into any adjoining stems. The exact number of trunks you leave will depend on the area your bush covers, and whether you want to shrink its size.

2 Cut away all the small, thick sucker growth at the plant's base. These stems crowd both the main bush and each other. Removing them will allow you to see which of the remaining larger stems (those shaded in drawing) may still need to be cut.

MASTER GARDENING TIPS

Maintenance Pruning for Lilacs

▶ Always cut off the fading blooms late each spring.

▶ Some lilacs are grafted on ash or privet roots that may send up some shoots that look quite different from lilac plants. Prune or pull out any foreign-looking sprouts before they can threaten the real lilac.

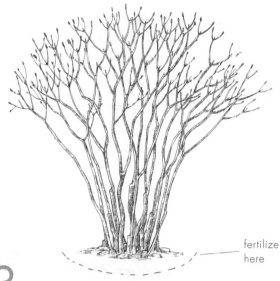

fertilize
here

3 Give the plant a good dose of fertilizer. After pruning, help the bush recover and thrive by feeding it a mixture of dried manure (about 20 pounds for the average-size bush) and 2 or 3 cups of garden lime. Scatter this in a circle a foot away from the bush, just before a light spring rain will wash it into the soil.

4 After the shrub blooms, cut off the spent flowers. Remove the fading blooms only; don't touch the stems and leaves. Clip just above the buds forming for next year's blooms. The farther you cut back, the more likely that you are picking off next year's blooms. If allowed to go to seed, the energy drain on a lilac bush is so great that it may bloom sparingly the following year. By pruning off the old blossoms, you help to ensure regular blooming. Of course, if you have a long hedge of tall-growing bushes, this snipping may be impractical, and you'll have to settle for heavy blooms whenever the lilacs want to provide them.

MASTER GARDENING TIPS

Thinning for Bouquets

▶ Whenever possible, choose blossoms growing toward the interior of the plant. This way, taking a bouquet will not be as noticeable, plus you'll be helping the plant to maintain a pleasing shape.

▶ Cut the stems to another branch without leaving a dead stub.

▶ Never tear off stems, or you'll damage the plant.

▶ Although heavy picking isn't likely to disturb an older, well-established plant, cut sparingly, if at all, from young bushes.

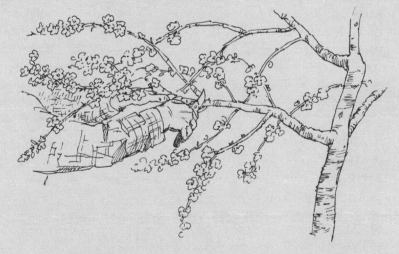

Picking beautiful flowering stems is one of the great pleasures of having a flowering shrub. When cut properly, the plant is not harmed and some of your pruning is done for you.

Restoring an Old Flowering Tree or Shrub

Often the question of how to prune an old, deciduous flowering tree or shrub comes up. Is it possible? Is it worth the trouble? How can it be done?

The answer depends on the variety of plant, its vigor, the care with which you prune, and your climate. You can slash back some tropical and semitropical plants mercilessly and they will quickly grow back into youthful, thrifty plants. Trees and shrubs in northern climates need to be treated more carefully, and in most cases it's best to spread out major pruning jobs over several years. Cut back only a few limbs at a time, and as they regrow you can remove a few more. In this way you can revitalize your tree. A gradual renewal is better for the plant's health, and its appearance is less drastically altered during the process.

Keep in mind that shrubs and flowering trees have definite life spans, and if they are nearing the end of their days, pruning often won't help them revive. Just as with fruit and shade trees that reach this stage, it is better to cut them down and plant new ones nearby.

> ### MASTER GARDENING TIP
>
> #### When to Do Restorative Pruning
>
> Early spring is usually the best time. The plant will be entering its period of most vigorous growth and thus be more resilient.

MASTER GARDENING TIPS

Restorative Pruning Strategies

Problem: The plant has become too large.
Solution: When a shrub gets overgrown, cut a few of the older stems completely to the ground and shorten the remaining ones to just a bit lower than the height you want the shrub to be. Then allow it to grow back enough to cover the pruning wounds. In future years, prune to keep it at the size you want. Prune back flowering trees such as mountain ash and tree hydrangea according to directions for proper pruning (page 46).

Problem: The plant's growth has become too tight.
Solution: Many low-growing shrubs, such as potentilla, hydrangea, and moss rose, become too dense after a few years of unregulated growth. You can thin these out by pruning at least half the stems to the ground the first year and the remaining half the second year. Or, if the bush is vigorous, cut it completely to the ground and allow it to grow back.

Problem: The plant's growth has become too loose.
Solution: Flowering quince, mock orange, some shrub roses, and many other shrubs and ornamental trees tend to grow tall, loose, and floppy. When plants begin to droop and touch the ground, it is time to shorten them. Cut back all the leggy branches, completely remove a few of the older ones at the base, and clip off all suckers.

Problem: The plant's growth has become too twiggy.
Solution: Honeysuckles, blueberries, dogwoods, and some viburnums are among the shrubs that are likely to grow many small branches at the ends of their limbs as they get older. As a result, the blooms are fewer and the berries smaller. In addition to thinning the old wood, clip off this dense outer growth to renew the plant and revive its earlier blooming and bearing vigor.

Turning a Shrub into a Tree

A Peegee hydrangea *(Hydrangea paniculata* 'Grandiflora') is an excellent candidate for this project, because it grows quickly and eagerly, and responds well to training.

1 In the first year, prune to a single stem.

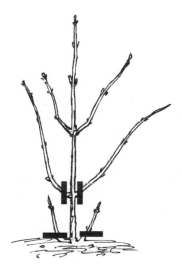

2 Cut off the lower branches in the second year.

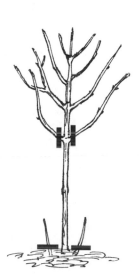

3 Continue to prune off bottom branches as the tree grows taller until the desired treelike form is reached.

4 The finished product — a handsome plant, in and out of bloom.

Pruning Shrubs That Produce Fruits or Berries

Most berry-producing shrubs, such as cotoneaster, pyracantha, and viburnum, need little pruning. If you consider the fruit important, prune them lightly to keep them in shape and to correct any damage caused by animals, weather, disease, or insects.

Note that some berry-producing shrubs, including bayberry and winterberry, are unisexual. This means that only the female plants produce fruit, so if you want berries you must plant both males and females.

Prune to Encourage Annual Cropping

Viburnum and others often produce an extra-heavy crop of berries only every other year.

Although you can encourage annual bearing by pruning, a better and easier way is to cut off some of the flowers in the summer during years when the shrubs are blooming heavily. This will prevent overbearing and encourage the bush to deliver a good crop the following year.

Cut for Decorations

My wife likes to cut branches of cotoneaster, red viburnum, and other berries for interior decoration in the fall, and she sometimes worries that this is detrimental to an ornamental plant. It's true that when the plant is small it isn't a good idea to cut off the branches, although a few berries can be snitched with no harm. As a bush gets older, however, you do no damage if you gather a moderate amount of the colorful berries to use for bouquets or holiday decorations. Naturally, it is better to cut off the branches with clippers rather than to break them off in jagged tears. Since most of next year's fruit buds are near the ends of the limbs, don't sacrifice too many of them.

MASTER GARDENING TIPS

When to Prune Fruit- and Berry-Producing Shrubs

▶ Prune in late fall after the berries either have been eaten by birds or have passed their prime.

▶ Or prune in early spring before any growth starts.

Fruit- and Berry-Producing Shrubs

Barberry *(Berberis)*

Bayberry *(Myrica pensylvanica)*

Burning bush *(Euonymus atropurpurea)*

Cotoneaster *(Cotoneaster)*

Cranberry bush, nannyberry, black haw *(Viburnum)*

Dogwood *(Cornus)*

Firethorn *(Pyracantha)*

Flowering quince *(Chaenomeles)*

Hawthorn *(Crataegus)* (best with a minimum of pruning)

Honeysuckle *(Lonicera)*

Rugosa rose *(Rosa rugosa)*

Russian olive *(Elaeagnus)*

Smoke tree *(Cotinus)*

Winterberry *(Ilex verticillata)*

Plants with Colored Bark

Certain dogwoods, maples, beeches, birches, roses, euonymus, brooms, and viburnums have distinctive bark color that can add beauty to an otherwise bare winter landscape. Although most of these are grown primarily for their summer beauty, a few are planted mainly for the color of their winter bark.

Plants with red bark include Tartarian dogwood (*Cornus alba*), Siberian dogwood (*C. siberica*), and red-osier dogwood (*C. sericea* or *C. stolonifera*). Try Japanese rose (*Kerria japonica*) for green stems. Golden- or yellow-twig dogwood (*Cornus sericea* 'Flaviramea') has yellow bark.

MASTER GARDENING TIP

When to Prune Plants with Colored Bark

Prune in late spring to keep wilder-growing varieties within bounds and to thin out growth so that remaining stems will be larger, showing the colored bark better. Every six or seven years cut some of the larger stems to the ground to renew the plant.

Shrubs and Trees That Need Special Care in Pruning

Shrub or Tree	Comments
Flowering dogwood (*Cornus florida*)	In cold areas it's unwise to prune off the lower branches of this large shrub to make it into a tree. The tender bark sunscalds easily, and it will crack and split in the winter sun.
Cotoneaster (*Cotoneaster*)	Requires little pruning except to shape. Some make excellent espaliers if properly pruned.
Deutzia (*Deutzia*)	Prune before flowers are completely gone so that new growth will start faster. Prune heavily for bushy growth. Prune off the suckers that come from the roots.
Big-leaf hydrangea (*Hydrangea macrophylla*)	Prune when flowers are fading, because it blooms on the tips of year-old wood.
Sweet gum (*Liquidambar*)	Plants branch from the ground, so pinching terminal buds won't induce bushy side branching. Allow to grow into natural shape, but prune to space branches.
Mulberry (*Morus alba*)	Tends to be brittle. Prune to shorten branches and to encourage a smaller, bushier tree that can better resist wind and other weather damage. Staking is usually beneficial to a young tree. Do not overfertilize mulberries.
Coralberry or snowberry (*Symphoricarpos*)	May grow leggy as it gets older. Prune the branches in very early spring, if necessary.
Small-flowered tamarisk (*Tamarix parviflora*)	Blooms on the previous season's wood, so, unlike other tamarisks, this one should be pruned immediately after flowering.
Blueberry (*Vaccinium*)	When grown as an ornamental, needs pruning to remove old wood and to shorten branches that are bending over. For fruit, thin the branches and cut back twig growth at the ends of the branches.
Weigela (*Weigela*)	Needs heavy pruning to get rid of deadwood and winter injury, which is often considerable.

Pruning Roses

If you were to ask anyone, young or old, to name the perfect flower, the answer would most likely be the rose. For centuries, in both legends and backyard gardens, the rose has been one of the world's most popular flowers. Modern horticultural science has developed roses in a wide range of colors, and there are varieties that bloom on bushes, vines, hedges, and even trees. The petals and hips are popular in teas, jellies, and numerous other culinary and aromatic concoctions. It's only right that the rose get special mention when it comes to pruning. Each of us wants our rosebushes to live up to their full, beautiful potential.

Pruning Roses at Planting Time

Roses are sold bare-root and potted. Don't prune back a potted rose; it's already established and growing. A bare-root one, on the other hand, may need a little attention, and because it is still dormant, you can cut safely.

MASTER GARDENING TIP

Planting a Rose

Remember that most roses are bud-grafted, and the big, burl-like spot just above the roots is the graft. In cold climates, plant so that the graft is just slightly below ground level; in milder areas, it should be an inch or two above.

1 Once you get your bare-root rose home, soak it in a bucket of water for a few hours or overnight to hydrate it.

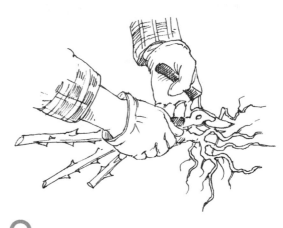

2 Check the root system, and trim off all damaged or dead growth.

3 If it is more than 8 inches high and has never been cut back or has been only partially cut back, cut your rose down to about 6 or 8 inches above the dark line that shows where the ground level was when it was dug. Be sure to cut to a live bud or branch each time so that you leave no dead stubs.

General Rose Maintenance

Most roses are thorny critters, and you'll appreciate a pair of heavy gloves when you're pruning and carrying away the clippings. Be especially careful to use sharp clippers, so that you don't crush the stems and cause cell damage. The kind of pruning you do, and when you do it, varies according to the classification of rose and your climatic conditions.

Although some polyanthas, floribundas, and hybrid tea roses are quite vigorous, others have been weakened by hybridization, and they need special care, especially the first year.

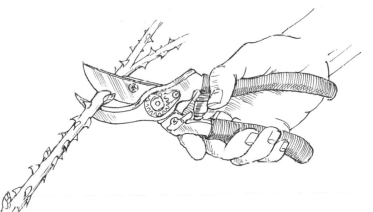

Always cut on a slant just above a bud or to a live branch, and retain enough leaves and stems to feed the plant. For cutting heavy branches, you may need a saw or loppers.

MASTER GARDENING TIPS

When to Prune Roses

▶ If you live in the South, you can safely prune roses in the fall or even during the winter, if temperatures don't drop below freezing that day.

▶ Cautious southern gardeners and those in colder parts of the country prune in early spring instead, just as the buds are beginning to swell. Hard frosts are usually over by this time, and the sap isn't yet flowing enough to cause a heavy loss from the cut ends.

MASTER GARDENING TIPS

Pruning Roses

▶ Hold off on cutting any blooms with long stems from hybrid teas during the first year. In future years, as soon as the plant has developed several strong, tall canes, moderate cutting of blooms will be perfectly safe.

▶ Cutting roses in full bloom, with long stems and some leaves, is actually summer pruning, so be sure that you don't scalp the plant.

▶ To grow a large exhibition flower, disbud: Pick off all the smaller buds along the stem, and leave only the large, fat bud at the top.

▶ Always snip off fading blooms, so that the plant will direct its energy into making buds for next year's show.

▶ Always cart away the clippings from the rose garden; they can become a breeding place for diseases and insects if left on the ground.

▶ You can prune heavily those roses that grow vigorously, but cut wood sparingly from the slower-growing, weaker kinds. Heavy pruning doesn't always stimulate a weak plant to grow faster. In fact, depriving it of necessary leaf area may make it lose vigor and produce fewer blooms.

Pruning a Hybrid Tea Rose

Hybrid teas are the most common roses in the United States. Hundreds of named varieties are offered in catalogs, garden centers, and supermarkets every spring. You can choose from recently introduced, patented varieties, or the old, reliable favorites such as 'Peace' and 'Mister Lincoln'. You must prune them each year to keep them blooming well. The flowers bloom on new shoots sprouting from canes that grew the previous year.

1 Thin out the old, weak, and winter-damaged canes and those that are crossed or too close together. If you prefer tall-growing roses, you may not want to shorten them at all except to make the drooping canes a bit stiffer. If short, bushy plants fit better into your garden scene, cut all the ends of the canes farther back.

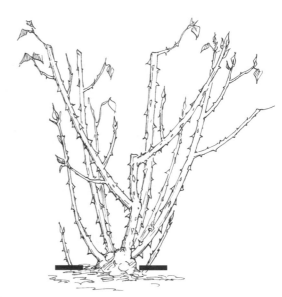

2 Remove all suckers originating from below the bud union. They detract from the bush's appearance and won't resemble the plant above the graft.

MASTER GARDENING TIP

Roses and Winter Damage

If you live in a cold-winter area (USDA Zone 6 and north), take steps in the fall to prevent winter damage. A few weeks before winter arrives, carefully lay tall canes down on the ground and cover the entire bush with several inches of soil, evergreen boughs, fiberglass insulation, or leaves. This should be done before the temperature drops below 15°F. Don't worry if all the leaves haven't yet fallen off.

In the spring you may find some winter injury in spite of the covering. By the time you have pruned it off, you may not have much bush left, so allow floppy branches on weak canes to stay — the bush will need all the leaf area it can get.

Other Rose Types

Floribundas resemble hybrid teas; however, they have several flowers in a cluster rather than one to a stem (so they are seldom disbudded), and they are generally shorter-growing plants. Prune them the same way as you would hybrid teas. When they are dormant, cut out nearly all the wood that is over one year old. Cut back slightly any younger wood and remove all weak branches.

Polyanthas produce clusters of small and medium-size blooms, and these, also, are seldom disbudded. The bush needs minimal pruning. Treat it much like a flowering shrub. The canes tend to stay small and may need some thinning out eventually. Remove any wood that no longer produces blooms.

3 Cut older main stems back to strong new shoots. Cut across the stems, not at an angle.

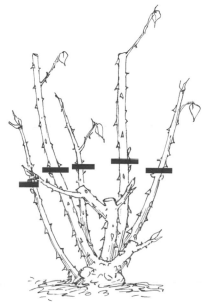

4 Cut back to five or so strong canes, each about 8 to 10 inches high. As spring arrives, the plant will burst into vigorous new growth, and it will regain its former height come summer.

Pruning Shrub and Species Roses

Modern shrub roses resemble old-fashioned roses and have a half-wild appearance. They can grow for years with no care at all, but they look their best with at least a little attention. They are usually allowed to grow tall for a hedge effect, but if you like shorter, heavier-blooming plants, you can cut back the bush to a foot from the ground early each spring before any growth starts.

Moss roses, sweetbriers, cabbage roses, and **rugosa roses** are all pruned in nearly the same way. All are quite vigorous, so if you don't prune them annually, cutting back heavily may be necessary to keep them in their place and to remove old, rotten wood.

Hedge roses need heavier pruning at planting time than do those grown as specimens in the garden. Set the plants 2 feet apart or slightly closer, and prune them to within 4 or 5 inches of the ground when you plant them. Each year, in late fall or early spring, cut back enough of each plant to produce a bushy, hedgelike effect. Then, during the summer when the bushes grow too tall or wide, snip back the ends to keep the hedge looking nice and even.

Multiflora roses are still planted as living fences in some areas; however, this type of hedge has many disadvantages. In addition to being very thorny, multifloras are wide, sprawling plants, which makes it difficult to get close enough to trim them, and it is nearly impossible to keep out the grass and weeds that spring up among them. In my opinion, the flowers are not attractive, and the birds scatter the seeds all over so that the plant sometimes becomes a pesky weed. If you decide to use them in spite of their drawbacks, prune as tightly as possible from their youngest days, and carefully restrain them in their rows.

MASTER GARDENING TIP

Rose Hips

Some shrub roses, especially rugosas, produce large numbers of red seedpods called hips. These are a rich source of vitamin C. Although it is better to cut off the fading blooms of most roses so that the bush won't produce energy-draining hips full of seeds, these roses are so vigorous that it doesn't harm them a bit if you let hips develop. Pick them off after a light frost, before they freeze hard and turn mushy.

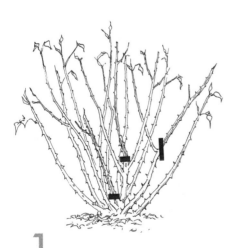

1 Remove dead canes and deadwood.

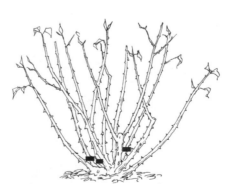

2 Thin remaining canes for better ventilation and form.

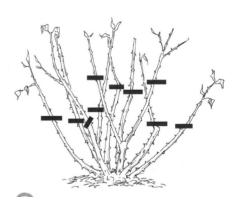

3 Cut back remaining healthy canes to various heights (between 1 and 3 feet) to keep the bush growing densely.

Pruning Climbers and Ramblers

Climbers differ from rambling roses in having a more upward habit of growth that better enables them to climb a trellis or pole. Many of the best hybrid tea roses are now available in climbing form. Their flowers are large, and they bloom for most of the summer, unlike the short blooming season of the ramblers. Climbing roses bloom mostly on wood that is two years old. Your plant should have a balance of current year's growth, year-old, and two-year-old wood.

    Ramblers usually are not grafted. All the new canes coming from the roots are part of the main plant, so you don't need to worry about wild suckers crowding out the good canes. They bloom best on year-old wood, so allow the shoots to grow freely the first year. Secure them to a fence or trellis the following year, and they will bloom. In the meantime, select three to five of the young shoots and allow them to grow for blooming the following year. In late fall, or the following spring if you live in the North, cut out all the canes that have previously produced blooms. Tie the new canes to the fence or trellis, and they will bloom that summer. Repeat this process every year.

1 Each year, cut out dead canes and canes that have bloomed recently, at ground level. If the remaining new, strong canes still seem to be too numerous, cut out a few of these also. Aim for three to five strong, husky canes to remain.

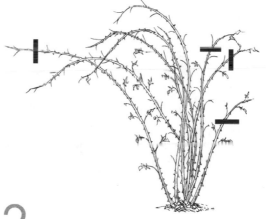

2 Prune off the top few inches of any nonbranching canes. Also, snip off any weak growth on the new canes.

3 Prune back branches that have flowered by one-third of their length, ending just above a healthy bud or shoot.

Pruning Tree Roses

Tree roses are usually hybrid tea, grandiflora, or floribunda roses that have been grafted or budded on top of a brier or rugosa rose rootstock that is 3 feet high or more. Although they have a beautiful, formal look, tree roses are much more difficult to grow and maintain than their bush counterparts, and often need staking. In the North, the whole plant must be bent over and buried during the winter in order to survive.

Remove all suckers growing on the main stem or from the roots as soon as they appear, or they will crowd out the grafted rose in a short time. Keep a close check to see that none of the wild rose suckers is growing among the regular rose branches. Although the foliage is similar, the wild invaders can be spotted by careful observation.

Lightly prune the top by thinning out any weak branches and cutting out old branches that are no longer blooming well. Cut back the rest to 5 to 10 inches from the graft. Do this in early spring before the green buds appear. In cold areas where the trees are buried for the winter, don't dig them up until all the hard frosts of 25°F or lower are over. Even though some sprouts may have already started, you should do any necessary pruning at that time. For shaping, you can snip during the growing season.

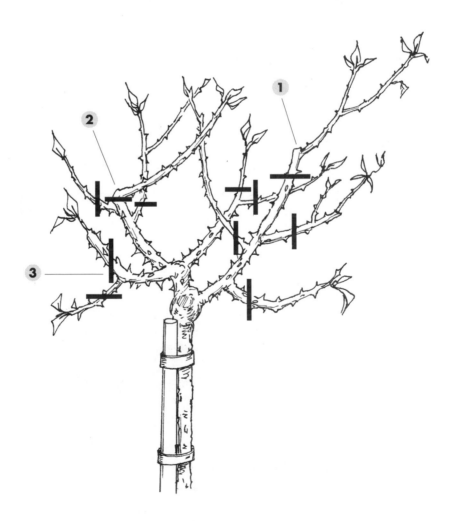

Keep the tree roses healthy and attractive by removing suckers; thinning out weak and/or old branches (**1**); removing crossing branches (**2**); and cutting back remaining branches to 5–10 inches from graft (**3**).

Choosing a Tree or Shrub

If you choose the right plant for the right place, you'll find that many flowering shrubs and trees don't need much pruning. Before you buy, consider your answers to the following questions.

Can it grow in my area? Although you naturally want to surround yourself with plants that you enjoy, it is equally important to choose the ones that are suited to your climate. Some plants are extremely hardy, but others do well only in places with long growing seasons and mild winters. The USDA Hardiness Zones are a helpful guideline.

Can it grow in the spot I have in mind?
Rhododendrons need an extremely acid soil, while lilacs prefer soil containing generous amounts of lime. A hemlock hedge might be ideal for a sheltered valley location, but don't subject it to cold, drying north winds in winter, or it will look beat up all summer.

Will it fit in the spot? Before you choose a plant, research its growth habits and ultimate size. For instance, many plants that would grace a large, old country home will be too large and coarse to complement a ranch house. And don't sign yourself up for years of constant pruning by planting something inappropriately big for the spot. If there's a plant you really must have — a blue ceanothus, for example — try to find a smaller-growing or dwarf variety of it, such as 'Joyce Coulter' or 'Skylark'.

Will it suit my lifestyle? If you don't like to putter in the garden, or if you are away for most of the summer, your plants should be the kind that need little pruning or other care. Likewise, if you garden only at a summer home you won't want plants that require winter pruning.

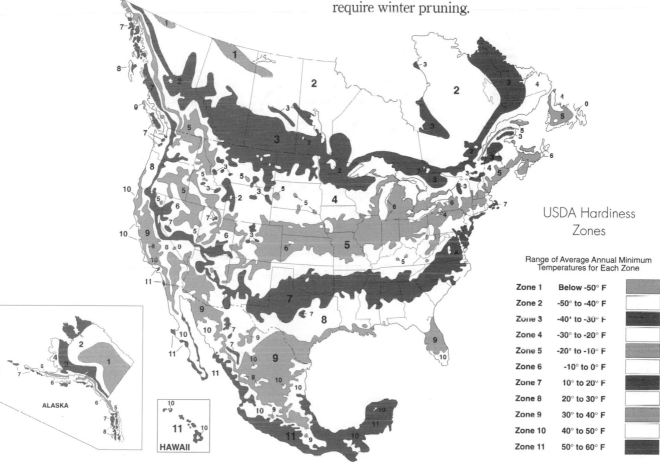

USDA Hardiness
Zones

Range of Average Annual Minimum
Temperatures for Each Zone

Zone 1	Below -50° F	
Zone 2	-50° to -40° F	
Zone 3	-40° to -30° F	
Zone 4	-30° to -20° F	
Zone 5	-20° to -10° F	
Zone 6	-10° to 0° F	
Zone 7	10° to 20° F	
Zone 8	20° to 30° F	
Zone 9	30° to 40° F	
Zone 10	40° to 50° F	
Zone 11	50° to 60° F	

A shade tree is a lifetime project, so choose a location where it can grow to its majestic stature without heavy pruning.

Shade Trees

Years ago, there were about a dozen large maple and elm trees growing around one of the older houses in our neighborhood. The family members could tell you during which year each one was planted, because each tree recalled a certain event.

This is Effie's tree, they would say, planted in 1887, the year she was born. One tree was Sarah's, and the other was George's, and so on. Trees commemorated when Grandma and Grandpa got married, and the year Grandpa died. One even marked the time that a younger son took over the farm. Long after the farm was sold, family members returned for picnics under their trees.

Trees are still used as living reminders. Each year our small nursery sells a large number of commemorative trees. Among the many uses I've heard about are for births and marriages, as tributes to admired teachers, to commemorate special events, as memorials for beloved friends or relatives who have died, and as gifts from a graduating class.

It isn't necessary to plant a tree as a memorial for you to establish a personal relationship with it. A large shade tree is especially solid, strong, and dignified. It is a place where youthful secrets can be shared in a tree house and where everyone can cool off on a hot summer day as a breeze rustles the leaves above. I know one delightful lady who likes to hug the huge trunks of shade trees! In short, trees are special, and like everything else we treasure, they deserve our care and protection.

The term *shade tree* usually connotes a deciduous tree, although evergreens can also be shade trees. Pruning evergreens will be covered in detail in the next chapter.

In This Chapter

- Basic Tree Shapes
- Choosing the Proper Tree
- Pruning at Planting Time
- Maintenance Pruning
- Basal Pruning
- Care of Mature Trees
- Tree Surgery
- Cavity Repair

Basic Tree Shapes

To avoid making major pruning mistakes when you're training a young tree, keep in mind what its mature shape would be naturally. As a rule, allow trees that grow in a pyramidal and columnar form to keep their lower branches. Spreading and ball-shaped trees look better and are more useful as shade trees if you remove their bottom branches. Trees with weeping habits, except possibly evergreens, need to be pruned enough so that the lower limbs do not flop on the ground. Light conditions and whether it has enough room to grow also affect a tree's mature form.

Columnar

Columnar maple (*Acer platanoides* 'Columnare')
Flowering crab (*Malus* x *robusta* 'Erecta')
Poplar (*Populus;* particularly upright is *P. nigra* 'Italica' — Lombardy poplar)
Pyramid arborvitae (*Thuja occidentalis* 'Pyramidalis')
Pyramid birch (*Betula pendula* 'Fastigiata')
Pyramid English oak (*Quercus robur* 'Fastigiata')
Pyramid hornbeam (*Carpinus betulus* 'Fastigiata')
Swiss stone pine (*Pinus cembra,* especially *P. cembra* 'Columnaris')
Upright beech (*Fagus sylvatica* 'Fastigiata')
Upright mountain ash (*Sorbus aucuparia* 'Fastigiata')
Upright Scotch pine (*Pinus sylvestris* 'Fastigiata')
Upright white pine (*Pinus strobus* 'Fastigiata')

columnar

Pyramidal

Alder *(Alnus)*
American arborvitae *(Thuja occidentalis)*
American holly *(Ilex opaca)*
Bald cypress *(Taxodium distichum)*
Black gum *(Nyssa sylvatica)*
Douglas fir *(Pseudotsuga menziesii)*
English holly *(Ilex aquifolium)*
Fir *(Abies)*
Larch *(Larix)*
Magnolia *(Magnolia)*
Pin oak *(Quercus palustris)*
Pyramid Austrian pine *(Pinus nigra* 'Pyramidalis')
Spruce *(Picea)*
True cedar *(Cedrus)*
Turkish filbert *(Corylus colurna)*
Upright yew *(Taxus cuspidata)*

pyramidal

Round

Ash *(Fraxinus)*
Japanese hemlock *(Tsuga diversifolia)*
Japanese maple *(Acer palmatum)*
Norway maple *(Acer platanoides)*
Sargent crab apple *(Malus sargentii)*
Saucer magnolia *(Magnolia* x *soulangiana)*
Umbrella catalpa *(Catalpa bignonioides* 'Nana')

round

Spreading

Balm-of-Gilead *(Populus* x *gileadensis)*
Basswood *(Tilia)*
Beech *(Fagus)*
Birch *(Betula)*
Cork tree *(Phellodendron amurense)*
Elm *(Ulmus)*
Honey locust *(Gleditsia)*
Maple *(Acer)*
Oak *(Quercus),* including live oak
Pine *(Pinus)*
Plane tree *(Platanus)*

spreading

Weeping

Beech *(Fagus sylvatica* 'Pendula')
Canada hemlock *(Tsuga canadensis* 'Pendula')
European white birch *(Betula pendula)*
Larch *(Larix decidua* 'Pendula')
Mountain ash *(Sorbus aucuparia)*
Norway spruce *(Picea abies* 'Pendula')
Peach *(Prunus persica)*
Weeping willow *(Salix babylonica)*
White pine *(Pinus strobus* 'Pendula')

weeping

MASTER GARDENING TIP

What's in a Name

Most catalogs list the botanical and horticultural names of a plant as well as its common name. Many of these describe the growth habit. When you see 'Fastigiata', 'Columnare', or 'Erecta', you can be sure the tree will take on an erect, upright form. 'Pyramidalis' indicates a cone shape. 'Globosa', like globe, naturally indicates a round shape. 'Nana' means dwarf, and 'Pendula' refers to a hanging or weeping growth habit.

Choosing the Proper Tree

It is important to choose a type of tree you like and one that is suitable for its location. For example, many small-growing trees are fine for tiny lots, whereas a large-growing tulip tree or an enormous balm-of-Gilead needs a more spacious area. Pick varieties that grow well in your climate and do not require more time than you have to give them.

The shade trees in the chart on the following pages succeed in many locations and are widely planted across the country. There are also hundreds of others that are popular in more limited areas. Often there are many varieties within a species, so your choice is wide and almost endless. Prune according to the rules for all shade trees, unless exceptions are noted.

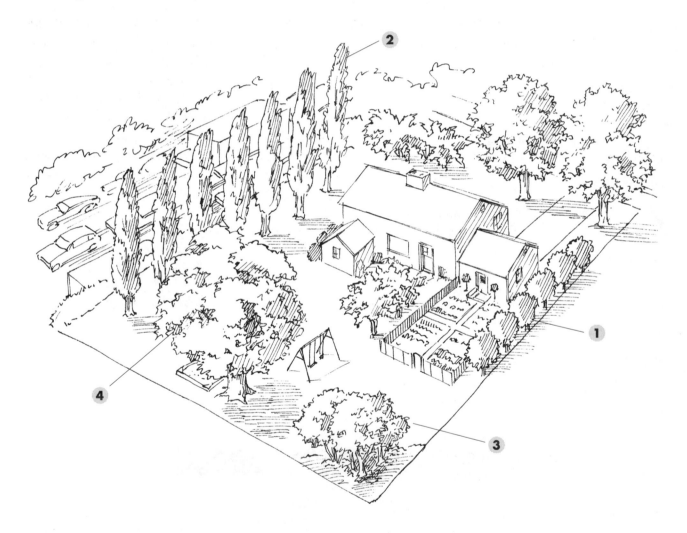

Don't take the term *shade tree* too literally. It also embraces trees like the Lombardy poplar that offer little in the way of shade. Shade trees can define borders (**1**), shield houses from noisy highways (**2**), provide a protected living or playing area (**3**), and offer autumn color (**4**), among many other practical and aesthetic purposes.

Since large trees are the kings and queens of the landscape, you should plan their locations with care. The rest of your garden, and your home and other buildings on your property, should relate to them as well.

Tree	Description	Pruning Needs
Ash (*Fraxinus*)	Of the numerous kinds of ash, green ash is one of the most popular. Attractive and tall, it makes a good street tree that needs little care. Leaves are fernlike. The tree produces an abundance of keys (seeds) similar to those of maples. It is inclined to leaf out late in the spring and drop its foliage early, showing very little fall color.	Prune the lower limbs to force the growth upward and to enhance the natural upright growth of the ash family. Other pruning is minimal.
Beech (*Fagus*)	The smooth, gray bark of the American beech and the interesting foliage of the European beech make both of these trees valuable in a landscape planting.	The American variety should be basal-pruned to show off its attractive bark in the winter landscape. Beech limbs are heavy, so it's best to train the tree early to grow with a central leader. However, eventually some limbs will probably grow into crotches.
Birch (*Betula*)	Although there are birches with white, yellow, or gray bark, the paper white (canoe) birch is most people's favorite. Birch leaves are small, so grass and flowers can grow well in the dappled shade below. The leaves of some varieties are attacked by leaf miners, and as they grow older these trees become unsightly unless you spray them often. Birch trees are attractive grown in clumps or groupings.	In addition to early training, prune them to show off the white-barked ones to their best advantage. Do this in late summer or early fall to avoid bleeding. Never pull the papery bark from the tree, because this will permanently disfigure the trunk.
Cork tree (*Phellodendron amurense*)	The cork gives a filtered-shade effect. It has a broad, spreading top, beautiful foliage, and attractive bark, and grows well in city conditions. Few insects and diseases bother it. Since it is not a tall tree, it should be allowed to branch close to the ground. The wide-spreading branches and furrowed bark add to its charm.	Needs pruning only to maintain a straight central leader.
Ginkgo (*Ginkgo biloba*)	A good street tree because of its resistance to disease, insects, and pollution. Grows tall and reaches well above wires and streetlights. Individual trees produce either male or female flowers. If they can be identified, plant only male trees, because the female blooms produce fruits with a strong, unpleasant smell. Ginkgo becomes more attractive as it matures.	Basal pruning can help emphasize this tree's height, but otherwise prune as little as possible.

Tree	Description	Pruning Needs
Honey locust (*Gleditsia triacanthos*)	Provides only light shade, so grass grows well beneath it. Only minor leaf accumulation in the fall. Some of the newer varieties add color and don't produce the messy pods formed by the older types.	High basal pruning makes the honey locust a good substitute for the American elm. Prune in late summer to correct the bad crotches that tend to develop. Keep this tree growing to a central leader for as long as possible.
Hornbeam (*Carpinus*)	There are several kinds of this long-lived tree, including the European, American, and Japanese. All are small-to-medium, bushy trees with attractive foliage. They are difficult to transplant, grow very slowly, and are sometimes clumpy.	Prune them only to keep them in a tree form, leaving their rugged, natural appearance undisturbed for as long as possible.
Horse chestnut (*Aesculus*)	Horse chestnuts and buckeyes have long been planted as street trees, although I feel there are certainly many better choices. The trees eventually grow too large for most street plantings and city lots, plus they are dirty trees: Throughout the year they drop flowers, inedible nuts, leaves, and twigs. As if these drawbacks weren't enough, they are also quite susceptible to disease.	Prune off lower limbs as trees grow. Later, remove any unsightly or dangerous limbs.
Linden, basswood (*Tilia*)	Some of the numerous varieties of this family are suited for one part of the country, and some for another. They are tall trees with beautiful foliage and bark, and they produce fragrant flowers that are especially attractive to bees. Some have large leaves.	Do high basal pruning to emphasize the tall growth and distinctive bark as they grow to their majestic size.
Maple (*Acer*)	Many varieties of this beautiful tree. Maples branch well, and produce an abundance of large, heavy leaves that have excellent fall color. They are also excellent shade trees. Sizes range from the small-leaved and dwarf-growing maples, such as the Japanese varieties, to the giant sugar maple and red maple, trees that may grow more than 100 feet tall. Norway maple: A nice tree for planting along streets, and varieties of it have been introduced with red and variegated foliage. Silver maple: Grows fast, but it requires considerable pruning. Its shallow roots sometimes present a problem in lawns and under sidewalks.	Prune all maples in late summer; they bleed badly if pruned in late winter or spring.

Tree	Description	Pruning Needs
Oak (Quercus)	Members of this large family of majestic trees typically grow more slowly than the maples, but like them, oaks are best suited only to larger properties because of their size. In certain areas they are somewhat susceptible to disease and insect damage, but live for decades nevertheless. They have excellent, long-lasting fall foliage.	Pruning should be limited to removing dead, diseased, and broken wood, and to training when young.
Plane tree, sycamore (Platanus)	Huge, spreading tree with large, maplelike leaves. Good street tree.	Both trees need careful basal pruning when they are young in order to develop a strong central leader. Large limbs are likely to develop, but since the trees are such strong growers, this creates no problem.
Poplar (Populus)	As most of the poplars are shortlived, they are useful wherever you need temporary, fast-growing trees. The most commonly planted is the tall, slim Lombardy. The large-leaved balm-of-Gilead is probably the largest and longest lived of them all.	Prune poplars in late summer.
Tulip tree (Liriodendron tulipifera)	A huge tree that needs lot of room, the attractive tulip tree has large flowers hidden among its leaves each spring, and sports golden fall color. It is also disease resistant, which makes it an ideal shade tree wherever room and climate permit.	Pruning is seldom necessary, and you'll see that it naturally develops a strong, straight main trunk.
Weeping willow (Salix babylonica)	This widely planted tree has little besides its graceful beauty to recommend it. The wood is very brittle and breaks easily, and the leaves are small. It's susceptible to insects and disease, and is short lived. It grows very fast, however, and leafs out early in spring. Some varieties are suitable for planting only on wet ground, and others do well only in dry areas.	Both pruning and staking are necessary early in the tree's life. This is to prevent it from weeping when it is too young, which would cause it to become a misshapen bush instead of a graceful tree. Later, constant pruning is necessary to prevent the long branches from dragging on the ground and becoming a nuisance. Remove deadwood as soon as you discover it, but avoid overpruning whenever possible, or you will stimulate too much regrowth. Prune in late summer, since weeping willows bleed badly if pruned in late winter or spring.

Pruning at Planting Time

When you buy a plant, its roots may have been dug with a tight ball of earth and wrapped in burlap or plastic, it may be growing in a pot of soil, or the bare roots may be surrounded only with moist moss. Each kind of packaging requires different care at planting time.

Balled-and-burlapped: If your new tree comes with its roots enclosed in a large ball of soil, you probably don't need to prune at planting time. Just be careful not to damage the root ball as you maneuver it.

Container-grown: The roots of some trees that have been growing for several years in a large container before being sold develop circularly. If this pattern continues after the tree is planted, the increasing size of the encircling roots can actually strangle the tree in later years. Check the outside roots to see if this strangulation is occurring. If it is, prune off or spread out the offending root. Then, plant the tree in a good mixture of soil and compost to encourage quick growth of new, outward-reaching roots.

Bare-root: If you purchase a small bare-root tree, or dig one up in a friend's yard or in the wild and transplant it, you should prune when you plant. If a lot of root damage was inflicted when it was dug up, severe pruning may be necessary. Remember to make your cuts on a slant, just above a bud, and cut to an outside bud on the side branches.

Pruning Bare-Root Trees

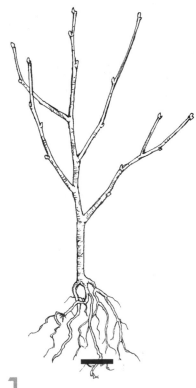

1 Prune any broken roots with a smooth cut.

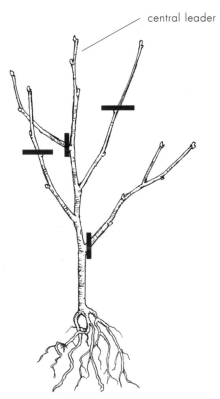

central leader

2 Prune branches as shown, leaving a central leader.

Maintenance Pruning

If your tree grows well, additional pruning may not be needed for many years. However, there are times when you should intervene. Remember the old saying that an ounce of prevention is worth a pound of cure.

Problem (1): Crossed branches develop or the top begins to grow crooked.
Solution: Do some snipping and pinching during the growing season. Wait until the dormant season to do any heavier pruning.

Problem (2): Abundant sucker growth appears from the base of the tree.
Solution: Use a saw or loppers to cut off the suckers and any weak lower limbs, close to the trunk, in late summer. Do not cut in spring, or the tree may bleed sap excessively.

Problem (3): Weak crotches collect dirt and water. The wood eventually begins to rot, and the rot will spread to the rest of the tree.
Solution: Cut out as much rotten wood as possible, back to healthy wood. Fill cavities as described on page 77. To prevent this problem from occurring in the first place, or if the plant is still young, you should have good luck encouraging the trunk to grow straight, with a strong central leader, by tying it at intervals to a tall stake.

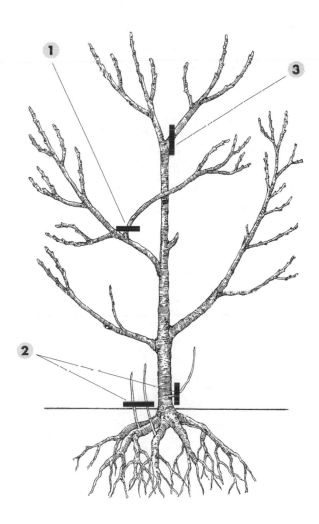

Basal Pruning

- **What is basal pruning?** It's the ideal way to shape a shade tree. Just clip off all limbs that start too close to the ground as soon as they appear, thereby directing more of the tree's growth upward.

- **When do I begin?** Start when a tree is 12 to 16 feet tall. Don't procrastinate. Not only is it easier to cut off the bottom limbs of the tree when they are still small, but you also leave smaller pruning wounds to heal over.

- **What if I start too late?** If you neglect to do this early shaping, and large limbs are growing too low on your young tree, be sure that it has developed a good top before you cut off any of the bottom branches. Never cut off more than a quarter to a third of a tree's branch area, because a certain amount of leaf area is always necessary to feed it. If several good-size limbs must be cut off, spread out the project over several years by cutting off only one or two each fall. By not being too hasty, you will allow the tree time to grow additional leaf area at the top to compensate for the loss of basal limbs, and you'll avoid shocking the tree.

- **How do I identify basal limbs?** Basal limbs tend to grow upright on most trees when they are young, so it often seems unnecessary to cut them off. However, as the tree grows larger and wider, these limbs spread outward and downward. Unless you remove them, they will become a nuisance by the time the tree is 15 or 20 years old.

- **How high should I basal-prune?** A few seasons of noting how the sun enters your house at different times of the year will help you to ascertain what that height should be. A distance of 8 feet from the ground to the first branches is the bare minimum for most lawn trees. Basal-prune street trees from 12 to 15 feet high, so they won't interfere with traffic.

MASTER GARDENING TIP

The Benefits of Basal Pruning

If your tree is growing as part of a screen you probably won't basal-prune, but if it is to grow into a large specimen tree — one you'll be able to picnic, play, and mow under easily when it is fully grown — you must do this. Basal pruning not only makes a tree look more treelike, but it also lets in additional light and air to make your lawn, flowers, and other plants grow better. And your house will be more comfortable and energy efficient year-round. Large deciduous trees are nature's air conditioners. They provide cooling shade in summer, and after their leaves have fallen in autumn, they allow sunlight through to warm your house when you need it most.

summer sun

winter sun

One of the benefits of basal pruning is that it opens up more light under a tree. If the tree is growing near your house, you'll then enjoy more light. Perennials or annuals will also thrive beneath its canopy.

Care of Mature Trees

Even if you gave your trees the best training and pruning care when they were young, they will probably continue to need pruning even after they've matured. Weather, disease, and insects will take their toll, no matter how carefully you planned a tree's location or performed its initial shaping. Or you may acquire a full-grown tree, having had no choice about its early training or location.

The Benefits of Fertilizing

In addition to pruning, proper tree care includes regular feeding with a good organic fertilizer containing nitrogen. This is a particularly wise practice for trees that are struggling. Trees deteriorate ahead of their time for many reasons: Roadway paving limits their growing area; erosion washes away the good topsoil from their roots; road salt washes onto the root system; their roots are near or grow into a drainage area from a septic field; air pollution; their bark is damaged by a lawn mower or string trimmer; the plant is damaged by animals, insects, or disease. Additional fertilizer can help compensate for some of these abuses and give a tree a new lease on life.

Removing Large Branches

Remove large limbs in sections, rather than all at once, to avoid having too much weight drop at one time.

Although opinions differ, I feel it is beneficial to paint these large cuts to seal out the weather and facilitate healing.

MASTER GARDENING TIP

Is My Tree Worth Saving?

If you own a tree that has become decrepit, or if you have acquired a sad specimen along with your new property, you should first consider if it is worth saving. Life span varies greatly according to species. Some of the giant redwoods are estimated to be 3,000 or 4,000 years old, and trees of many other species in this country are older than the Republic. However, some members of the poplar family, for example, are over the hill by the time they have reached the age of 30.

This mature cherry tree has a black-knot-infested limb that must be removed. It's important to cut carefully, so that you will do as little damage as possible to the tree and the surrounding plants and structures.

Tie a rope around a limb before cutting it, make large cuts as directed on page 30, and then ease it gently to the ground.

Tree Surgery

Natural and man-created environmental hazards may shorten a tree's life considerably. If it is near the end of its days, the best tree surgery in the world won't add many months to its life, and you'd be better off cutting it into firewood and replacing it with a young, healthy specimen.

However, a tree that looks bad is not always ready to die, and taking down an old tree is a difficult and often expensive operation, especially if buildings, streets, or power lines are nearby. A tree that is only a little battered can benefit greatly from some surgical care.

Tree surgery involves the removal of major parts of a tree and the healing of bad wounds. It is a specialized job that usually requires extensive training and equipment. Even so, you can perform minor tree surgery by yourself and save a considerable amount of money.

MASTER GARDENING TIPS

A Tune-Up

▶ If you use a chain saw, be extremely careful not to cut into any healthy limbs accidentally, including your own.

▶ Cut out all dead- or rotten wood, as well as any wood that has been damaged by woodpeckers, ants, or other creatures.

▶ Saw off smoothly, to the nearest live juncture, any limbs that are broken or partially broken.

▶ Seal all the cuts with a good tree paint or dressing.

Bracing. Use this technique to secure a heavy, weak limb or one that is beginning to split.

1. Drill holes through trunk and limb.

2. Join them with a strong, threaded bolt and nut, with large washers at each end, to prevent damage to the tree. Alternatively, attach a cable to bolts through both limbs. Sometimes a large chain or wire rope is wrapped around both limbs to prevent splitting, but this could cut into the bark of the tree and make ugly wounds, so I don't recommend this method.

Cavity Repair

Trees of any age may develop openings or cavities as a result of a wound. If the opening is not covered, it can develop into a canker or accumulate dirt and grime and begin to rot. That rot will gradually spread to the rest of the tree, making it a place where insects and disease proliferate.

1 Clean out the cavity carefully. Remove all dirt, old bark, insects, and rotten wood right down to solid wood, much as a dentist cleans out a tooth prior to filling it. If possible, flush out the area with clean water.

2 Smooth out the rough edges with a heavy-grit file.

3 Fill the hole with a good tree-cavity sealer. Asphalt compounds, such as those used in patching driveways and roofs, are suitable, but avoid any compound containing creosote, since it is poisonous to trees. The commercial tree sealers made by Treekote are good because they usually include an antiseptic that discourages reinfection of wounds.

Check back now and then to make sure that the filler hasn't slipped out during hot weather or shrunk and ceased to fill the opening. Add more material whenever necessary so that new wood can eventually grow neatly over the filled cavity.

By intensive shearing, you can keep a tall-growing species of evergreen small practically forever. We have a white spruce in our backyard that is more than 50 years old. If we had allowed it to grow, it would probably now be over 50 feet tall. But I've sheared it to stay 3 feet tall and can keep it that size for another 50 years if I tend to business.

Pruning Evergreens

When I first became interested in home landscaping many years ago, I was impressed by the hundreds of beautiful, bushy balsam firs and white spruces that dotted the pastures of many northern New England dairy farms. These evergreens were obviously quite old, but the cows had kept them trimmed to a neat, compact size, and many looked strikingly better than the conifers that graced the manicured lawns in town.

Since they were free, I moved a few from our cow pasture to our front yard. I watered them often and sheared them carefully, but they soon grew out of shape, got too big, and lost their beauty.

So I began to watch more closely as our hungry herd of Holsteins did their shearing. Obviously they were doing something right! I noticed that they began eating the pale green, soft new growth as soon as it appeared in the spring, and that they always chewed the trees on dewy mornings or during a rain. As soon as the short growing season was over, the cows stopped snacking on the evergreens and went on to other fodder, which allowed the cut ends to heal rapidly.

As soon as I began to imitate the shearing techniques of our bovine botanists, my landscaping efforts began to improve. In fact, it wasn't long before one of the town's best gardeners stopped by to ask what my pruning secret was, and where I had learned it.

When you prune correctly, it is possible to keep an evergreen at a certain size, or allow it to grow so slowly that it hardly seems to be growing at all. In fact, it will look as if it grew that way naturally.

In This Chapter

What Is an Evergreen?

Trees and shrubs in general are usually divided into the deciduous and evergreen categories. Deciduous trees lose their foliage during the winter, while evergreens keep theirs year-round. Although we tend to think that all evergreens are conifers, a few members of this large family do not bear cones. Yews and junipers, for example, produce berries instead. To add to the confusion, some conifers are not evergreens. Larch (tamarack) and taxodium both look like they belong in the evergreen family, but they shed their needles every winter. There are also a considerable number of shrubs that are deciduous in the North yet evergreen in the South.

MASTER GARDENING TIPS

Evergreen Varieties

▶ *Needled evergreens* (or, more correctly, narrow-leaved evergreens) include fir, hemlock, juniper, pine, spruce, yew, cedar, and arborvitae.

▶ *Broadleaf evergreens* include azalea, boxwood, camellia, holly, laurel, pieris, and rhododendron.

Evergreens come with a wide variety of foliage and seeds, and some — such as the broadleafs — produce attractive blossoms and fruits. Some pines, such as the sugar pine, produce large (20 inches) cones; others, such as the hemlocks, tiny ones.

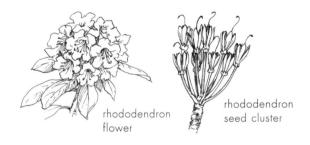

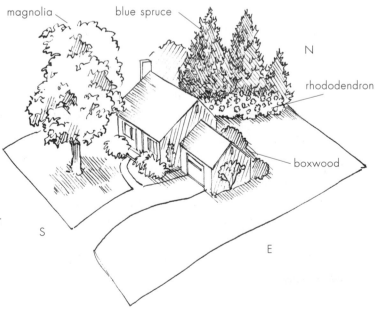

Evergreens offer a home landscape many advantages. Here, someone wisely situated large blue spruces to the northwest, where they block cold winter winds; rhododendrons and the more tender boxwood can grow in their shelter. On the south side of the house, summer shade is provided by a magnolia.

Needled Evergreens

Many people think that trees grow just as children do — all year-round and without a pause. Unless you've observed them carefully, you may not have noticed that needled evergreens have a briefer, faster growing season than do deciduous trees and shrubs, which grow throughout most of the summer. For most needled evergreens, new growth occurs for only about three weeks, although some, such as hemlocks and junipers, have a longer season, and yews make a small additional growth in late summer where the climate permits.

You need to watch for this fleeting period, because it is the ideal time to shear your evergreens. Pines, most spruces, firs, and yews begin to grow about the time that freezing nights are over and the ground is warming up (this may vary from April or even earlier in the South to mid-June in the colder sections of the country). Arborvitae, cypress, hemlock, and juniper start their growth a little later.

HINT FOR SUCCESS

Your shearing, even when the tree is tiny, should conform to the shape you want it to be when it finally reaches the desired height. It is difficult to change the shape of a tree once it is well established. If you allow it to grow too wide at the base, for instance, it will be very difficult to decrease the width later on without spoiling the appearance of the tree.

Fortunately, because evergreens have a built-in dormancy that is well adjusted to their locality, they seldom start to sprout much ahead of schedule each season. Even during an unusually early warm spell in winter, they are likely to wait until the proper time to start growing.

Terminal buds (1) are the fat, brown buds that were formed the preceding year. You can spot them at the end of each twig from midsummer to the next spring. Cutting the ends of this new growth will create a denser appearance.

Dormant buds (2) are the thousands of nearly invisible smaller buds that develop on an evergreen's twigs and branches. Ordinarily they do not grow, but shearing at the proper time stops the active growth of the terminal buds and stimulates the sprouting and growth of many of the dormant buds.

MASTER GARDENING TIPS

Shearing Tools

▶ **Long-handled hedge shears** are the best tools for shearing, because they're easy to control and safe to use.

▶ **Thin-bladed shearing knives** are good for fast work and are widely used in Christmas-tree plantations, but are not well suited to the precision work required in home landscaping, and can be dangerous, too.

▶ **Electric clippers** can be a big help when you're doing a lot of shearing that must be completed early in the growing season, because they are so much faster than hand shears. We've found them especially good for shearing hedges.

▶ **Fingers.** If you have only a few small evergreens, you can give them a light pruning by simply pinching off the ends of the soft, new growth with your fingers. This pinching is especially effective on the stiff, upright candles of dwarf pines.

Shearing Basics

When you shear off new growth, the tree's energy, which normally could cause a few limbs to make active growth upward and outward, is redirected into the numerous smaller twigs. The result? You force the plant to grow bushier.

Whether you shear more than once a season depends on the amount your evergreens grow that year and on the size and shape you want them to be. Shearing only once gives a more natural look, since the new growth is uneven. Many gardeners prefer this unshorn appearance, although eventually the tree may grow too large. Two or three shearings may be necessary if you want to confine it to the tightest, neatest, most compact form.

If you prefer not to shear severely, you can shear lightly and let your tree gradually increase in size throughout its life. However, the advantage of severe pruning is that the plant can be kept small for a lifetime, getting thicker and more beautiful all the time. In fact, the branches will become so dense that you can even lay your ladder against the strong, thick branches of a larger tree while you prune its top.

The Four Principles of Prudent Shearing

1. For best results, start small. I often hear people say, "When that tree gets to the height I want it, I'm going to start shearing it." This is a mistake. It is difficult, if not impossible, to get a tall, loose-growing tree to tighten up and look nice if you start shearing too late in its life.

2. Never take off more than a third of an evergreen's total green material. If you are planning to top, basal-prune, or cut greens for Christmas, bear in mind that removing more than this is likely to cause severe shock.

3. Shear every year. It is important that shearing be an annual event, because if you miss even one year's clipping, it is difficult to get some trees back into shape. (So don't take a vacation during the brief evergreen-growing season!)

4. Shear when the new growth is wet, early in the morning or after a rain.

MASTER GARDENING TIPS

Advantages of Shearing in Early Spring

▶ The small interior buds will start growing at once.

▶ The cuts you make on the new growth will heal quickly.

▶ New buds will form where the cut was made and completely hide any shearing wounds. The tree will look for all the world as if growing that way was its own idea.

Results of Cutting Too Late

▶ If you wait till later in the season, the small buds you hoped to stimulate will remain dormant.

▶ You'll cut off the newly formed buds, and unsightly cut stubs will show all year.

How to Shear

A good shearing takes only a few minutes per plant — time well spent. Look over your plantings every day or two when they are making their most active growth. By observing the beautiful, soft, light green growth, you'll not only keep abreast of how they're doing, but I've a hunch that the plants will respond to your presence, too, and thrive because of it.

Think of shearing as giving the tree a haircut. Cut off the ends of all the branches on the outside of the tree, much as you would shear a sheep or a dog. Each type of evergreen makes a different growth: New growth on hemlocks tends to be droopy; that on spruce or fir is stiff.

MASTER GARDENING TIP

When to Shear

Begin soon after growth starts in the spring, while the new sprouts are still short.

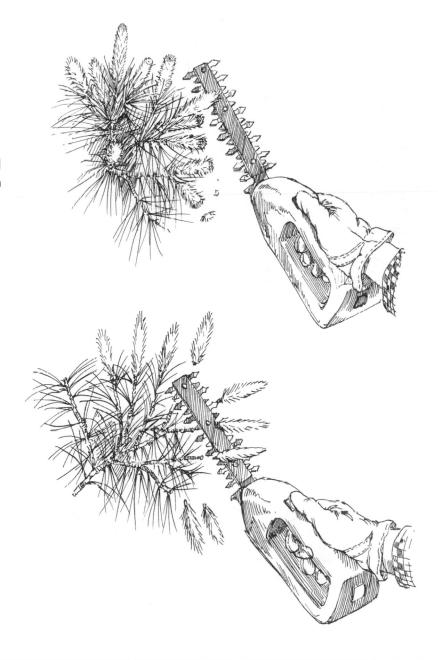

When pines are growing, they send out numerous little upright shoots called candles. If you want the tree to grow a little, wait until the candles are 2 to 4 inches long, and then pinch or clip off only the very tips.

If the tree is large enough, let the candles grow to about an inch, then shear them off completely. To maintain a compact appearance on a red, white, or Scotch pine, trim the candles on the plant's top and sides.

Shearing Specimen Evergreens

Chances are good that the beautiful, tight blue spruce you admire in your neighbor's yard was sheared last spring and several springs before that, as were the bushy hemlock in the public garden and the globe arborvitae on the church lawn. Specimen trees attain a special beauty through proper shearing. It is important that you not only choose the right kind of tree, but also shape it to complement its natural growth habit once it is established.

Ordinarily an evergreen grows about a foot each year. By shearing annually, you can shorten this growth to no more than a few inches per year, which appreciably lengthens the time you can enjoy your tree before it gets too big and has to be replaced. Or you could also, by intensive shearing, stop growth at any stage.

Well-sheared, tight-growing trees make a favorite nesting place for birds, as they like the protection of the dense branches for raising their young. More than once we've had to refuse to sell a tree that a mother robin had claimed for her nursery, and occasionally we've been thrilled to find a nest among the boughs of our Christmas tree; according to tradition, this is an omen of good luck for the next 12 months.

MASTER GARDENING TIPS

What Kind of Evergreen Is Best for Shearing?

▶ *Pines* are not ordinarily a good choice for specimen trees, because they grow too fast and tend to lose their lower branches. They really look best when allowed to grow into magnificent, full-size trees.

▶ *Firs* also lose their lower branches after a few years, although they make attractive temporary plantings.

▶ *Arborvitae, hemlock,* and *spruce* trees make medium-size, stately specimens that will last a long time. They hold their branches to the ground very well, especially if you shear them regularly.

Note: Hemlock and American arborvitae grow as cone-shaped, narrow pyramids and look best when they are sheared to this form. Spruces tend to develop a cone shape, too, but are a bit more spreading at the base.

Prune to the natural shape of the tree, if possible. A tall-growing hemlock is best pruned to a pyramid shape; a globe arborvitae to its natural round shape.

A Shearing Timetable

When you buy a young tree for a specimen, choose one that is bushy and well shaped so that you get your project off to a good start. Here's what to do when you get home.

1. Planting day: If the tree is thin and ill shaped, prune it severely at planting time to get it into a more compact shape. Otherwise, clip off only the newest, light green growth.

2. A week after the first shearing: Give the tree another light clipping if it is growing out of shape or to remove any extra tops.

3. The first few seasons: Allow your tree to grow a little each year in its early life. One or two shearings each growing season are enough, unless you are trying to achieve a highly formal look.

4. After the tree has reached the desired size: Severe shearing will probably be necessary to keep it from getting any larger, and several shearings may be necessary during the growing weeks. Although these will in no way hurt the tree, it's better to do several light clippings than to take off too much at once.

MASTER GARDENING TIPS

Shearing Guidelines

▶ *Keep the top of each tree sheared to a point* (or at least rounded off). Not only does this shaping make a natural-looking tree, but also a pointed tree is less likely than a flat-topped one to be damaged by ice storms or crushed by heavy loads of snow.

▶ *Don't let the upper branches get any wider than the bottom ones.* All parts of evergreen trees need sunlight, and shaded twigs will die.

▶ *Shear needled evergreens when they are wet,* if possible, just as cattle do. An ideal time is after a rain or when the trees are covered with early-morning dew. This way, the sheared ends will not turn pinky brown right after they are cut. (Don't worry if you can't, however. The browning is only a temporary discoloration, and will soon disappear. Only the evergreens with needles seem to have this browning problem, so wet shearing isn't necessary with cedars, cypress, junipers, arborvitae, or the broadleaf evergreens.)

▶ *Work when you're angry!* If you go into the yard singing or whistling, you won't cut off enough. The secret of good shearing is to snarl as you slash, at least until you get the hang of it.

Shearing Dwarf Evergreens

With the popularity of the one-story ranch house and the necessity for small lots in crowded areas, there is an increasing demand for small landscape plants. Many species grow short and shrubby naturally, like the spreading yew, some mugho pines, and trailing juniper. Other dwarf evergreens are freaks of nature — that is, runts that failed to grow into large trees. A dwarf tree can be propagated by grafting and by cuttings, and many new varieties of conifers have been introduced by these methods. There are now named varieties of dwarf white pine, dwarf Scotch pine, dwarf Norway spruce, dwarf balsam fir, and so on. These undersize trees are so popular that horticulturists tramp though woods and pastures looking for even more interesting mutations of nature to propagate.

In addition to the natural dwarf evergreens and the freaks of nature, there is another source of small evergreens. A whole industry is at work crossing the various dwarf plants now in existence, thereby creating even more varieties. And botanists are busy trying to classify and name all of these diminutive evergreens.

Although miniatures range from rock garden–type trees that grow only a few inches high to varieties that may grow several feet tall, most of them still need some shearing. Nearly all need to be clipped around the sides occasionally if they are to retain their compact shape. A spreading yew that is 2 feet tall and 10 feet across may be an interesting sight on an open hillside, but it will look out of place beside the front steps. Light cutting is best. Shear a plant only enough to keep it within bounds and looking good. Refer to the chart below for advice about specific plants.

SHEARING DWARF EVERGREENS	
Evergreen	**Pruning Advice**
Creeping junipers	Snip outer ends only and remove dead branches.
Scotch pine (*Pinus sylvestris* 'Fastigiata')	Allow to grow to its natural tall, skinny shape, usually without any pruning.
Weeping pines and hemlocks	Permit to droop.
Spreading, creeping, or globe evergreens	Clip according to the natural growth habit. Shear only when an evergreen starts to get out of shape or out of bounds, and only during its active growing season, so that the cut ends will heal over quickly.

Creating a Dwarf Evergreen

If you want to grow dwarf evergreens, it is much better to buy and plant true dwarfs than to continually shear taller-growing specimens. Not only do these look more natural, but they're also easier to care for, and there's less danger that they will outgrow the spot you've given them.

If you live in the country, however, you might like to experiment and create your own dwarf evergreens. Native wild trees have the advantage of being both dependably hardy and free. If you're careful to shear them severely each year, wild trees personally dwarfed by you can make excellent low-cost landscaping.

If you want to keep a spruce, fir, pine, hemlock, or arborvitae to a height of 1 or 2 feet for a lifetime, simply follow the instructions for shearing specimen trees. Instead of one or two light shearings each year, however, you will probably need to give the tree even more — sometimes four or five passes. This translates to giving the tree a tight clipping every four or five days during the growing season. Your shearing must be especially severe once the tree reaches the desired height, so that it will never get any larger. Root pruning every few years is another way to slow down the top growth and make shearing easier and more effective (see page 35).

When a plant exceeds its allotted space — like this juniper, which has wandered into the sidewalk area — you will have to prune it back. Just do it at the time that will cause the least trauma to the plant: early spring.

Shearing Windbreaks and Screens

Spruces, arborvitae, and hemlocks make ideal screens or windbreaks because they grow slowly and tightly and hold their lower branches to the ground, even late in life. Pines and firs grow faster, but because they tend to lose their bottom limbs eventually, they are less desirable for this purpose.

Clip the tops and sides each year for the first two or three years. This will help the plants grow in a tight pattern and close to the ground.

Keep the sides sheared so the width will be manageable. Make sure that the top part of each tree is never wider than the lower, because bottom branches need all the light they can get.

MASTER GARDENING TIP

Can Older Evergreens Be Rejuvenated?

People often ask me if they can renew an evergreen tree or hedge that has grown too large and out of shape by cutting it back nearly to the ground. Although you can do this to a lilac bush with good results, it will not work with an old and tired evergreen; you will have to replace it. Evergreens cannot tolerate having more than a third of their bulk removed in any one season. (Yews are an exception: You can cut back even an older plant heavily and it will recover and begin to grow again.)

Pruning Needled Evergreens

Although evergreens are more likely to be sheared than pruned, there are times when woody limbs need to be removed — when one dies, for instance, is diseased, or becomes damaged in a storm. Sometimes basal branches or even the entire top may have to be removed, again due to storm damage or disease.

Always cut a damaged branch back to a crotch.

MASTER GARDENING TIPS

When to Prune

▶ To shorten or remove limbs, cut in late summer, fall, or winter when the tree is dormant. If you prune during the growing season, they are likely to bleed badly. And if you cut in very cold weather, the frozen, brittle wood may break in the wrong places, thus injuring the trunk.

▶ To shorten limbs only slightly, do it in the very early spring, so the new growth will cover your cuts within a few weeks. The amount you cut should be very small, however, because at this time of year it is harmful for the tree.

Tall-growing evergreen trees look best when growing with one strong, central leader. Fortunately, this is their natural tendency. Occasionally, however, a competing leader or two will develop. To save the tree's appearance, remove the interloper, shorten it, or, if feasible, bend it down.

MASTER GARDENING TIPS

Basal Pruning

▶ You may wish to take out some limbs for the sake of appearance. When spruce trees and some other evergreens are young, they have beautiful lush branches that grow to the ground. But as the trees grow larger, some people like to cut out a few of these lower branches so that the handsome trunks can be seen. They may even prune off all the lower limbs to feature a trunk. Consider this decision carefully before you cut, because once the branches are off, you can't put them back!

▶ If you basal-prune a very large evergreen, you may find that sometimes a lower limb has a large, fat, burl-like growth where it joins the trunk. If so, cut the limb just outside the burl rather than close to the trunk as you ordinarily would. Cutting too close makes an unnecessarily large wound.

Broadleaf Evergreens

The list of broadleaf evergreens is so long that I'll make no attempt to cover them individually, with the exception of the most common. Compared to the needled evergreens, these generally need little pruning, and the pruning they do need is similar for all of them.

Azalea, holly, mountain laurel, and rhododendron are grown over much of the United States, while bay laurel, holly, grape, jasmine, leucothoe, oleander, and olive are grown in the warm South and along the Pacific Coast. In addition to these, there are many shrubs that are deciduous in the North and evergreen in the South, such as certain varieties of abelia, andromeda, azalea, barberry, cotoneaster, daphne, euonymus, pyracantha, privet, and many viburnums.

Most of these are sold potted or with their roots in a ball of soil, so no pruning at planting time is necessary. Early pruning to train the plant is important, however.

Snip off the terminal, or end, buds of the new sprouts to force the latent buds to develop and grow along the sides of the branches. After the plant reaches blooming size, if the branches are growing too long, you may pinch off the small end buds. Be careful to leave the big, fat blossom buds that will be next spring's blooms.

If you want your bush to stay compact, continue this type of pruning for the life of the plant. You will be the proud owner of a handsome, bushy, vigorous shrub.

MASTER GARDENING TIPS

When to Shape

Early summer, when the plant has finished blooming and is actively growing, is best.

▶ *Azaleas, mountain laurels,* and *rhododendrons* are closely related, so their early training is much the same. Often they have a loose habit of growth. If you want a tight, compact bush, some pinching or cutting back of the new growth is necessary.

▶ *Camellias* and *hibiscus* also need some pinching of the end buds in early summer if you want to the plants to grow bushy. If you prefer a tall, vine-like growth, or choose to espalier them, cut out the shoots that are growing in the wrong direction. Train the longer shoots by carefully bending them and tying them to the lattice or trellis in the way you want them to grow.

▶ *Holly* needs very little pinching when it is young, since it tends to grow tight naturally. You may need to shear Japanese holly for shaping. If you are growing a holly hedge, it will need an annual clipping during the growing period. If you prefer your holly to grow tall, however, prune it as little as possible until it reaches the height you want. This may take a few years, so be patient.

Renewal Pruning

As broadleaf evergreen shrubs grow older, they occasionally need rejuvenation. In the South, rhododendrons, azaleas, mountain laurels, and hibiscus are often cut back completely to the ground to renew them. Usually they are fertilized heavily with cottonseed meal and manure a year or two before this operation to help them to withstand it.

It works best to spread out any heavy cutback over two or more years, especially if below-freezing temperatures are common where you live. Do heavy pruning of this type in late winter or very early spring.

azalea

Remove fading flowers immediately after they have bloomed so that the plants won't waste any energy producing seeds (this process is called deadheading). With azaleas in particular, you need to be extra careful, so that the newly forming buds — next year's show — are not damaged.

MASTER GARDENING TIPS

Maintenance Pruning

► Shorten any branches that are too long in spring.

► Cut off winter injury and broken branches anytime.

► Thin out growth that is too thick.

► Cut back all the remaining branches.

► Go easy on picking flowers for bouquets from small plants during the first few years, but you can cut them safely from mature plants in moderate amounts with no damage to the plant.

MASTER GARDENING TIPS

► **Hibiscus** blooms on new wood, so even if you cut back a bush to a foot or so from the ground, it will still bloom well during the following season.

► Where there is no frost, you can grow a **poinsettia** into a large shrub. To get it and similar plants to bloom well, cut back all the branches in early spring. Or you can renew the whole bush by cutting it down to about a foot from the ground.

► **Camellias, magnolias,** and **gardenias** seldom need pruning. Some shaping in their early years is practically all that is necessary. Avoid making any large cut unless conditions absolutely require it, because cut ends seldom heal well.

► Some of the smaller-leaved broadleaf evergreens, such as **Japanese holly, boxwood,** and **evergreen privet,** are widely planted for hedges and topiary. Shear these during the summer to the shape you want.

► **Holly** branches can be cut from a mature bush at Christmastime for decoration.

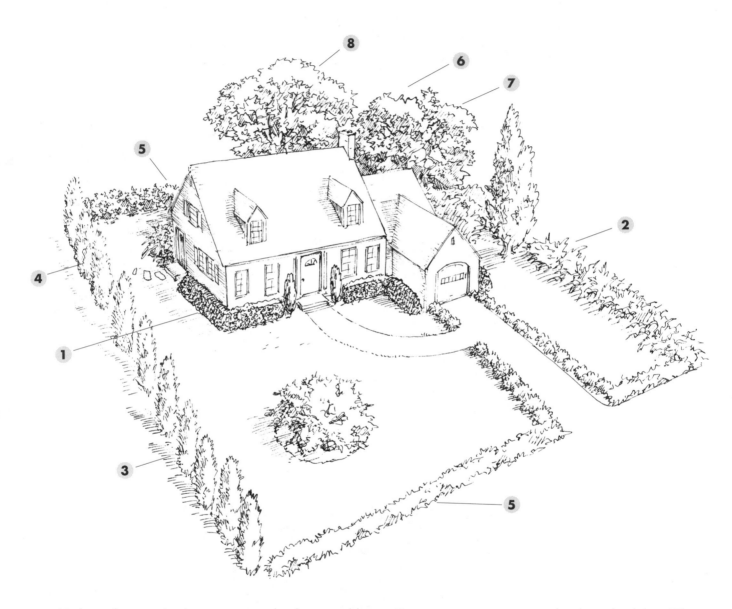

Hedges of various kinds are important landscape additions. You can create an attractive border or backdrop (**1**); mark property lines (**2**); shield out traffic noise and fumes (**3**); hide unattractive views (**4**); discourage trespassing (human and animal) (**5**); ensure privacy (**6**); form windbreaks or snow traps (**7**); shelter nesting birds (**8**).

Pruning Hedges

Recently a friend of ours sold his home. An avid gardener, he had added a few dollars' worth of plants to his property each spring, and since he always bought small and medium-size specimens, his entire investment over a 10-year period probably wasn't more than $300. As soon as he got home from work each day, he would putter away in his garden, pruning and shearing his flowering plants and fruit trees. His particular pride and joy was a beautifully sheared hemlock hedge.

His neighbor's identical house on the same street was still unsold, even though he was asking $8,000 less for it. That fellow had only a few anemic-looking bushes growing around his place. "I'm sure the landscaping sold my place," our friend told us. "And I'm pretty sure I got $10,000 more for it because of the landscaping."

Our friend was delighted about the success of his modest investment, but more important, his gardening hobby had given him pleasure and relaxation over the years. As soon as he moved, he started to landscape the grounds around his new home, and the first thing he planted was a long hedge of tiny hemlocks. He has already begun to shear it.

The way you shear a hedge varies according to its purpose. You can trim it into a tight and formal shape or allow it to grow loose and natural. You can make it tall, medium, or short — or, if you want, you can sculpt the top into towers and turrets. You can have an evergreen or deciduous hedge, or one that produces fruit or flowers.

Caring for a hedge is not difficult, yet as you drive around it's obvious that many gardeners are not very skilled in the art. Perhaps the old English expression "Homely as a hedge fence" refers to one of these unkempt rows of bushes. Just as barbers probably felt during the long-hair era, keen gardeners sometimes feel an almost uncontrollable urge to stop their cars, grab their shears, and start clipping whenever they see an untidy hedge.

Starting a New Hedge

It is particularly important to get your hedge plants off to a good start. Each one should grow in a bushy form at about the same speed as all its companions. Start with healthy, compact, small plants, if possible.

Begin shearing while the plants are still young, just as soon as they start to grow noticeably — sometimes in the first year, and certainly by the second. Even if you want your hedge to grow to 4 feet, don't wait until it gets to that height before you start to shape it. In order to have a tall, tight hedge, you should first develop a *small*, tight hedge, then let it grow larger gradually. Just as it is difficult to make a single, tall, loose-growing tree compact and bushy, it's no easy job to tighten up a large, loose-growing hedge.

1 You can dig a hole for each individual plant, but it is easier to get the plants in a straight line and equally spaced if you plant your hedge in one long trench.

2 If you are planting a straight hedge, use a string stretched taut to mark the line, just as if you were getting ready to plant peas in a garden row. Unless you're installing a mass planting, never plant a hedge more than one plant wide. For easier shearing, set the plants in a single rather than a staggered line, unless you plan to use your hedge only as a high windbreak or snow trap.

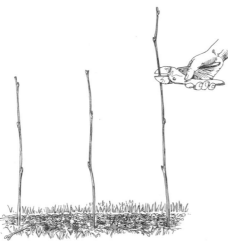

3 Set out the plants 2 feet apart, measuring from the center of each plant. Plant tall-growing hedges, such as a lilac hedge, several feet apart, but the exact distance depends on how quickly you want a tight hedge. The farther apart you place them, of course, the longer it will take for the plants to intermingle. Prune the new plants.

MASTER GARDENING TIPS

For bare-root, nursery-grown hedge plants and plants dug from the wild: Cut back about a third of the top, just before or just after planting. This compensates for the roots that were lost or damaged when the plant was dug up. Another reason to trim back spindly or tall hedge plants is so that you will have a dense, symmetrical hedge.

For plants with intact rootballs and pot-grown plants: You probably won't need to do any pruning at planting time.

Shearing a Hedge

You'll need to trim an informal hedge only once or twice a year, although more vigorous growers, such as privet and ninebark, may need additional clippings. Formal hedges need more attention to look their best. Cut them every few days during their growing season. See the box for additional advice.

MASTER GARDENING TIPS

When to Shear a Hedge

The best time is when the plants are making their fastest growth.

▶ Trim your hedge as soon as it looks like it needs it. Just as you wouldn't wait for your lawn to become a field before mowing it, you should trim your hedge throughout the growing season. Not only will it be thicker and better looking, but it will also be healthier, because it will expend less of its energy on useless growth.

▶ Most needled evergreens make their growth early, so you won't need to shear them after midsummer. (See chapter 6.)

▶ Most deciduous plants, like privet, ninebark, and barberry, grow for a longer period, so you must trim them off and on for most of the summer.

▶ Broadleaf evergreens such as boxwood and Japanese holly also grow over a long period, so they will need some shearing throughout the season.

▶ Prune flowering plants directly after the blooms have faded so that new buds can set for the following year. (Rose hedges are the exception, and are best pruned in early spring or late fall. Shear them in the summer months only if they are growing too tall or too wide.)

Don't shear off the top of a hedge and ignore the sides. Soon it becomes irregular and too wide, and sags under the weight of heavy rains, ice, or snow. If anything happens to an individual plant, you can replace it much more easily if your hedge is slender.

Unless you have an excellent eye for such things, you should put up posts and a string as a guide when you're shearing long, straight, formal hedges, so that you don't end up with a lopsided row.

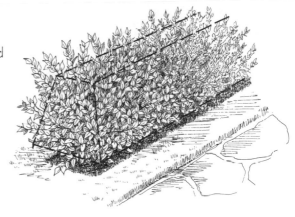

Always shear a hedge so that the bottom is wider than the top. The difference may be barely noticeable, but it is extremely important. Hedges that are even slightly wider at the top always look top-heavy, and the lower branches, lacking their full share of sunlight, become thin and soon die.

Making an Arch in Your Hedge

MASTER GARDENING TIP

Arch Care

Whether you choose a hedge archway or one made of vines, you should shear it every year so it grows thick and bushy. If you keep the sides narrow enough to allow light to enter, the branches on the underside of the arch will stay green and growing.

The simple method. Plant two tall-growing trees 4 to 6 feet apart to act as the sides. (*Note:* They should be far enough apart so that by the time they have grown thick and full, you will still have enough room to walk or push your lawn mower through the opening.) In the spring, when they are starting to grow actively, bend them over carefully to the desired height, and tie them together to form the arch. Within a few years they will grow together.

A grafted arch. After planting (see the note above about spacing), graft the two trees together. Hemlock, arborvitae, and most other tall-growing evergreens — and some deciduous plants — fuse together well.

Cheating. Build a wooden trellis in the proper shape, and plant a vine to cover it. If you choose a compatible vine, it will look very much like a part of the hedge.

Reviving an Old Hedge

You may be faced with an overgrown hedge, with plants that are too tall, too wide, or growing out of kilter with each other. If the plants are thrifty and healthy, you can sometimes cut them back nearly to the ground and allow them to start over. Your chances for success are best with a deciduous hedge — privet, ninebark, pyracantha, potentilla, lilac, barberry, bayberry, spirea, or buckthorn, for example.

You can also cut back and renew certain evergreens. Yew, boxwood, and holly will often respond well to a severe pruning. But spruce, pine, fir, and hemlock can seldom be rejuvenated in this manner, and arborvitae will survive a hard pruning job only if the plants are young. You can either shape overgrown evergreens into a tall, informal hedge or take them out altogether and start over with new plants.

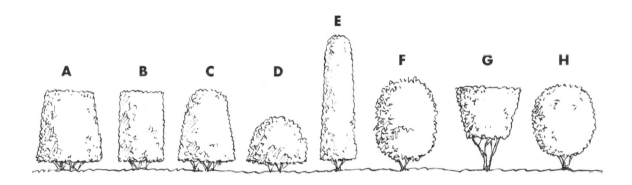

Hedge shapes. A box effect (**A**) is good where snow loads are not too heavy. The sides here (**B**) are too straight, so the lower branches may not get enough sunlight. Shapes **C, D,** and **E** are suited to areas with heavy snows. **F** is an untrimmed hedge. The top of hedge **G** is too wide, making this shape undesirable — the sun can't reach lower limbs and snow will crush the top. The canopy hedge (**H**) is best suited to sunny climates with mild winters (that is, no heavy snowfalls).

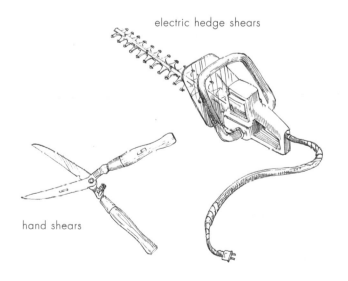

electric hedge shears

hand shears

I've found electric hedge shears are easiest (I use them on my long arborvitae hedge), since the job has to be done quickly, while the plants are making their fastest growth. They're fast, easy to handle, precise, and less tiring to use than hand shears. However, hand shears with long handles and blades are excellent if you don't have to shear a great deal. A shearing knife is handy for informal shearing, but it isn't easy to do accurate work with it.

Formal Hedges

Although the formal, English-garden style of landscaping is rarely used around American homes these days, tightly clipped hedges are still popular. The chart below lists some favorites.

FORMAL HEDGE FAVORITES		
Plant	**Characteristics**	**Maintenance**
Arborvitae, Eastern white cedar *(Thuja)*	An ideal, fast-growing, tall hedge. A good windbreak and snow barrier, and an excellent choice for mass plantings. You may find it too coarse for short, small hedges. If your soil is acidic, add lime for the best color and good growth.	Choose the pyramidal variety for tall, narrow hedges that need shearing only on top.
Boxwood *(Buxus)*	For most of the United States, boxwood is synonymous with hedge. The tightly sheared hedges and formal topiary gardens of Long Island and Washington, D.C., are usually boxwood, a shrub introduced from Europe during Colonial times. It shears beautifully and is healthy and long lived.	Shear several times a season to get a tight effect. In heavy-snow country, shear the top rounded or pointed to prevent crushing.
Canada hemlock *(Tsuga canadensis)*	A lacy-looking evergreen that can be sheared into a beautiful hedge. Young seedlings and transplants are inexpensive. Although not fast growers, trees will form a long-long-lasting hedge. The Carolina hemlock *(T. caroliniana)* is a good choice for urban areas; it grows even more slowly.	Shear in early summer.
Chinese elm *(Ulmus parvifolia)*	Widely planted in years past, the Chinese elm is not so popular today: It grows fast, but the wood is weak and breaks easily; it is short lived; and it tends to attract insects that then spread to other plants.	Shear severely throughout the summer.
Holly *(Ilex)*	Wherever it grows well, holly (particularly Japanese holly) makes a beautiful, tight evergreen hedge. Choose the best variety for your region, because hardiness can be a problem.	Holly needs just enough shearing to keep it well shaped.
Ninebark *(Physocarpus)*	Not usually a great hedge plant, but in northern New England, the upper Midwest, and Canada it is a satisfactory one. Attractive white flowers in early spring with dense foliage that turns reddish in the fall.	If you want a low-growing hedge, save yourself considerable shearing and plant a dwarf variety.
Privet *(Ligustrum)*	Members of the privet family are among the most popular hedge plants. Varieties are available for every region except the coldest parts of the country. Plants are inexpensive and can be raised from cuttings. Foliage is dense, with small leaves.	Shear by hand or with light electric hedge clippers. Shear in summer while the plants are making rapid growth. Frequent shearings are necessary for a tidy look.
Spruce *(Picea)*	Comes in many varieties of dwarf and full-size trees. All can be sheared into hedges, but those with shorter needles look best. Choose a variety suitable for your area and one that will grow to the height you want.	Shear spruces tightly or they will grow too large eventually. Usually at least two clippings a season are necessary.
Yew *(Taxus)*	Many varieties of yew are available; you'll find one suitable for your region unless your winters are cold and lack snow cover. Plants grown from cuttings are likely to be more uniform in color and growth habit than are those grown from seeds. Red berries on female plants add color to the autumn landscape. Upright-growing varieties are best for hedges.	Shear once or twice during the growing season.

Hedges for Barriers

We once planted a row of Colorado blue spruces for a customer who wanted to stop trespassers from using her private yard as a shortcut to the public beach. The prickly trees were perfect for the purpose. No one in a bathing suit has yet been known to push through those sharp-needled plants.

Sometimes hedges are planted solely to keep out unwanted visitors, human or animal. Living fences are often cheaper to establish and maintain than real fences, and they appear less hostile.

In time, and with careful pruning, most plants can be grown into a barrier hedge, but thorny, rugged plants are best if you have a choice. Shear your plants in the summer when they are actively growing. Do it once over lightly — just enough to produce a thick, informal hedge — or frequently and severely, to achieve a neater, more symmetrical, and more formal appearance. In either case, follow the general rules for shearing, and never allow the plant to grow wider at the top than at the bottom. The plants listed below are excellent barrier hedges.

HEDGES FOR BARRIERS

Plant	Characteristics	Maintenance
Barberry *(Berberis)*	Barberries have long been used for this purpose, and you know why if you've ever tried to grasp a sprig. The thorns are tenacious. In areas where these plants do well, they are ideal barriers.	When they begin to deteriorate, cut them to the ground and they'll renew themselves. In places where they are short lived, or suffer winter injury or insect trouble, choose another plant.
Crab apple *(Malus)*	The wild varieties make the best hedges. 'Robusta' is a good prickly one in the North.	Plant them 2 or 3 feet apart, and shear heavily in early summer for thick bottom growth.
Hawthorn *(Crataegus)*	Hawthorns make very effective barriers.	Choose a variety that is especially thorny and will grow to the height you want. Shear the plants tightly whenever necessary.
Plum *(Prunus)*	Native plums make a good barrier fence if they're sheared tightly.	Plant them 2 or 3 feet apart, and treat them as you would hawthorns and crab apples.
Rose *(Rosa)*	Shrub roses are most common for this use, and there are many to choose from. Generally speaking, they have denser foliage and less refined blossoms than hybrid teas.	Keeping them uniform may be difficult because of their informal growth habit, although their flowers can be beautiful (look for the deliciously fragrant rugosas). If weeds and weedy shrubs seed in and grow among them, they'll be a problem to remove.
Spruce *(Picea)*	When spruce is used as a barrier hedge, the pricklier the plant, the better. Colorado blue spruce *(P. pungens)* is one of the best choices, since it is fast growing and adapts to a wide range of soils and climates. Because this spruce varies from bright green to blue-white in color, choose colors that are uniform or you'll have an unattractive mottled effect.	Tight shearing is necessary to make it impenetrable.
Thorny honey locust *(Gleditsia)*	Use a thorny variety when planting a barrier, since the thornless kinds aren't as effective.	Plant them 3 feet apart and shear heavily.

Flower- and Berry-Producing Hedge Plants

Ordinarily, plants don't produce flowers or fruit well when they're sheared into a tight hedge pattern. So allow them to grow naturally, pruning to encourage denser growth and to remove weak or crossing branches rather than shearing. The following plants produce well when grown as an informal, lightly pruned hedge. Except where noted, prune directly after flowering.

FLOWER- AND BERRY-PRODUCING HEDGES

Plant	Characteristics	Maintenance
Barberry (Berberis)	Choose a variety that will grow to the size you want. The upright-growing kinds are best.	Prune or shear it to keep it from growing too wide.
Buckthorn (Rhamnus)	The tall, upright variety is often used as a hedge. The plants are attractive and produce berries over a long season for the birds.	They tend to get thin at their bases, so prune closely when they're young to encourage bushiness at the bottom of the hedge. In some areas birds cause a problem by dropping buckthorn seeds all over, which will grow up as weedy plants.
Cotoneaster (Cotoneaster)	Choose the upright-growing varieties.	Most varieties need little shearing. Prune in early spring if it's necessary to control the size.
Firethorn (Pyracantha)	Choose upright, thorny kinds for hedges. Shear loosely in order to get fruit.	Cut off the old wood in late fall to promote heavier crops of berries the following year. You can shape many varieties into espalier and other unusual forms.
Flowering plum (Prunus)	Most don't bear any fruit.	If necessary, prune right after blooming, and shear as needed during the summer to keep it in shape.
Honeysuckle (Lonicera)	These are excellent for attracting flocks of birds to your yard.	Prune the hedge to remove old wood and any dead branches. Shear it to keep it in shape.
Hydrangea (Hydrangea)	The fall-blooming 'Peegee' is best for tall, informal hedges.	Cut back the top severely in early spring. Cut nearly to the ground, or cut according to how much you want it to grow the following summer. Cut off the flowers right after they have bloomed.
Lilac (Syringa)	Choose dwarf varieties, such as 'Miss Kim'.	Prune to remove fading flowers and suckers right after blooming. For any major pruning, see "Pruning a Lilac," page 50.
Mock orange (Philadelphus)	The white, fragrant blooms make this a worthy choice if you're looking for a tall, beautiful hedge plant.	Prune directly after blooming to shape and to remove old wood.
Rose (Rosa)	Rugosa varieties produce large, colorful hips.	Cut out dead flowers and older canes right after blooming. (See "Pruning Roses," page 56.)
Saint-John's-wort (Hypericum)	The bright yellow flowers of this low-growing hedge are a gay spot of color in the summer.	Prune in late summer to remove the seedpods and, if necessary, renew old wood.
Viburnum (Viburnum)	Choose the kind that grows to the height you want to save clipping and to get the most berries.	Prune lightly right after blooming to keep it in shape. If you need to prune heavily, do so in fall or late winter.

Hedges Needing Careful Maintenance

There are a few plants that demand extra care to keep them looking nice. This doesn't mean that they require full-time professional care, but you will need to spend a little more conscientious time to maintain them.

HEDGES NEEDING CAREFUL MAINTENANCE	
Plant	**Maintenance**
Most evergreens, including pines, firs, spreading yews, and blue spruces	Require heavy, meticulous pruning.
Mugho pine	A low shrub with coarse limbs; needs occasional clipping with hand pruners.
Spreading deciduous shrubs, including spreading barberry *(Berberis)*, flowering quince *(Chaenomeles)*, winterberry *(Ilex verticillata)*, beauty bush *(Kolkwitzia)*, and honeysuckle *(Lonicera)*	Need attention throughout the growing season to keep them under control.
Large, coarse trees, including the larch *(Larix)* and oak *(Quercus)*; fast-growing trees, including poplars *(Populus)* and willows *(Salix)*; prolific growers, including ninebark *(Physocarpus)*	Need attention throughout the growing season to keep them under control.

Annual Hedges

I'm often asked for the name of my beautiful little evergreen that turns bright red in late summer. It's sometimes difficult to convince gardeners that the Mexican firebush *(Kochia scoparia)* isn't a formally sheared evergreen at all and that it grows easily each year from seed. Although this plant seldom needs pruning if it is well spaced and gets plenty of sunlight, many annuals do need a bit of pinching and shaping to get them to grow as a tight, informal border. You can grow cosmos, dahlias, marigolds, petunias, geraniums, ageratums, impatiens, and zinnias as low summer hedges. Remove their fading blooms regularly to encourage continuous blossoming.

Mexican firebush grows in one season and needs no shearing.

Low-Maintenance Hedges

Gardeners with limited time, or those who don't especially like to putter around the garden, may prefer to have hedges that require little care. "Low maintenance" means that a hedge needs only a few clippings per season, or that you can clip it quickly and easily.

Ordinarily, upright-growing shrubs with fine twigs and small needles or leaves are easier to care for than the coarser-limbed, spreading varieties, or those with larger leaves or longer needles.

A young, growing hedge needs less attention than it will when it has reached the size and shape you want. Often one annual pruning is enough for evergreens in their formative years, but after the hedge is mature, one heavy pruning and an additional three or four light ones over the course of a season may be necessary to keep it looking good.

LOW-MAINTENANCE HEDGES

Plant	Characteristics	Maintenance
EVERGREEN CHOICES		
American arborvitae, white cedar (*Thuja occidentalis*)	Choose dwarf-growing cultivars to minimize shearing.	One or two easy shearings will control this favorite in northern gardens.
Canada hemlock (*Tsuga canadensis*)	Lacy foliage produces a beautiful hedge.	One or two easy annual shearings will keep this beauty looking nice for years.
Holly (*Ilex*)	Buy both male and female plants to get berries.	Upright-growing varieties need two or three relatively easy shearings each season.
Spruce (*Picea*)	If you plant species, clip them hard to keep in control.	Dwarf-growing varieties of Norway spruce (such as bird's nest, *P. abies* 'Nidiformis') need only one easy shearing on the sides each year, however.
Upright yew (*Taxus cuspidata* 'Capitata')	A beautiful hedge needing little care. Choose both male and female plants to get berries.	This variety and other upright-growing yews need one to three easy shearings each year.
DECIDUOUS CHOICES		
Barberry (*Berberis*)	Choose the upright-growing kinds for the easiest maintenance — for example, mentor *(B.* x *mentorensis)* or true hedge *(B. atropurpurea* 'Erecta').	Clip tightly for a neat-looking, dense hedge.
Buckthorn (*Rhamnus frangula*)	The columnar varieties, such as tall hedge ('Columnaris'), are best.	Careful early shearing is sometimes necessary to keep the plants tight at the bottom.
Crab apple (*Malus*)	It is better not to use grafted varieties, because the suckers are difficult to control.	The various crab apples can be sheared into tight hedges that are easily maintained, although some additional care is needed initially to shape them.
English laurel (*Prunus laurocerasus*)	A common sight in the mild-climate areas of the South and West, this handsome plant is valued for its fast, lush growth and glossy leaves. It is not fussy about soil. It can be hard to control, so many gardeners use it as a tall, loose screen.	Clip to keep looking neat, and to the height you want.

Plant	Characteristics	Maintenance
DECIDUOUS CHOICES (cont'd.)		
Five-leaf aralia *(Acanthopanax)*	Good foliage plant that does well in shade.	The two to four clippings necessary each year are easily accomplished.
Forsythia *(Forsythia)*	The dwarf varieties make an easy-to-care-for, informal, blooming hedge.	Prune after blooming to shape and remove old wood.
Hedge maple *(Acer campestre)*	Even though the foliage on this plant is large, it is attractive.	Prune mostly to shape.
Hornbeam *(Carpinus)*	Both the native and European varieties make a tight, slow-growing, easy-to-maintain hedge that will grow fairly tall, if you wish.	Prune to keep to the height you want, and to make a dense hedge.
Korean boxwood *(Buxus microphylla* var. *koreana)*	A rich green plant for Zone 5 and warmer. Tends to be expensive.	This low-growing plant with fine foliage shears easily. With power clippers, large plantings can be beautifully maintained.
Privet *(Ligustrum)*	Upright-growing kinds such as dwarf border privet (*L. obtusifolium* var. *regelianum* or the cultivar 'Constitution') are easy to care for.	Even though these are classified as easy care, several prunings are still needed during the summer.
Winged spindle tree *(Euonymus alata* 'Compacta')	The dwarf size of this plant makes it easy to care for.	Prune to shape.
Wintercreeper *(Euonymus fortunei)*	A fast-growing, easy-care hedge plant. The foliage comes in a variety of colors as well as variegated patterns.	Prune to shape. Cultivars are semi-evergreen to evergreen.
Viburnum *(Viburnum)*	Sheared or unsheared, many of the viburnums make neat hedges. Some are dwarf naturally, so choose the mature height you want to ensure the least care and to make berry production more certain.	Prune to control size and shape. Occasionally cut out old wood.

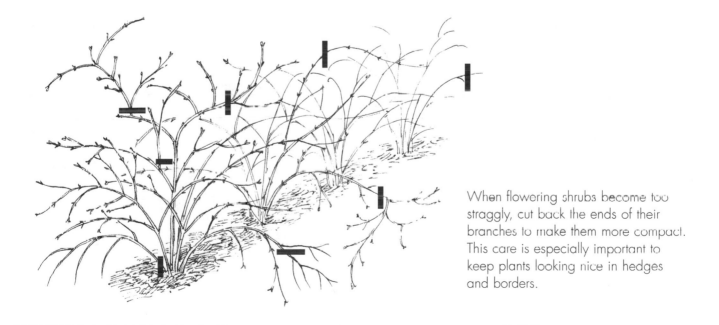

When flowering shrubs become too straggly, cut back the ends of their branches to make them more compact. This care is especially important to keep plants looking nice in hedges and borders.

Artistic pruning requires your time during the growing season. Most of the shearing must be done in early summer when the trees are growing rapidly, so if you like to scuba dive in Aruba or fish in Alaska in May or June, this hobby isn't for you. You'll need to be in your garden several days a week when the plants are growing, if only for a few minutes each time.

Artistic Pruning

When I was very young, my family occasionally shopped in a neighboring town. Although there were several routes we could take to get there, I always begged my parents to drive by the "umbrella tree." On a small patch of land in his neat pasture, a local chicken farmer had sheared a dozen or so native spruce and arborvitae trees into balls, umbrellas, cones, eggs, and other shapes. It was a novel sight in the North Woods, and many people went out of their way to look at his topiary. Locals still speak fondly of those trees, and I wonder if he ever realized how much his work was appreciated by the young and old who passed by his farm. I'm sorry that I never had the chance to tell him how much I enjoyed them — long before I grew up he either died or moved away, and the exciting shapes I admired so much became ordinary large trees.

His creations inspired me because I learned that you don't have to be an English gardener working with yew or boxwood to grow fancy shrubbery. I also learned that a planting doesn't have to be 200 years old to look good, and that artistic pruning is possible even in the North where snow sometimes gets 8 feet or more deep.

Many of the artistic forms of pruning were developed in Europe or Japan, where small lots made necessary the *multum in parvo* concept. In this country, espaliers and topiary are usually created more for aesthetic reasons than because of space limitations.

Although fancy topiary and other artistic prunings demand patience and skill, the simple shearing of evergreens and the shaping of flowering shrubs and fruit trees are so easy that anyone can have fun with the process. Many varieties of dwarf plants developed recently are ideal for artistic shaping, because they grow so slowly. Nor do you have to sacrifice practicality. I've seen commercial fruit orchardists growing their trees as sheared hedges, cordons, and fences — forms that are traditionally considered more ornamental than useful.

The pruning of an artistic form must go on throughout the life of the plant. Frequent snipping and shearing will be part of your summer chores, just like mowing the lawn and pulling weeds in the vegetable garden. If you have spent years creating a horticultural masterpiece and then neglect it as you go on to other projects, you'll find, within a year or so, that it has become overgrown and is probably past help. But such is the life of a gardener — a thing of beauty is a job forever.

In This Chapter

- Topiary
- Topiary Frames
- Espalier
- Creating a Cordon
- English Fences
- Pollarding and Coppicing
- Pruning a Japanese-Style Garden

Topiary

Shearing reaches its zenith in topiary, the art of trimming trees and shrubs into geometric forms, arches, animals, and many other shapes. Two centuries ago this art form became so popular that it was overdone in many European gardens. It has never been common in America, except in some formal or exhibition gardens, probably because most of us prefer an informal and unstudied look — and because we don't have hired gardeners to do the work.

On a modest scale, though, creating a topiary can be a lot of fun. The potential shapes are limited only by the patience and imagination of the gardener, and sometimes by climate.

Getting Started with Topiary

1. Start with small, tight-growing plants. Plant them in an area where they will receive a full day of sunlight.

2. Begin shearing as soon as growth starts, and continue as long as necessary throughout the summer. Evergreens usually need only two or three shearings a year; deciduous plants have the advantage of growing faster and producing quicker results, but they need more shearing.

MASTER GARDENING TIPS

Successful Topiaries

▶ Begin shaping when the plant is still small. You can't take a large tree and sculpt it into an artistic shape like an artist chiseling away at a block of marble.

▶ Shear it often when it is growing, to create a closely grown, tiny-leaved (or needle) effect.

▶ Shear your basic shape (for example, a cone or pyramid), and allow bulges to appear gradually. Shape a bulge into a head, or leg, or other part of your design.

Start with a tall, slender tree. Shear it all around.

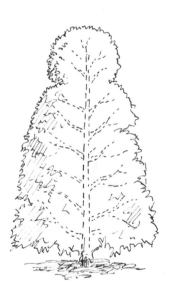

Begin to remove unwanted branches between sections.

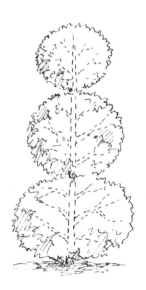

Clip remaining branches into globes or cubes, the largest ones on the bottom.

Topiary Frames

More complicated forms — four trees that form the legs and finally the body of an elephant, for instance — require careful planning and usually a framework of wood or metal. My wife saw such an elephant in Thailand — it was massive and arched over a driveway, tall enough for a car to drive beneath.

MASTER GARDENING TIPS

Cold-Climate Topiary

Most topiary is grown in the warmer zones where snow can't crush it. If you live in the North and want to experiment:

▶ Use only the hardiest plants (native specimens are usually best).

▶ Select topiary shapes that are pointed or rounded on top and narrow in width, so that they won't collect heavy loads of snow and ice.

▶ When winter comes, build a wooden tepee around more fragile pieces, or simply shovel the snow off after each big storm.

Buy a preformed frame, or make your own.

Plunge a stake or pole into the ground as close as possible to the middle of the young plant, then secure the frame to it at some point. Otherwise, the frame may shift over time and make it difficult for you to keep to your original plan.

Wait for stems to emerge beyond the frame's bounds, then clip them back neatly, or, if you want them to expand laterally to fill in the shape, tie them loosely to the frame with soft twine.

MASTER GARDENING TIPS

Choosing a Suitable Plant

Evergreen choices. Boxwood, holly, and yew varieties are the most popular, but arborvitae, cypress, hemlock, and spruce also may be used. Pines, Colorado spruces, and most of the firs are a bit coarse for topiary.

Deciduous choices. Try Chinese elm, cotoneaster, ninebark, privet, pyracantha, Japanese and Amur maples, and similar trees and shrubs. Sometimes even the coarser-growing trees such as maples, birches, and hornbeams can be sculpted into bowers, arches, unusual shapes, and haunted-forest forms.

English ivy can be trained to grow over wire shapes into giraffes, camels, and hippos, as in the topiary garden of the New York Botanical Garden Conservatory.

Espalier

The espalier is one of the most familiar artistic pruning forms and is just the thing if you wish to grow trees or shrubs in an extremely small space. It is a plant grown flat, like a vine, against a wall, fence, building, or trellis.

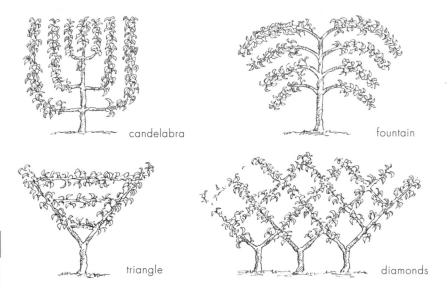

fan

candelabra

fountain

triangle

diamonds

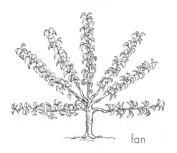

MASTER GARDENING TIPS

Regional Considerations

In warm climates:

- ▶ Grow your espalier in a spot that does not receive direct sun all day, because a wall reflects heat that will cause the leaves and fruit to suffer on hot days.

- ▶ A white wall is preferable as a growing background, because it absorbs little heat.

In cool climates:

- ▶ The more sun, the better.

- ▶ A dark-colored wall attracts heat and is a better backdrop.

- ▶ A fruit tree or vine may grow as an espalier when it would struggle growing in the open. Grapes, for example, can often be grown in cool areas if trained against a dark, south-facing building, whereas it would be impossible to ripen them only a few feet away from the building.

Getting Started with Espalier

1. Select a tree that branches in a way that fits into your espalier plan. If you are unable to find a well-shaped specimen, it's better to start with a whip, or prune all the limbs off a small-branched tree and start training each new branch as it grows. A few nurseries sell small espaliered trees and shrubs that have already had their early training. Although a head start should make things easier for you, there are benefits to starting your own. You can use the kind of plant you want, choose your own design, and save money.

2. Provide your espalier with a support structure. You may be tempted to drive nails into a wooden surface and tie the branches to them, but this is not a good practice. It's difficult to prune when the branches lie flat, and repainting the building is nearly impossible. Instead, install a lattice, trellis, or wire fence at least 6 inches away from the wall or fence. Wire is easiest and usually the most practical for fruit trees. Shrubs are easier to train on a trellis or lattice.

Set two sturdy posts, 7 or 8 feet tall, at the expected outside spread of the espalier. Brace them to prevent the wires from sagging. Next, staple smooth wire from one to the other like a wire fence. Place the first wire about 3 feet from the ground and the others about a foot apart.

3. Plant the tree or shrub just in front, roughly midway between the posts.

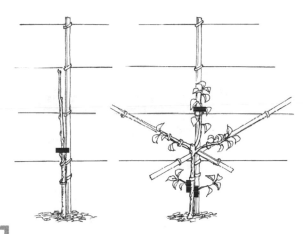

1 When growth begins on your new plant, allow to remain only those branches growing in the right direction. Clip or pinch off all the others throughout the growing season.

MASTER GARDENING TIPS

A Successful Espalier

▶ In addition to the regular pruning of a fruit tree, you may need to prune off some of the fruit buds in late winter to prevent overbearing. If too many fruits set anyway, thin them out in early summer when they are still small so that the tree will produce a crop annually.

▶ When you're trimming, don't cut off the short, stubby spurs that bear the fruit! Flowering crabs and hawthorns need to have their older spurs thinned out occasionally, as they get too numerous, but always leave enough to produce a good crop.

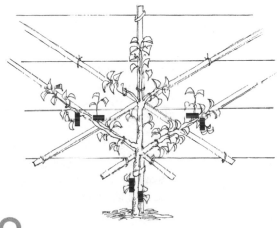

2 Bend the branches as they grow — while they are still pliable — and secure them with twine or vine clamps to the supporting wire or trellis in the pattern you want.

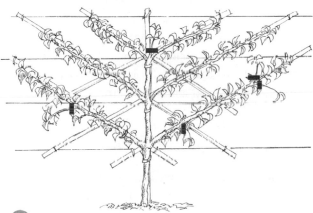

3 It may take several years of growing and shaping to "finish" a complicated pattern. Even after your tree has become an artistic triumph, you must continue to prune through the summer to keep it looking attractive.

MASTER GARDENING TIP

What Sort of Plant Can I Use?

Fruit trees are often chosen for espaliers because they are both productive and pretty, in leaf and in flower. Dwarf apples, pears, quinces, citrus fruits, and figs are most commonly used. Plums, cherries, peaches, and apricots are more difficult to train, as are the bush fruits and nut trees. *Note:* Sheltered espaliered fruits ripen earlier than those grown in the open, which are subjected to cooling winds.

Camellia, cotoneaster, flowering crab, flowering quince, forsythia, fuchsia, hawthorn, laurel, magnolia, pyracantha, yew, and viburnum are among the ornamental shrubs or small trees that can also be grown in this manner. Those plants that grow vigorously, such as lilacs and hydrangeas, are unsuitable for espalier planting. You'd only get frustrated trying to keep them pruned.

Creating a Cordon

You have a number of design options when you create an espalier: Fans, candelabras, fountains, diamonds, and triangles are only a few of the possibilities. Many shrubs can be trained as beautiful espaliered forms, especially in the areas of the country that don't get severe winters. One popular form is the cordon. Cordon is the French word for "cord" or "rope," and refers to a planting (usually of a dwarf fruit tree) that extends in ropelike fashion, either vertically or horizontally. When a tree or shrub is trimmed to grow in a tall, slender shape, it is often called the beanpole method. Europeans have used this technique for centuries, but only recently has it become popular in America.

Traditionally, cordons have been grown mostly as ornamental trees, and the style was not widely used by fruit growers. However, some commercial orchardists are now experimenting with growing fruit trees as upright cordons because they are discovering — as you will in your backyard planting — that a cordon doesn't take up a lot of space and comes into production faster. Fruit growers, for instance, are planting as many as 60 dwarf cordons to the acre, versus 35 full-size trees. The initial cost of buying, planting, and training is high, but subsequent pruning, insect and disease control, and harvesting costs are lower, and the planting starts producing good crops many years sooner than would a regular orchard.

Getting Started with a Cordon

1. Start with a branchless tree. Plant as usual, then prune back the top from a third to a half, cutting to a good fat bud. If you are working on a tree that is already branched, cut off all the side branches close to the trunk, leaving a single, straight whip.

2. Place a sturdy stake close to the newly planted tree. Tie the tree to the stake with soft cloth at regular intervals.

3. Clip or pinch all the new growth coming from the sides to 4 or 5 inches in length. Always snip off any growth beyond the 4- or 5-inch limit on the side branches.

MASTER GARDENING TIPS

A Successful Cordon

▶ Choose an upright-growing tree or shrub that will not grow too tall or too fast. Dwarf apples and pears are good candidates; the stone fruits (peaches, plums, and cherries) and citrus fruits are more difficult to train as cordons.

▶ Allow the main trunk to grow to a height of about 6 feet — for easy reach.

▶ Cordons must be kept to a manageable size, but as the roots grow, this tends to become more difficult. Slow down the growth by pruning the roots (by cutting around the tree; see page 35).

▶ In addition to regular pruning of a fruit tree, you may need to prune off some of the fruit buds in late winter to prevent overbearing. If too many fruits set anyway, thin them out in early summer when they are still small, so that the tree will produce a crop annually.

▶ To grow a cordon horizontally or obliquely — angles even more contrary to the plant's normal growth habits — you'll have to prune heavily to keep the plant attractive.

English Fences

English fences are part espalier and part horizontal cordon. Like both, they need frequent pruning and pinching all summer — and throughout their life — to keep them looking like a fence. They're basically freestanding espaliers; that is, they grow without the aid of a wall or building. The branch ends of each tree are grafted to the branch ends of the neighboring tree. The process is demanding and time consuming, so you should attempt it only if you can devote enough time to keep it looking finished and manicured.

MASTER GARDENING TIP

What Sort of Plant Can I Use?

Dwarf fruit trees, especially apples and pears, grow well in this fashion, as do flowering crabs and similar flowering trees, such as redbud, mountain ash, and hawthorn.

Getting Started with an English Fence

1. Plant small trees in a row about 8 or 9 feet apart.

2. Allow three or four branches to grow on each side of the tree in a method that resembles the Kniffen system of growing grapes (see page 150).

3. Pinch and trim frequently to maintain the form.

4. Graft the ends when the limbs of each tree grow past those of its neighbor. Make a slanted cut at the ends of both branches and join the cut ends together, lining up the inner bark layers so that the sap can flow freely between them. Wrap the juncture with freezer tape or rubber (not plastic) electrical tape. In a year or two, the ends will grow together into one long branch.

Trees can be forced to grow in artistic patterns by regular, severe pruning.

MASTER GARDENING TIPS

A Successful English Fence

▶ Put in wires, pipes, or boards, secured to heavy posts, to train the young trees and to hold up the heavy fruit on the fruit trees until the limbs are sturdy enough to do the job on their own.

▶ The plants that make up an English fence will probably need a root-pruning job every three or four years, to keep them from growing too fast.

Pollarding and Coppicing

Pollarding is a tree-shaping technique that results in a highly mannered look. Coppicing, on the other hand, is a technique whereby you regularly cut down a tree almost completely to ground level, resulting in a multistemmed plant. Just don't attempt this on a young plant, or it may not survive; older, established plants, however, can get a new lease on life and a new look. Coppicing is seldom practiced in this country, except to renew hedgerows, especially those grown for firewood.

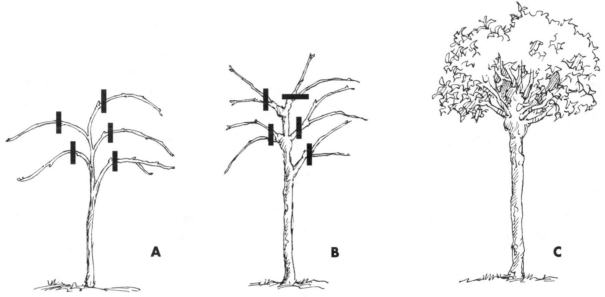

Pollarding. Remove the lower limbs and chop off the remaining ones for a clublike effect, which will soften when the plant bursts into fresh growth each spring. Spread this operation over several years to get started, as shown in **A, B,** and **C** above, then cut back the branches each year in early spring. This method was formerly used to prune catalpas into ball and umbrella shapes. Once popular in Europe, it is little used today.

before coppicing

after coppicing

Coppicing. To avoid shock to the plant, cut only when the tree is completely dormant. Poplars, willows, wild cherries, wild plums, and locusts stand this treatment well. Coppicing is often used to grow firewood. When harvested in their dormant season, the trees grow a new crop of wood within a decade or so. You can also apply this technique to some shrubs, such as this hydrangea, in order to give them renewed life.

Pruning a Japanese-Style Garden

A Japanese-influenced garden is almost always built on uneven land. It usually features running water and distinctive, small trees that greatly resemble very old, full-size trees.

The skillful pruning process that makes this kind of landscaping possible is similar to that used on bonsai plants grown in shallow dishes (see chapter 14 for more details). If you were to shear a 5-foot Colorado blue spruce in the usual manner, it would be an attractive, stiff, formal specimen. However, a similar 5-foot tree grown and pruned in the Japanese method can resemble a 100-foot spruce that has been growing for a century or more on a windswept Colorado mountaintop.

Getting Started with Japanese-Style Pruning

1. Thin the limb area rigorously. Cut off some of the branches at the trunk, particularly any long or large limbs. Part of the charm of an ancient-looking specimen is being able to see its trunk.

2. Train the remaining branches by wrapping wire around them in a manner similar to making a bonsai (see page 207). Stick the base of the wire in the ground, bend the tree carefully, and spiral the rest upward at about a 45-degree twist.

For evergreens, this is best done when they are dormant (fall or winter); for deciduous plants, wrap in early summer when they are most flexible. Heavy trunks and branches require 8- or 9-gauge wire, and 18- to 20-gauge wire can be used in most other cases. Remove the wire after a season's growth.

3. During the growing season, snip and pinch frequently — do not shear the ends.

4. Do an annual heavier pruning during the dormant season in late fall.

Almost any tree can be dwarfed in the Japanese manner, but some are more attractive and easier to prune in this fashion than others. The slow-growing conifers and dwarf trees or shrubs make the best choices for this kind of landscaping.

MASTER GARDENING TIPS

A Successful Japanese Garden Look

► Occasional root pruning may be necessary to get a bonsai effect. (See chapter 14.)

► To add to the ancient, weathered look, grow the tree in soil that is covered with several inches of moss. In a few years, remove the moss and let the gnarled roots become a part of the tree's trunk.

► Position a few carefully selected rocks that have interesting shapes to complete the picture.

► If you can manage to get a brook to wend its way through the landscape, or to construct a natural-looking fountain, all you'll need is a kimono and a cup of sake as you relax in your masterpiece.

Neglected

Well-pruned

A well-pruned apple tree bears annually over all its branches and can support the weight of a moderate-size harvest, whereas a neglected tree is likely to produce only biennially and the fruits will be small.

Pruning Fruit Trees

I'm always surprised at the modest yields gardeners expect from their orchards. I have a friend who always has a superb vegetable garden, a wonderful bed of roses, and the best strawberry patch in town. Each tomato is a jewel. Every stalk of corn produces two large ears, and every flower in his perennial bed looks as if it is posing for the cover of a garden magazine. Yet in spite of his gardening skill, he seems to be perfectly satisfied to take whatever his fruit trees hand him. And often this isn't very much. He has good fruit during the rare years when conditions are perfect, but usually he gets fruit that is small, misshapen, poorly colored, and infested with insects. Furthermore, he typically gets a crop only every other year. It seems that pruning fruit trees is a neglected art, one that novice growers often don't completely understand.

I'm sure that when my friend's trees were young, they were full of vigor and produced excellent fruit. Young trees almost always bear large, colorful fruit because they still have few limbs, and the fruit gets lots of sunlight. However, as fruit trees mature and grow more branches, you must prune to keep them producing well. Most naturally produce a large crop every other year, but pruning can change that to annually.

Pruning fruit trees need not be confusing. One thing that helps is to know that your fruit tree almost always consists of two parts. The roots usually belong to a type of tree that produces low-quality fruit but grows vigorously and is winter-hardy, whereas the grafted top is a named variety like 'Delicious'. The two have been joined because this is the most efficient way to produce large numbers of quality fruit trees. Fruit trees grown from seed seldom resemble the parent tree even slightly, and growing trees from cuttings or layers is a slow and extremely difficult process.

Pruning a Bare-Root Fruit Tree at Planting Time

Some gardeners enjoy pruning their fruit trees and consequently do a good job. However, no one should prune simply for the fun of it — you should understand the reasons for pruning.

Although it isn't easy, you should cut back any bare-root young tree at planting time. When we prune trees for customers at our nursery, they wince and say that it looks as if we are slaughtering the poor things, but we assure them that this is one of the best things to do to ensure good growth and early crops.

Most mail-order plants are sold bare-root, and unless the directions you receive with the tree indicate that it has already been done, you will have to prune. (If your new tree comes enclosed in a ball of soil or growing in a pot, no cutback is necessary.)

MASTER GARDENING TIPS

Reasons for Pruning Fruit Trees

▶ To get the tree off to a good start

▶ To encourage good crops of quality fruit

▶ To manage your tree's size

▶ To keep your tree healthy

▶ To repair a tree that hasn't been pruned properly or at all

1. Cut off any jagged edges or broken roots. Because bare-root fruit trees have probably been dug mechanically, chances are good that some of the roots have been seriously damaged in the process. This pruning helps them heal smoothly.

2. Cut back the top area to make it equivalent in size to the root. Always cut on a slant just above a bud. If you've purchased a whip — a young fruit tree with no side branches — cut it back by at least a third. For example, if your tree is 6 feet tall, cut it back at least 2 feet. If your new plant has branches, first cut off those that are weak, dead looking, broken, or too close to the ground. Then cut back the top by a third, and each strong, healthy limb by at least a third also. Cut to an outside bud so that the next branch will form toward the outside and the tree will spread outward rather than inward toward the trunk.

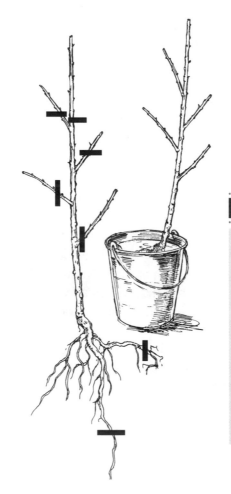

HINT FOR SUCCESS

Keep in mind that these directions are only for pruning. Don't neglect the other steps in proper planting, like soaking roots for several hours after arrival, using lots of good soil and water while planting, and planting at the right depth. Most fruit-tree failures are due to the lack of proper planting as much as the failure to prune properly at planting time.

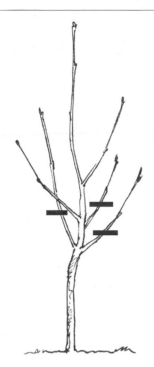

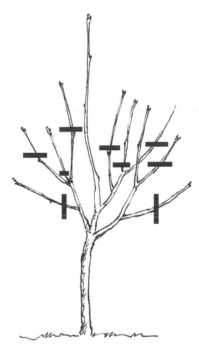

At planting time: Pruning a new, bare-root fruit tree begins its very first year. Shorten all branches by one-third. It is not necessary to prune potted trees or those bought with their roots wrapped in a ball of soil.

Year two: Begin training. Encourage the central leader to be strong by thinning out the vertical branches growing along it.

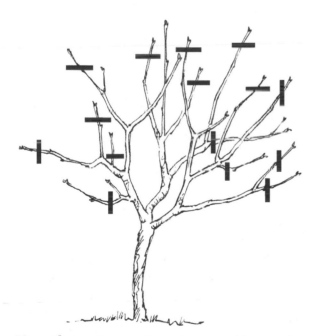

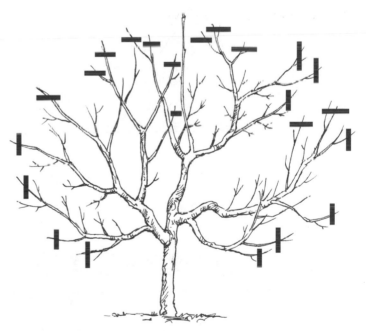

Year three: Prune only to shape, and keep only one central leader. Pruning before bearing spurs are established delays fruiting.

Year four and beyond: Prune lightly to shape the tree during the first years of its life. The old saying "As the twig is bent, so the tree is inclined" is unquestionably true. A little snipping and pinching here and there while a tree is young will save you a lot of heavy pruning later. Also, heavy pruning can delay the tree's first crop; prune just enough to help shape it. In later years, you will cut more aggressively, aiming for one of three forms: central leader, modified leader, or open center (see page 119).

Pruning a Young Fruit Tree

Apples, pears, and peaches produce fruit loads much heavier than those on plums and cherries. Since plums and cherries are apt to grow into a bushy form no matter what you do, early shaping is important mainly to keep them from getting too wide — and to prevent the branches from growing too close to the ground. When you are growing apples and pears, you will find that some need more shaping than others. Many apples, such as 'Wealthy' and 'McIntosh', seem to grow into a good shape quite naturally. Others, like the 'Delicious' and 'Yellow Transparent', tend to grow very upright, forcing lots of tops with bad crotches (see drawing below).

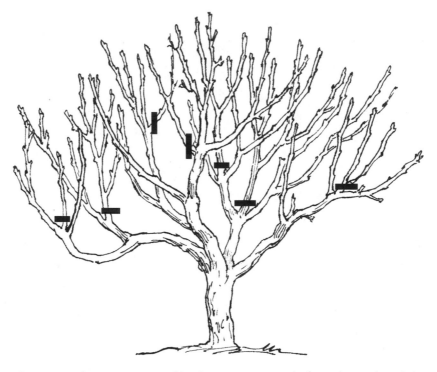

Prune upright-growing trees like this one to get rid of weak crotches that are likely to break under a heavy load of fruit.

MASTER GARDENING TIPS

Pruning Principles

▶ *Train the young tree to grow in a spreading shape.* The heavy pruning at planting time sometimes results in too many branches close to the ground. Pinch or clip off all undesirable new sprouts.

▶ *Keep in mind an image of the mature tree* as you clip or snip off the buds or tiny twigs. Aim to develop a strong tree with a branch structure sturdy enough to hold up the crop.

▶ *Prune in accordance with the tree's natural growth habit.*

▶ *Thin!* Keep the branches sparse enough for fruit to get enough sunlight to ripen. Some trees grow twiggy naturally; certain apple varieties, such as 'Jonathan', and many varieties of cherries, plums, peaches, and apricots, need additional thinning of their bearing wood to let in sunshine.

Fruit-Tree Pruning Styles

Pruning for a central leader

Recommended for: Trees that bear heavy crops of large fruit, including apples and pears, are usually best pruned to grow with a central leader, or trunk, at least in their younger days. With only one strong trunk in the center of the tree, branches come out strongly from it at fairly wide angles and can safely bear abundant loads of fruit.

How-to: Thin out the branches growing from the central leader as necessary to allow open space between the limbs. Thin also the branches that come from these limbs, and so on, out to the outermost branches. Eventually you will have to cut out the top of the tall central leader, because it will gradually sag under a load of heavy fruit, forming a canopy over part of the tree and shutting out needed light.

What it achieves: Sunlight produces colorful, flavorful, vitamin-enriched fruit. Sunlight and circulating air also help to prevent scab, mildew, and a host of other diseases that thrive in shade and high humidity.

central leader

Pruning for a modified leader

Recommended for: Although the central-leader method is preferred by most orchardists for growing apples and pears, the modified-leader method is easier to maintain simply because most fruit trees grow that way naturally.

How-to: The modified-leader method is initially the same as the central-leader method, but eventually you let the central trunk branch off to form several tops. Cut back the tops of tall-growing trees from time to time to shorten the trees and to let in more light.

What it achieves: This training ensures that the loads of fruit at the top of the tree are never as heavy as those at the bottom, where limbs are larger.

modified leader

Pruning for an open center

Recommended for: Since this method, also known as the open-top or vase method, produces a tree with a weaker branch structure than if it had a strong central leader, lightweight fruits are the best subjects: quinces, crab apples, plums, cherries, peaches, nectarines, and apricots.

How-to: Prune so that the limbs forming the vase effect do not all come out of the main trunk close to each other, or they will form a cluster of weak crotches. Even with the whole center of the tree open, you'll need to thin the branches and remove the older limbs eventually, just as you would with a tree pruned with the central-leader method.

What it achieves: This is an excellent way to let more light into the shady interior of a tree.

open center

Prune for Quality Fruit

When your first objective is quality fruit, follow these guidelines:

• **Let in the light.** To produce good fruit a tree needs plenty of sunshine, and a fruit tree has a potentially large area to produce fruit: A full-size, standard tree can be well over 30 feet wide and 35 feet high. However, only 30 percent of an unpruned tree, because of its tight branch structure, gets enough light, while another 40 percent gets only a fair amount of light. As these percentages indicate, when only the top exterior of the tree produces good fruit, you are getting the use of but one-third of your tree, and all that fruit is grown where it is most difficult to pick! Even the most careful pruning won't bring the light efficiency to a full 100 percent, but you can greatly increase it. (See the bottom illustration on page 119.)

• **Remove surplus fruits** when your tree sets too many. The production of too many fruits (and therefore seeds) taxes a tree's strength, and certain varieties of fruits, unless you give them a helping hand, seem bent on bearing themselves to death. Although regular pruning will cut down on the number of fruits produced, a tree may still bear a greater number than it can develop to a large size. *Note:* When a tree bears too many fruits in any one year, it usually bears few, if any, the following year.

MASTER GARDENING TIP

Fruit Trees as Ornamentals?

Fruit trees are not usually recommended as ornamentals, because there are many other flowering trees that need less care and have fewer disease and insect problems. But many people feel a fruit tree doesn't need much special attention when grown for its appearance rather than for its produce. This isn't totally true; all fruit trees need occasional pruning to remain healthy, even if you never eat their produce.

If at any time your tree, regardless of it size or age, appears to be setting too many fruits, thin each cluster of small fruits to a single fruit. Thin apples, peaches, nectarines, and other large fruits to 6 inches or more apart.

Prune judiciously to admit more light to the center of the tree.

Repair Pruning

Sometimes you inherit a relatively young fruit tree that has gotten off to a poor start due to lack of pruning or incorrect pruning. It's usually not too late to fix it.

Problem: The tree has a weak, U-shaped crotch. It will collect water, begin to rot, and eventually split or break off at this point.

Solution: Cut out one of the forks. The result will be a crooked leader, but that is nevertheless a big improvement, and later the crook will straighten out considerably.

Before

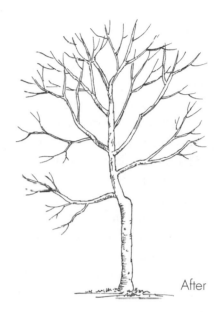

After

Problem: The tree has several tops.

Solution: Prune back to a single top. Any remaining side branches may be removed later as the top grows taller.

Before

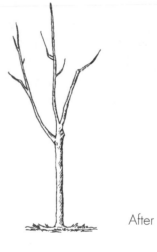

After

Problem: The tree is tangled with growth.

Solution: Simply removing all unnecessary growth may make a world of difference. Cut weak and dead branches, branches that compete with each other, and those that have strayed too far from the rest of the tree.

Before

After

Prune to Manage Your Tree's Size

What's wrong with a large tree? Standard-size fruit trees can grow to 30 or 40 feet or more, but a large specimen is difficult to manage and dangerous to work in. And because so much of it is shaded, it often produces poor fruit.

In suburban and urban settings, trees (particularly the lower, outside branches) are deprived of light as buildings, high or tight fences, and other trees crowd them. They respond by growing too tall — and require a lot of drastic pruning later on. The problem also occurs in rural settings. Farmers let their cattle or horses chew off all the lower branches, forcing the growth upward. (Pigs, however, can be allowed to clean up the unused fruit at harvest time.)

What can you do if you have excessively tall fruit trees? You can remove them — though cutting down healthy trees, just because you or someone else planted too many, is a traumatic experience. Still, thinning is often the only way to achieve a good orchard.

Of course, it's best to prune regularly so that a tree doesn't get too tall in the first place, but if this advice comes too late, consider shortening it. Make sure the tree in question is healthy enough to stand major surgery, and that there will be enough lower branches left to sustain it after its upper level has been removed. The leaf surface remaining must be adequate to supply nutrients to the tree. Like an obese person, the tree got into its overgrown condition over a period of many years, so don't try to correct all its problems at once.

MASTER GARDENING TIPS

How to Prune Back a Too-Tall Fruit Tree

▶ Begin the project in late summer or early fall.

▶ Cut off the top in stages — prune off only small pieces of limbs at any one time. This way, the weight will be lightened before you begin the heavy cutting. Also, these small cuts lessen the danger of splitting limbs, and help ensure that you won't drop heavy pieces of wood onto the lower branches. (If possible, have a helper handy to catch the limbs as they fall or to guide them away from the tree.) See the directions for cutting off heavy limbs detailed on page 30.

▶ Don't remove more than one large limb in any one year. Make sure that some regrowth has started on the lower branches before you make any further cuts.

Prune to Keep Your Tree Healthy

Even a young fruit tree occasionally needs to be pruned because of some mishap. Limbs get broken, tent caterpillars build nests, and as the tree gets older, rot and winter injury often take their toll on its branches.

Rejuvenation is vital to a tree's health, especially when your goal is to produce good crops of high-quality fruit over a number of years. Many trees that produce handsome specimens while they are young or middle aged often bear only small, poor fruit as they grow older. By replacing and renewing the old bearing wood, you encourage the tree to continue bringing forth large red apples or big crops of juicy plums or peaches.

MASTER GARDENING TIPS

A Mature Fruit Tree's Annual Tune-up

As with every other kind of pruning, you'll get the best results from rejuvenation pruning when you do it on an annual basis rather than as an occasional event.

▶ **Remove damaged wood.** Clip or saw off the injured part back to a live limb or the trunk. Even one deteriorating limb is not good for the tree's health, and the accumulation of several sick limbs will speed the decline of the tree.

▶ **Thin out and open up the tree** to permit sunshine to enter and ripen the fruit. Air will circulate to discourage disease, and it will be easier for birds to spot and pick up preying insects.

▶ **Remove a few of the older limbs.** If you do this each year, the whole bearing surface can be renewed every six or eight years, which is like getting a whole new tree. In addition, because you will seldom need to do any drastic pruning of large, heavy limbs, the tree will suffer less. Large limbs should grow only as an extension of the tree trunk itself, and as a unit from which the smaller limbs grow. These overlarge limbs are a tremendous strain on the tree, so the fewer, the better.

▶ **Cut off crossed branches** or branches that might rub to cause wounds in the bark.

▶ **Remove water sprouts promptly.** (These are those upright, vigorous-growing branches that appear in clumps, often from a large pruning wound.) They are usually unproductive, and can weaken the tree by causing additional, unwanted shade.

Managing Suckers

- **What causes suckers?** A lot of sucker growth occurs on fruit trees when a slower-growing variety is grafted onto a vigorous-growing rootstock.

- **What's the difference between water sprouts and root suckers?** Water sprouts emerge from branches and root suckers emerge from the ground.

- **What should I do when I spot them?** Mow or clip them off at ground level as soon as they appear, while they're still on the small side and succulent.

- **What if I don't remove them?** If they appear from below the graft, they'll grow into a wild tree or bush that will crowd out the good part of the tree within a few years. They will also sap valuable energy from the tree.

- **Can I transplant them?** Because suckers look like new, young trees, it's tempting to think you can transplant them to form a new fruit tree of the same variety. But such trees usually produce fruit of inferior quality because they have come from the rootstock rather then the named variety.

- **Can I use them for grafts?** Certainly, give it a try if you like to experiment. You can produce new trees that are of good quality by cutting a small, pencil-thin limb or bud from a named variety — say, a 'Delicious' or 'Rome Beauty' apple — grafting it onto one of your wild sucker trees, and planting the result where you'd like a new tree to grow.

MASTER GARDENING TIP

Seedlings in the Orchard

In some unmowed orchards, trees sprout and grow from seeds of unused fruit that fall on the ground. Treat them like suckers and remove them as soon as they begin to grow. Like any weed, they sap energy from the orchard by depleting the water and fertility of the soil — and eventually they crowd out the good trees.

Although seedlings can often resemble the named varieties, their appearance is deceptive, and almost always the fruit is of inferior quality. Don't allow them, or any other weed, to compete with the vast root system your trees need to support the large crops of fruit you're anticipating.

Suckers are fast-growing shoots, usually vertical and erect. They tend to appear as a cluster of branches close to the base of a tree trunk, but sometimes (especially on plums and cherries) they pop up from the roots anywhere under a tree, even a distance away from the trunk.

Dealing with Sunscald

Sunscald is the most common type of winter injury to fruit trees. You'll recognize it if you see bark that looks blistered, with small cracks or even large slits that run up and down the tree.

- **What causes it?** Sunscald can take place in any climate when the bright, warm sun shines directly on a young tree's bark. It is especially hard on trees with little foliage to shade them. It often occurs in the North on late-winter days when the sun warms the bark to temperatures far above the surrounding air. Then a cloud suddenly covers the sun, or the sun drops behind a hill, or perhaps a quick, cold breeze comes up. The sudden cooling of the tree's surface, and the subsequent tightening of the bark and freezing of the cells, causes the damage.

- **What should I do?** If you spot the damage early, stick the loose bark back onto the limb with large thumbtacks or small nails with large heads. After tacking, cover the whole area with tree dressing.

- **What happens if I don't treat it immediately?** If you don't repair sunscald damage at once, the wood and loose bark separate and the wood around the wound dies, sometimes necessitating a major pruning job in the spring.

- **What can I do to prevent sunscald?** We like to spray a thinned white latex paint on our trees every two or three years, paying special attention to covering the trunk and lower branches on the southern and eastern exposures, where the sun shines brightest in late winter. This helps keep the tree sap cool. Whitewashing the tree stems is useful in the South, too, where excessive sun often blisters the bark during hot summers.

MASTER GARDENING TIPS

Other Types of Winter Injury

Sometimes a tree doesn't stop growing early enough in late summer to harden up its wood properly, and it isn't able to withstand the first cold spell or the extreme cold in winter. Or untimely warm spells in late winter may stimulate bud activity, and the trees lose moisture that the frozen roots can't replace. Occasionally, extreme cold or chilling winds during cold periods can cause cell damage. Also, during a cold, windy period or a prolonged cold spell, the insulating bark may be penetrated by the low temperatures, causing damage to the interior of the tree and the roots.

Treatment:
- ▶ Cut out damaged wood early in the spring. If the winter damage is severe, a heavy pruning of damaged wood will probably be all that a tree can stand, so don't do any additional pruning that year. (When this happens, avoid fertilizing for a year or so to prevent overstimulation of growth in an already weak tree.)

  Note: Make sure that the wood is really dead before you start pruning. Sometimes it is difficult to tell which limbs are really dead and which are merely slow about leafing out. If in doubt, postpone the pruning for a few weeks, just to be sure.

Prevention:
- ▶ Choose varieties that are suitable for growing in your region (that is, hardy in your USDA Hardiness Zone).
- ▶ Prune carefully and at the right time.
- ▶ Fertilize only in spring and early summer so that you don't stimulate late growth.
- ▶ Before winter arrives, cover tree roots with a heavy mulch of hay, shredded bark, or leaves so that the ground doesn't freeze deep or warm up suddenly. This mulch will help to prevent root injury and also keep the tree from running out of moisture.

When to Prune Fruit Trees

When is the best time to prune fruit trees? This is a subject of ongoing debate among pomologists. Magazines often run articles supporting one season or another, and each professional orchardist and experienced home grower has a favorite time. Meanwhile, beginners can get confused listening to the controversy.

Perhaps the best way to help answer the question is to describe what happens when you prune at different seasons. Seasonal conditions vary greatly throughout the country, so your location is an important factor in determining when you should prune.

Spring

Most people agree that pruning a fruit tree when it is just beginning to make its most active growth is one of the worst times. The tree will probably bleed heavily, and it may have trouble recovering from the loss of so much sap. Also, infections such as fire blight are most active and likely to spread in the spring. If a book suggests pruning in early spring, the author often means late winter — that is, before any sign of growth begins.

The only pruning you should do in the spring is to remove branches that have been broken by winter storms or injured by the cold. Immediately tack bark that has split from the trunk back onto the wood, and seal the wound with tree dressing to prevent air from drying the bare wood.

Early Summer

Although I don't recommend major pruning in early summer, this is a good time to pinch off buds (fruit buds are plumper than leaf buds) and snip off small branches that are growing in the wrong direction or in the wrong place. Also remove suckers, water sprouts, and branches that have formed too low on the stem as soon as you notice them.

Fruit trees grown in planters or tubs, espaliers, and other artistically shaped trees should be clipped regularly to keep them looking their best. Clip or pinch back new growth on tight hedges, "beanpoles," or fences as soon as they begin to grow, and continue throughout the summer to maintain them in the intended size and shape.

MASTER GARDENING TIP

Lorette Pruning

Developed in Europe by M. Lorette, this is an excellent but complicated method for intensive fruit growing. It is especially useful on dwarf fruit trees and on trees grown as espaliers, cordons, hedges, and fences. (See chapter 8.)

To prevent useless limb growth, begin pruning in early summer and continue until early fall. No dormant pruning is done at all. By frequent clipping and pinching, you'll direct the tree's energy into producing fruit buds near the trunk or on a few short limbs, rather than out at the ends of long branches.

This technique is somewhat like shearing a hedge, and results in small, easy-to-care-for trees that bear fruit at an early age. Each part of the tree is in full sunlight because there is so little leaf area. Therefore, the fruit is of superior quality.

In cold regions, the Lorette method is risky, since trees pruned in summer tend to keep growing later in the season, and this growth may be injured during the winter. For the same reason, even in areas where the growing season is long, vigorous-growing trees such as peach and apricot are often difficult to grow by the Lorette system.

Late Summer

Late summer is a favorite time for many people to prune their fruit trees. By pruning after the tree has completed its yearly growth and hardened its wood, yet before it has lost its leaves, you'll stimulate less regrowth. You still have to take care of any frost injury in late winter, but late-summer/early-fall pruning works well if extensive winter damage is not likely.

Wherever growing seasons are short and you expect extreme cold or heavy snow and ice loads to cause injury to your trees, late-winter pruning is best. Don't cut back a tree in late summer if there's a good chance that the remaining branches will be winterkilled — you'll have to prune away too much of the tree.

Late Fall and Winter

Late fall or winter is a favorite time to prune in the warmer parts of the country. Orchardists have more spare time then, and the trees are bare, so it is easier to see what needs to be done. Choose days when the temperature is above freezing, however, to avoid injury to the wood. Frozen wood is very brittle and breaks easily when accidentally hit by a ladder or pruning tool.

If you live in a cold part of the country, or if you're growing varieties that are inclined to have winter injury, wait until the coldest weather is over before pruning.

Late Winter

This season is probably the most popular time for northern gardeners to prune. As in late fall and winter, the tree is completely dormant, and since the leaves are off, it is easy to see where to make the cuts. You can repair any winter injury and the weather is usually warm enough during the day to avoid cutting frozen wood.

If you prune your trees regularly each year, late winter is a satisfactory time to prune, because you don't have to remove large amounts of wood. However, if your trees have been neglected for a few years and are badly in need of a cutback, late winter is not the best time. Excessive pruning in late winter usually stimulates a great deal of growth the following spring and summer, because the tree tries to replace its lost wood. Branches, suckers, and water sprouts are likely to grow in great abundance. If a major pruning job is necessary, you're better off doing all or at least a large part of it in late summer or early fall so that you won't encourage a burst of regrowth.

MASTER GARDENING TIP

Pruning in Snow Country

You may need to prune differently if your fruit trees are growing in an area where snows are heavy and the average accumulation is 3 feet or more, or if the snow drifts that high around the trees.

Although in most regions it's best to allow a fruit tree to grow its branches quite close to the ground, this isn't the thing to do in deep-snow country. Heavy ice crusts sometimes settle as the snow underneath melts, breaking lower limbs in the process. This causes ugly wounds in the tree's trunk. Don't plant dwarf fruit trees, because their branches are practically all low growing.

Pruning Dwarf Fruit Trees

Many of the fruit trees sold today are the dwarf or semidwarf type, rather than full-size trees. Although the tops of these small trees are the same variety and produce the same size fruit as ordinary trees, their special rootstocks keep them from getting large. Dwarf and semidwarf trees vary from about 5 to 12 feet high when fully grown, depending on the kind of rootstock.

Dwarf trees require some pruning just as full-size trees do, but their height needs no control, and, since they grow more slowly, the pruning is needed less often. You may also, just as on standard trees, need to do some thinning of the fruit to encourage a better-quality harvest. Miniature fruit trees grown in tubs or planters for ornamental purposes also need some shearing or snipping back during the summer to keep them in an attractive shape.

Dwarfing a Full-Size Tree

In some areas, regular dwarf fruit trees are not entirely satisfactory because of their lack of hardiness, a tendency to break in high winds or heavy snows, and their susceptibility to insect and disease damage. Full-size trees can be dwarfed by surgery without much trouble — an interesting, though not common, practice.

The surgery slows down the growth of a tree, and also usually makes it bear at a younger age. It is, however, not a permanent fix — after many years the inverted bark cells are replaced by those that are headed in the right direction, and the tree resumes growing at its normal rate until it reaches full size.

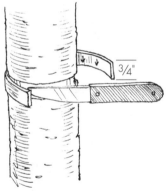

1 In early summer, cut a strip of bark about ¾ inch wide completely around the tree by making two rings. Cut to, but not into, the wood. Precision cutting is important because a careless cut with a sharp knife could kill the tree.

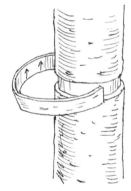

2 Remove the bark, turn it upside down, and replace it, with the green side still inward.

3 Cover the whole thing with grafting wax, tree dressing, or rubber electrical tape (not plastic) to seal out the air. Let the covering wear away by itself.

Pruning to Make Trees Bear

When a Tree Bears Too Much, Too Soon

The time required by a young fruit tree to begin bearing is generally from 2 to 12 years, depending on the kind of fruit, the variety, and your growing conditions. Don't allow a tree to bear fruit while it is still small, or it will be weakened and won't bear again for many years. It's difficult to say exactly when a tree is strong enough to bear its first crop, but you can make that judgment by evaluating the strength of the limbs, the height, and its general health.

What to do:

If you feel that your tree is too small to mature fruit without weakening the tree, pick off its first blooms or small fruits.

When a Tree Is Slow to Bear

Sometimes, instead of bearing early in life, a tree will do just the opposite. Some varieties naturally take a long time to produce, such as the 'Baldwin' apple and certain pears; others, in spite of your careful pruning, are so comfortable and growing so luxuriously that they forget to settle down and bear fruit. Delayed bearing can also be the result of overly rich soil.

What to do:

You need to find a way to slow down overactive growth and thereby get the tree to produce. Some old-timers used unconventional methods, like putting a good-size rock in the first crotch of branches. Others bent branches toward the ground and fastened them with ropes, like pegging down a tent, to make the tree produce faster. Not long ago, a gardening friend of mine who believes strongly in the secret life of plants told me he got excellent results by showing his delinquent tree a chain saw and voicing loud threats!

If you're skeptical of these methods, you could try the one described on page 128, "Dwarfing a Full-Size Tree." If you don't want to dwarf the entire tree, it's possible to reverse the bark on only a limb or two. Root pruning (see page 35) is another method used to slow down tree growth without injuring the tree.

As a last resort, you can try "ringing." Just bear in mind that this is a harsh operation and it isn't likely to do the tree any good. In early summer, cut a single slit three-quarters of the way around one or two limbs. Use a sharp knife and don't scar the bark any more than necessary. Cut through the bark, but not into the wood. Theoretically, ringing thwarts new vegetative growth and forces the tree to turn its energy to flowering and bearing.

Occasionally we hear of healthy, rugged trees, a dozen or more years old, that have yet to produce a single bloom. On them, ringing is worth a try.

The Old Orchard

Not long ago, a newlywed couple we were visiting asked me to look at the old orchard they wanted to rejuvenate. It was an interesting experience. Walking through a decrepit orchard that provided bountifully for a family three or four generations ago is a bit like wandering through a ghost town. Our friends wanted to know if they could salvage it. Many people ask the same question when they're faced with an old tree or orchard. Sometimes, unfortunately, it is better to clear the land, stack up a big woodpile, and start over — but not always.

Recovery Mission

If the neglected trees are in sound condition, and the fruit looks as if it could be improved by thinning, fertilizing, and pruning, by all means clean up the orchard and prune the trees. It will certainly be time well spent. Although it may never look like a model orchard, you should reap lots of good fruit and enjoy the happy knowledge that you have taken a sad, old fruit grove and made it into something worthwhile.

The following steps can be accomplished over the course of several years, as indicated. However, if the trees are not in desperate condition, or if they respond well to your initial cleanup pruning, you may accelerate the process.

Year one:

• With your saw and scythe, remove all the brush and weeds, all trees other than fruit trees, and any fruit trees that look decrepit or produce worthless fruit.

• Knock off all the loose bark on the remaining good trees, being careful not to open new wounds.

• Cut off dead limbs and all broken branches, making sure to cut each one back to a live branch or to the trunk without leaving a stub. Follow the directions for cutting large branches (see page 30) so that the wood doesn't split back into the trunk.

• Cut out limbs with woodpecker holes and those that have suffered weather damage or show signs of insect or disease infestation. This may be all the pruning you'll want to do the first year on those trees that needed severe pruning. On trees that required little surgery, however, you can begin some removal of the smaller limbs around the top of the tree to let in more light. Don't cut out too many live limbs in any one year, though, unless their weight seems to be threatening the tree.

• Paint over the cut areas with a good tree paint.

• Haul away all debris — wood, bark, and brush — so that insects and disease won't reproduce in it.

(see page 30)

MASTER GARDENING TIPS

Straight Answers

Before you decide to try to save an old orchard, ask yourself these two questions and answer them honestly:

▶ *Are the trees too far gone?* If their trunks are full of rot and large holes, or if they're half dead and splitting apart, they're probably on their last legs, and any pruning might finish them off.

▶ *Is the fruit the trees produce any good?* If it is green, hard, sour, and small, the trees are probably of a poor variety. Perhaps they grew as suckers from the roots of other trees now gone, or from seeds that grew out of fallen, unused fruit. Unless the fruit is worth cooking or making into cider, it's just as well to get rid of such trees.

Year two:

• Begin a light pruning at the top of each tree so that more sunlight can reach the interior. Remove no more than one-third of a tree's limb area at one time.

• Cut out a few older, medium-size, weak, and unproductive branches.

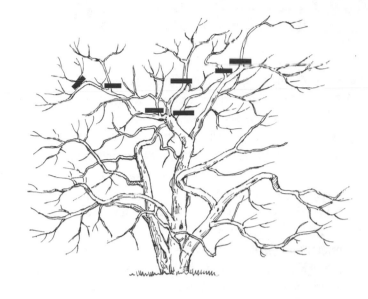

Year three:

• Thin out the branches even more.

• Begin to remove a few of the larger branches, to renew the tree.

Year four and beyond:

From now on, prune in a normal way. If a tree appears to be in good physical condition, with lots of lower limbs and adequate new growth, begin to cut back the top to make it lower. Your orchard, thanks to all your careful pruning, should now look much better, and begin producing tasty crops once again.

Pruning Sanitation

Some of the most serious diseases are carried by pruning tools. For example, fire blight, a bacteria-caused disease that's lethal to fruit trees, especially pears, has spread around many orchards through tools.

If you suspect disease, think of yourself as a tree doctor as you prune. You wouldn't expect a surgeon to take out your gallbladder with the same dirty instruments she used to remove her last patient's appendix. Your tree deserves careful treatment, with tools that have been disinfected.

Disinfect your tools after pruning each tree. Professional orchardists often use a mixture of bichloride of mercury and cyanide of mercury for this purpose, but both of these chemicals are poisonous and are not recommended for home use. For the home gardener, it is safer and quite effective to soak the tools in a pail containing a chlorine bleach solution (1 part bleach to 9 parts water) as you go between branches or trees. With these germ-free tools, you can approach your patients with a clear conscience and not feel that they are drawing their limbs about them in fear and trembling.

Disease also spreads around the orchard via the wind and insects. A good way to keep fungi, germs, and insects out of your trees is to seal up all cuts and open wounds with an antiseptic paint. Most infections are especially active in the spring, so do your painting and sealing early in the season before they get started.

Finally, always remove all of the pruning debris from the area. Don't put it on your compost pile: Either burn it or take it to a landfill.

MASTER GARDENING TIP

What about Decrepit Trees?

There is usually no way to get a sprawling, crotchy old tree back to growing with a model central leader without serious shock to the tree, and you can't top tall ones safely if they are past their prime. Usually, opening up a tree's center and thinning the wood is all the pruning you can hope to do on an elderly tree.

In addition to pruning, however, you can help rejuvenate it by fertilizing the soil generously and thinning the fruit during the years when it sets too large a crop.

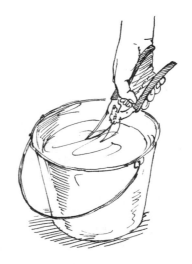

Dip pruning shears and saws into chlorine bleach solution (1 part bleach to 9 parts water) after each cut, before going on to the next one.

Pruning Spur-Type Fruit Trees

Trees bear their fruit either on the limbs or on short, stubby branches called spurs between the branches. Pears, plums, and cherries grow mostly on spurs, peaches grow on one-year-old limb growth, and most varieties of apples are produced both on spurs and on limbs.

Because spur-type fruit trees grow more slowly, they need less pruning. Since this means considerably less labor for the orchardist, scientists have worked on breeding trees that produce mostly on spurs, and there are now many varieties of this type of fruit tree available.

When too many fruit spurs develop along a branch, cut out some of them to encourage bigger and better fruits on the rest. After a few years of experience, you'll be able to judge about how many spurs are right for your tree. Each spur will usually produce for several years, but then you should cut it off to allow a replacement to grow. You'll be able to spot the older spurs by their aging appearance.

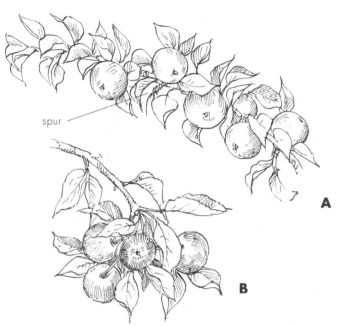

Some trees flower and fruit on especially short, stubby branches called spurs (**A**); others produce their crops at the tips of the branches (**B**).

MASTER GARDENING TIPS

Pruning a Five-in-One Fruit Tree

As a novelty, some nurseries sell three-in-one or five-in-one apple trees, and some even feature specimens with plums, cherries, peaches, nectarines, and apricots all growing on the same tree. Some home gardeners like to graft several varieties of fruit on their own single tree, too, either for the fun of it or because they have a small growing area.

These multiple-variety fruit trees are difficult to prune. However, if you have one or feel you must buy or graft your own, you can prune them if you take some precautions.

▶ *Mark the varieties.* You will have to remember each year where the different varieties are located, or else you may cut off the only limb bearing a certain kind of fruit. If you don't have a good memory, tie ribbons of various colors to identify each one.

▶ *Grow your multiple-fruit tree with an open center* (see page 119), since there will be three or more strong limbs. Each different kind of limb will grow at its own rate and in a different manner, so corrective pruning will be necessary to produce a well-balanced tree. It's a big job, but if you keep at it, you can avoid bad crotches, water sprouts, and lopsided growth.

▶ *Be careful not to inadvertently remove branches you wanted to keep.* We once had a tree growing in our backyard with red, yellow, and green apples. Each year I grafted some new varieties on it, but unfortunately, I also mistakenly pruned off a few others, so the tree never became the masterpiece I had hoped it would be. Still, I had fun, and intend someday to do another.

Apple

To prune apple trees, follow the general directions for pruning fruit trees. Keep the tree growing with a central leader, if possible, and correct any bad growth habits common for your variety of tree. Since apples are the most commonly grown fruit in home gardens, the following list of popular varieties includes growth characteristics to help you with your pruning.

Tree	Description	Pruning Needs
'Cortland'	Spreading, somewhat drooping growth habit.	Don't allow to branch too close to the ground. Prune and thin to encourage large fruit. Open top for good color, and brace drooping limbs.
'Delicious'	Dense grower; will form many weak crotches if left alone.	Prune carefully to remove weak crotches. Without overpruning, allow in plenty of sunlight. Thin heavily for giant-size fruit.
'Duchess of Oldenberg'	Rugged, semiupright, medium-size tree. Bears on limbs and short spurs.	Prune and thin regularly for annual heavy crops for a long time.
'Early McIntosh'	Semiupright, large tree. Tends to bear small- to medium-size fruit biennially.	Prune and thin to correct its natural habit of forming bad crotches.
'Empire'	Semiupright; small- to midsize, dark red fruit of excellent quality. Bears on short spurs.	Benefits greatly from regular pruning and thinning.
'Granny Smith'	High-quality tree; requires long growing season, so grow only in warmer areas. Annual bearer.	Requires ordinary pruning.
'Jersey Mac'	Large tree with spreading habit. Annual bearer of good-quality, early-ripening 'McIntosh' fruit that tends to drop early.	Heavy thinning helps prevent early dropping.
'Jonagold'	Large, semiupright tree. Bears large and excellent-quality fruit when well cared for.	Prune heavily to correct its twiggy habit of growth.
'Jonamac'	Semiupright tree, less twiggy than 'Jonagold'. Larger fruit than many 'Jonathan'-type trees. Excellent-quality apples stay on the tree well.	Prune in the usual way, and thin out part of the short bearing spurs if they are becoming too numerous.
'Jonathan'	Tends to produce many small branches. Produces naturally small apples.	Needs regular thinning out of small branches. Thin fruit heavily for larger apples.
'Lobo'	Large, semispreading, 'McIntosh'-type tree. Bears good-quality fruit that ripens somewhat earlier than regular 'McIntosh'.	For annual bearing, prune; thin if necessary.
'Lodi'	Produces apples similar to 'Yellow Transparent' but with somewhat firmer fruit.	Prune to correct its upright growth habit. Thin to prevent an overlarge crop every other year.
'McIntosh'	A nearly ideal tree. Strong, spreading grower.	If pruned adequately, fruit will need little thinning. Brace limbs to support heavy crops.
'Macoun'	Upright-growing tree that bears small- to medium-size high-quality fruit biennially. Excellent choice for conscientious home gardener.	Long, lanky branches must be pruned regularly.
'Melba'	Early-bearing tree with high-quality 'McIntosh'-type fruit that tends to ripen over a long season. Good for home use.	Prune and thin to discourage biennial bearing.

Tree	Description	Pruning Needs
'Mutsu'	Semiupright, late-maturing variety from Japan. Grows large fruit. A heavy producer, yet seldom weakens itself by overbearing.	Thin heavily for large fruit.
'Northern Spy'	Produces long-keeping, superior fruit. Difficult to prune. Tends to grow very upright.	Prune heavily but carefully to avoid affecting the crop. Thin the apples to get largest fruit and to ensure annual bearing.
'Prima'	Vigorous, spreading tree. Resistant to scab and other fruit diseases. Fruit is good.	Requires ordinary pruning.
'Priscilla'	Semispreading tree. Resistant to mildew, fire blight, and scab — excellent choice for organic gardeners because little spraying required.	Requires ordinary pruning.
'Quinte'	Semispreading tree. Excellent early apple with beautiful color. Not always a heavy bearer.	Pruning and thinning will increase fruit size and promote regular bearing.
'Red Astrachan'	Semispreading tree. Produces excellent, early, old time apple.	Needs regular pruning and heavy thinning, or it will bear biennially.
'Red Duchess'	Semispreading tree.	Benefits from pruning and thinning. Needs topping or it will grow too tall.
'Regent'	Semiupright tree. Fruit grows singly, not in clusters, hangs on well, and usually bears annually.	Needs little thinning. Requires ordinary pruning.
'Rhode Island Greening'	Very spreading tree.	Limbs need bracing under heavy fruit loads. Prune heavily. Thin to encourage annual bearing.
'Rome Beauty'	Very upright growing.	Difficult to prune to central leader, so prune early and carefully to develop a strong tree.
'Spartan'	Large tree with semispreading growth. Bears heavily. Tends to bear biennially. Fruit is excellent but often drops early and tends to be small.	Requires careful pruning. Thinning helps avoid biennial bearing and early fruit drop.
'Spijon'	Spreading, drooping tree is an annual bearer. Quality of fruit is only fair.	May be grown with an open center.
'Stayman Winesap'	Tends to produce long, leggy branches.	Prune back long branches. Be sure to correct any bad growing habits early.
'Twenty Ounce'	Large, upright-growing tree.	Prune to central leader and allow to spread.
'Viking'	Semiupright, hardy tree. Excellent early apple.	Prune and thin to encourage annual bearing.
'Wealthy'	Tends to overbear its high-quality fruit in alternate years.	Prune and thin regularly to get annual crops and prevent fruit from getting smaller as it gets older.
'Winesap'	Like 'Delicious', forms weak crotches if not carefully pruned.	Thin to allow in sunlight and to increase size of fruit.
'Yellow Delicious' or 'Golden Delicious'	Tends to grow upright and crotchy, with long, leggy branches.	Prune to correct bad crotches and to prevent limbs from breaking under heavy load of fruit. Thin heavily for giant-size fruit.
'Yellow Transparent'	Upright grower. Bears while still young. Tends to bear too heavily. Unusually susceptible to sunscald.	Prune and thin carefully for larger apples and a longer-living tree. Correct bad crotches so branches don't split under weight of fruit. Whitewash trunk to avoid sunscald.
'York Imperial'	Tends to bear a large crop every other year.	Prune fruit spurs heavily in late winter each year. Thin out small fruits to even out yields. Prune to keep top of tree open.

Apricot

Pruning apricots *(Prunus armeniaca)* is similar to pruning peaches (see page 140). Heavy pruning is necessary to produce good fruit.

- **The open center method is best.**
- **You may need to thin out the bearing spurs.**
- **Root pruning is beneficial** to help prevent excessive growth and, where the growing season is short, subsequent winter injury.

Prune heavily to get the best crops and so the tree will bear annually. Some growers prefer to prune in the fall because it results in less vigorous regrowth.

Cherry

Cherry trees *(Prunus cerasus, P. avium)* need less pruning than other fruit trees.

- **Start pruning to a central leader** when your tree is young to encourage a strong tree, especially if it is one of the larger-growing types. Because of the tree's natural habit of growth, you probably will have to change to a modified leader or open center as it gets older.
- **You'll need to do some pruning to let in the sun** to color the fruit, and to thin out the bearing wood.
- **Beware of overpruning,** which can lead to winter injury and premature aging.

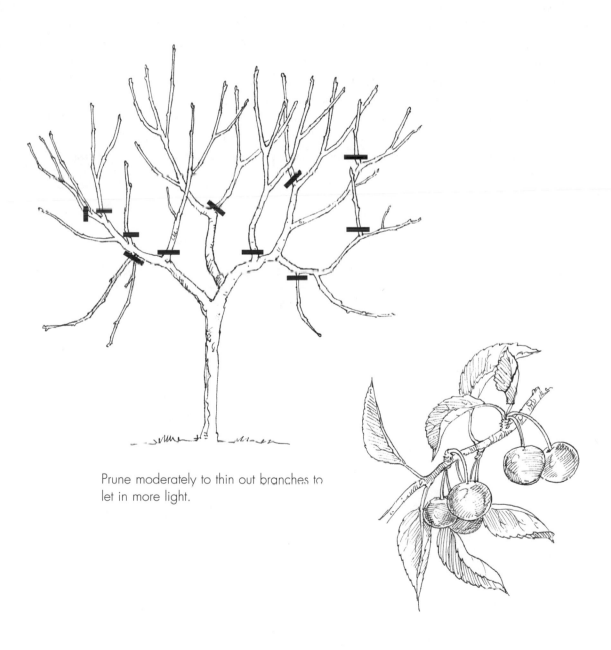

Prune moderately to thin out branches to
let in more light.

Citrus

Since oranges, grapefruits, lemons, and limes *(Citrus)* grow in the hottest parts of the United States, they usually need less pruning than fruit grown in the North, where we need to let sunlight into the trees. However, bare-root trees need a severe cutback at planting time, and you should train young ones early to grow in the shape you want. As the tree grows, you'll want to continue the shaping.

Both dwarf and full-size citrus trees may lose their vigor as they get older, so a rejuvenation pruning may be necessary to help them bear well again. Citrus trees can stand a more rigorous cutback than can peaches or apples, because winter injury is rarely a problem.

If you cut back a tree severely, do some clipping and training of the new branches to make sure that the tree grows back into a good shape. It will probably take at least two years before it begins to bear well again. The hot summer sun can easily blister tender citrus bark, so be sure to cover with white paint any bark that you suddenly expose to the sun through heavy pruning. Also, paint any bark that has become exposed because of winter injury.

You can prune all citrus trees into fancy shapes, such as espaliers, cordons, and fences, if you do it with care. As with the cool-weather fruits, the dwarf varieties are usually more suitable, and they can also be grown in large pots or planters.

MASTER GARDENING TIP

When to Prune

Since many citrus varieties tend to grow unevenly, some pruning back of overlong limbs is usually necessary. You can do this at any time of year, but in areas where frost is likely, wait until all danger is past in the spring. Dwarf citrus trees are becoming popular now for backyard planting, and just like other dwarf fruits, they need a lot less pruning than standard trees.

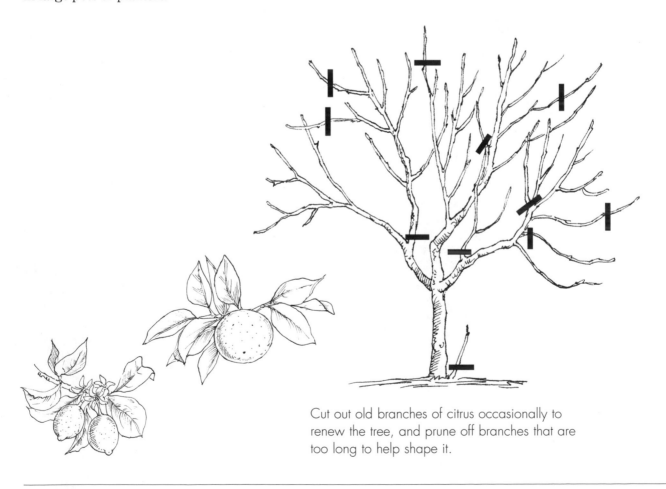

Cut out old branches of citrus occasionally to renew the tree, and prune off branches that are too long to help shape it.

Fig

Since fig trees *(Ficus carica)* bleed badly, it is important to prune them only during their dormant season. Figs grow from 25 to 40 feet tall. They can stand heavy pruning and make good espaliered trees. When you're growing them for an attractive landscape effect, keep them in balance by snipping and pinching. Don't allow them to branch as close to the ground as they would if being grown for their fruit.

- **White and brown figs** bloom and bear only on new wood, so the usual practice is to cut these back severely each year for better production.

- **Prune black figs** more like other fruits, by cutting back the wood that is over a year old.

- **Root pruning** is sometimes necessary to promote fruiting if they are growing in overfertile soil — in fact, fig trees do better where the soil isn't too rich.

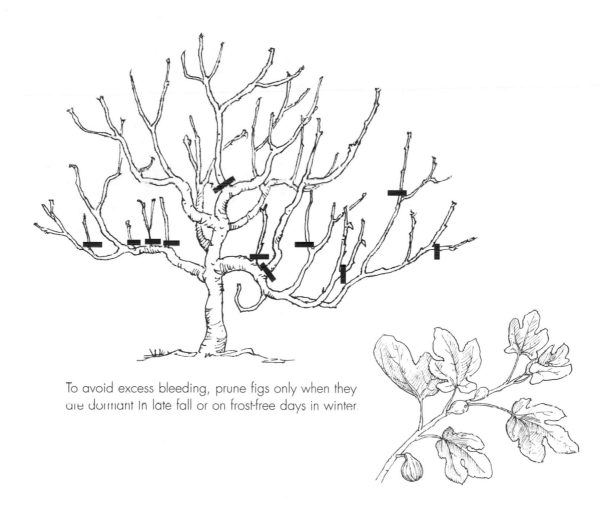

To avoid excess bleeding, prune figs only when they are dormant in late fall or on frost-free days in winter.

Peach and Nectarine

The peach *(Prunus persica)* has always represented a real challenge to dedicated gardeners. It is fussy about soils and climate, sensitive to spring frosts, and grows so vigorously that plenty of pruning is needed. Yet the juicy, tasty peach is so enticing that even northerners keep trying to grow it. Those fortunate enough to live where the peach grows well naturally want to grow it to perfection. Proper pruning plays an important role in peach culture, and an unpruned tree is a sorry sight, bearing fruit only at the ends of its branches.

MASTER GARDENING TIP

When to Prune

The best time to prune is in late winter, so that you can cut away wood injured by low temperatures. In years when winter damage is heavy, this pruning may be all the tree can stand. Never feed a tree after you've had heavy winter damage or pruned it severely, because you don't want to stimulate a rapid regrowth.

- **Usually both the peach and the nectarine** should be grown with an open center.
- **The trees tend to grow fast** and late in the season, and pruning makes them grow even faster. In areas where winter damage often kills improperly hardened wood, root pruning may be the only effective way to check excessive limb growth late in the season.
- **Don't allow peach and nectarine trees** to branch close to the ground, or you won't be able to keep trunk borers under control. Inspect the trunks frequently, and if you spot a borer's hole, use a wire and dispense with the fat grub at once. Then seal up the hole with either tree sealer, caulking compound, or plastic wood.
- **Even if you faithfully prune and thin,** peach trees tend to set such a heavy crop that broken branches may be a danger. Help your tree by propping up the weighty limbs with wide planks.

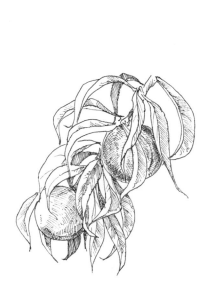

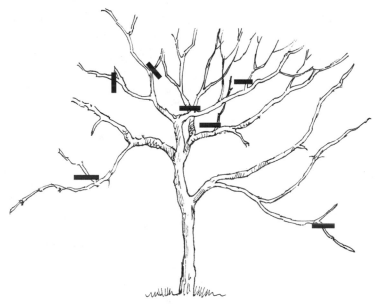

Like all fruit trees, peaches often set far too many little fruits — even when you have pruned the tree carefully. As a result, the tree produces a large crop of small peaches. To get large, luscious fruits, thin when they are about the size of marbles, spacing the ones that remain about 7 inches apart. This may be tedious and time consuming, but the results will be well worth your effort.

Peach, nectarine, and apricot trees are likely to grow tall, and since the best fruit often grows at the top of the tree, keep the tops low and accessible. The best method is to cut back the tall-growing limbs each year, but if you haven't done this, you can remove the top of the tree during the dormant season with no trauma to the tree. However, the fruit crop may be less the following year.

Pear

Pears *(Pyrus communis)* are not as difficult to grow as peaches, but in past years fire blight has killed off many of the trees. Now, thanks to more resistant varieties and a better understanding of the disease, this fruit is coming back in both large orchards and backyard gardens. Like most fruits, pears need a partner for pollination purposes, so always plant at least two different varieties.

Always be on guard for signs of fire blight. Early detection is important so that you can bring it quickly under control. You'll be able to spot it easily, because the limbs, leaves, and twigs look as if they have been held over a flame. Cut off diseased limbs completely back into good, healthy wood. Remove them to a safe distance and burn, bury, or otherwise destroy them, so that the disease doesn't spread. Sterilize your gloves and all tools in bleach solution after pruning each tree.

Fortunately for us pear lovers, quite a few blight-resistant varieties have been introduced in recent years. If you are making a new planting, consider 'Magness', 'Moonglow', 'Morgan', and 'Starking Delicious'.

MASTER GARDENING TIP

When to Prune

An annual light pruning is preferable to an infrequent heavy one for two important reasons: Heavy pruning delays bearing, and it encourages fire blight.

- **Pruning back bare-root pear trees at planting time** is important, and the rules are the same as for any other fruit. Usually, two-year-old, branched trees are the best kind to start with.
- **The training of pears in their early life** is quite similar to that of apples. Prune the tree to a central leader for the first few years. After that, grow it with a modified leader, if you wish.
- **The growth of most varieties tends to be upright,** so direct your early pruning toward thinning excess branches and encouraging a spreading tree.
- **Pears bloom and bear their fruit on the short, sharp spurs** that grow between the branches. Spurs need regular thinning, and occasionally you should remove older ones so they may be replaced by more vigorous young ones. Thin out the small fruits, also, if too many are set in any year.

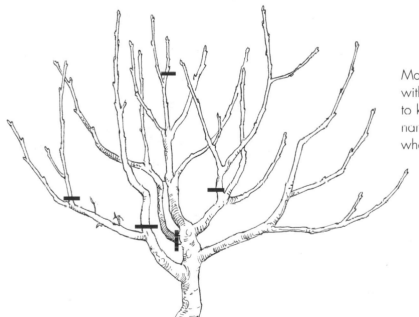

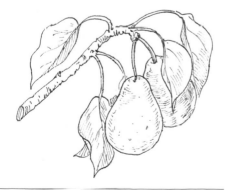

Many varieties of pears tend to grow upright with several tops, so prune out extra tops both to keep a strong central leader and to avoid narrow crotches that tend to break easily when loaded with fruit.

Plum

The plum *(Prunus)* is one of my favorite fruits. It comes in reds, blues, purples, yellows, and greens and is available in a wide range of sizes and flavors. The trees produce abundantly, and though I eat them by the bushel, I never tire of them. The years when the crop is poor are sad indeed, so I always hope for warm nights while they're in bloom.

Some varieties, especially the Europeans, are quite susceptible to a disease called black knot. Thick excrescences form along the twigs and are particularly noticeable in winter. As there is no spray available to control this problem, pruning is necessary. Attack a diseased tree with your pruning shears whenever the infection appears during the summer. Disinfect the tools as you work, and burn or dispose of the diseased parts promptly to prevent any spreading of the trouble. It is also a good idea to remove any infected wild plums or cherries growing nearby.

• **Prune plums carefully** to help them produce well and to allow the sun to ripen the fruit before the first frost hits. Due to their scraggly habit of growth, plums are best grown with an open center.

• **Follow the usual directions for pruning when planting.** One-year-old whips, from 4 to 7 feet tall, are the best choice if you're planting European or American plums, and two-year-old, slightly branched trees are preferable if you are planting the Japanese varieties. Cut back the whips by about a third, to a fat bud, and cut off any side branches until you've removed from one-third to one-half of the total wood area.

MASTER GARDENING TIPS

When to Prune

▶ *Japanese plums* require a lot of pruning, and you should do this annually in late winter.

▶ *European plums* need very little; an occasional thinning of older wood is usually all that is necessary.

▶ *Most American plums* and their hybrids need only moderate pruning to keep them bearing well. Some varieties, including some of the cherry-plum hybrids, grow very long branches that hang on the ground and should be shortened. Prune the tree to keep it in balance.

▶ *Many plum roots* sucker badly, so periodically cut off the small shoots growing from the tree's roots unless you keep the area under the tree well mowed.

Trees that produce large plums especially benefit from thinning. For best results, pick off the extra fruits when they are still tiny, in early summer, so that the remaining plums are 5 inches apart.

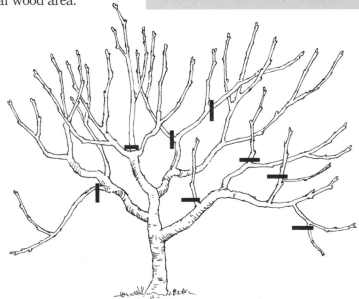

If your plum trees have a habit of bearing a large crop every other year, thin out some of the fruit to limit the large crop, to increase fruit size, and to encourage annual bearing.

Quince

Quince *(Cydonia oblonga)* is one of the few fruit tree varieties that need almost no pruning, although you should remove any broken, dead, or crossed branches as a matter of course. Do any necessary basal pruning to get the tree growing into a good treelike shape. Thin out the limbs only if they get so thick that harvesting of the fruit is difficult.

Like pears, quince trees are extremely susceptible to fire blight. Follow all the precautions recommended for pears should this disease strike your quince.

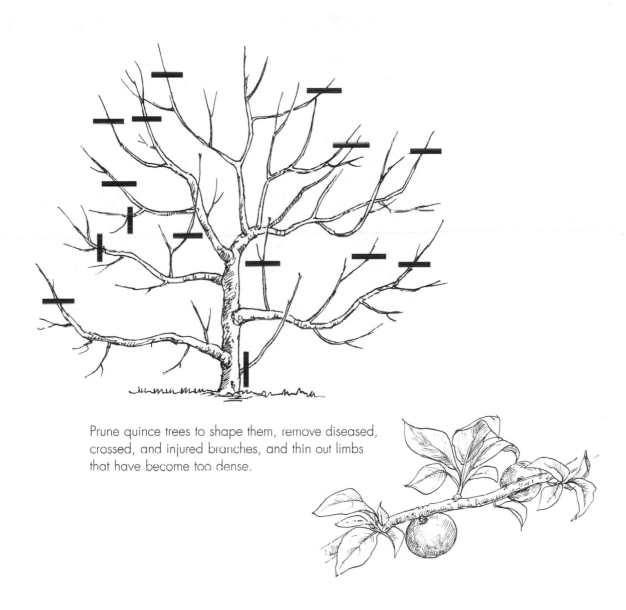

Prune quince trees to shape them, remove diseased, crossed, and injured branches, and thin out limbs that have become too dense.

Tropical and Semitropical Fruits

Only gardeners in completely frost-free regions can safely grow tropical fruits outdoors. Elsewhere, you can grow them in heated greenhouses and conservatories.

Plant	Characteristics	Maintenance
Avocado (*Persea*)	In tropical climates, any opening up of the tree will cause sunburn on tender bark.	For fruit: Allow tree to grow naturally. For beauty: Pinch and clip back lightly.
Mango (*Mangifera*)	Beautiful, shiny foliage.	In South: No special care outdoors. In North: Grow as pot plant; pinch back and root-prune (see page 35) occasionally to keep from growing too large; repot from time to time. Grow in ordinary garden soil; keep moist but not soaking wet.
Olive (*Olea*)	Needs more pruning than most other tropical plants. Usually grown as a tree, but may be pruned to grow as a shrub or tall, thick, hedge plant. If pruned carefully, olive trees can be very productive to a ripe old age.	For tree: Prune off basal suckers frequently and remove occasional older branch. Thin fruit by removing some blooms.
Papaya (*Carica*)	Grows only where frosts are unlikely. In cooler climates, melonlike fruits are sometimes grown in greenhouses. Resembles a large perennial more than a tree. Tends to grow tall with no lower branches.	Cut back top in early spring to encourage branching and greater productivity. For better appearance, remove old brown and yellow leaves that often hang on the tree during winter.
Pomegranate (*Punica*)	An ornamental tree that grows to an attractive shape with little care. For food production, best grown in tree form.	As an ornamental: Prune as you would a tall Japanese bonsai or espalier (see chapters 8 and 14). For food production: Remove suckers.

Cutting Grafting Wood

In recent years, there has been a renewed interest in home grafting of fruit trees. Just as our ancestors did a century ago, gardeners are growing their own trees, creating varieties that nurseries don't sell. It's also fun to propagate choice old varieties that are nearly obsolete.

Grafting is not a mysterious operation, and nearly any good fruit-growing book or encyclopedia will show you how it is done. Basically, you take a branch from a tree that bears good fruit and surgically transplant it to the root of a wild or unimproved tree. Bud grafting is similar except that you use a single dormant bud.

1 Cut a grafting branch — called a scion — very early in the spring, before any growth starts. Look for a branch that grew the previous year, one that is filled with nice, fat buds. Cut a piece about 1 foot long. You can cut it into shorter pieces when you get ready to use it. Cut on a slant close to an outside bud, and don't leave a stub. There is usually no shortage of scions available on young trees and on mature trees that have been kept pruned. Make sure this operation fits into your pruning program for that tree.

2 Wrap the branch in a plastic bag and store it in a cool place until you're ready to use it.

MASTER GARDENING TIP

Finding Good Young Branches

Some people, including us, are trying to rescue old varieties of fruit trees by grafting, but we often run into difficulty finding any young growth when trying to get a branch from an elderly tree. Often such trees have never been pruned and make only a small amount of new growth each year. Check the top of the tree. Or encourage the tree to generate a limited amount of fresh new growth by moderately pruning a few limbs in late winter.

Learn the proper pruning methods for your grapes and berries and you will get larger fruit and better crops, help the plants resist disease, and make it easier to pick berries; in addition, proper pruning extends the useful life of a small fruit patch by many years.

Pruning Small Fruits

Much of our family's best winter eating comes from the berry patch. Each year we stock a large portion of the freezer with dozens of packages of strawberries, raspberries, blueberries, currants, gooseberries, and elderberries. By late fall, jars filled with preserves and colorful juices line our pantry shelves, standing by to help us struggle through the winter blizzards. Small fruits come in a wide assortment of colors, flavors, shapes, and sizes. There are red, pink, and green varieties of gooseberries; black, purple, red, and pink raspberries; and many different kinds of grapes, blueberries, blackberries, and currants.

Small fruits are not only colorful, tasty, and full of healthy vitamins, but most of the plants are easy to grow as well. They are very productive, most bear a year or two after planting, they take very little room in the garden, they're usually inexpensive, and they need surprisingly little care.

You should prune small fruits for the same reasons you prune fruit trees, but the methods for pruning small fruits are somewhat different from those of the tree fruits, and different terminology is used. For instance, the word *cane* can mean a stem or stalk of a raspberry, blackberry, dewberry, or elderberry; the term is also sometimes applied to grapevines.

In This Chapter

- Grapes
- Pruning Bare-Root Grapes at Planting Time
- The Kniffen System
- Pruning an Old Grapevine
- The Bush Fruits: Blueberry, Cranberry, Currant and Gooseberry, Elderberry
- The Bramble Fruits
- Maintenance Pruning of Brambles
- Strawberries

Grapes

The grape *(Vitis)* is one of the oldest fruits in cultivation. Early Greek, Roman, and biblical writings refer often to "the vine" and the wine that was made from it. Many centuries before orange juice and apple pie became household staples, horticulturists were busy trying to figure out how to prune this remarkable plant so that it would produce bountifully. When you prune a grapevine, you are joining in an ancient tradition and using a skill developed millennia ago.

Over the years, many varieties of grapes have been introduced, and gardeners are growing hundreds of old and new varieties today. You may choose to develop your own little vineyard for delicious, fresh grapes or grape jelly, or to grow grapes for wine or unfermented juice. You may even decide to grow them simply for their beauty — some vines have especially handsome foliage.

Since many varieties of grapes are rank growers, an unpruned plant can spread quickly over a large area, forcing the plant's energy into the vine rather than into the production of grapes. To get good crops of this superb fruit, you must prune.

MASTER GARDENING TIPS

Pruning Grapes

There are many methods for accomplishing the results you want, and the system you use to prune will depend on a lot of things, including where you decide to grow your grapes. Keep in mind the reasons for pruning:

▶ Prune to keep the vine to a manageable size.

▶ Prune to direct the energy of the vine into producing fruit rather than stems and leaves, and to keep the crop growing close to the main stem so that the sap doesn't have to travel far to produce grapes.

▶ Prune to allow in sunlight, so the fruit can ripen. Grapes must ripen on the vine because, unlike most other fruits, they do not continue to ripen after they are picked.

Grapes grow mostly on one-year-old wood. As an unpruned vine matures, it carries more and more wood that is much older, and thus becomes not only tangled but unproductive as well. Allow the canes to grow one year and bear fruit the next, then prune them off. This means that each summer your plant should have canes at two stages of growth: canes that grew last year and are now bearing, and new canes that will bear next year.

Pruning Bare-Root Grapes at Planting Time

Because pruning at planting time is so important to a grapevine's future success, most nurseries prune the vines before they sell them. If yours hasn't done this for you, do it yourself, unless the vine is potted with its roots intact. You must steel yourself and prune heavily, so the roots will grow faster than the top and stimulate the vine to get off to a strong start. It will begin bearing heavy crops in two or three years.

1 Prune off all the side branches.

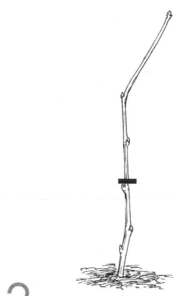

2 Cut back the main stem so that it is no more than 5 inches tall.

MASTER GARDENING TIPS

Grapevine-Pruning Methods and Timing

Grape-pruning methods vary because different varieties of grapes grow at different rates and the pruning must be adjusted accordingly. Pruning also varies with different soils and climates; look over your neighbor's shoulder when he is pruning his vines, especially if he seems to be having exceptionally good luck.

In any event, always prune when your vine is dormant — anytime after the leaves drop in the fall but before the buds begin to swell in the spring, provided the temperature is above freezing. Most northern gardeners choose early spring pruning so that they can cut off any winter injury at the same time.

▶ **Ornamental:** If you want a thick, shady vine with a few grapes hanging on it for effect, you'll need to prune only to keep it from becoming too overgrown.

▶ **Ornamental and productive:** If you want grapes as well as beauty, prune annually to get rid of all wood over one year old. Cut back part of the year-old wood, too, leaving only enough to cover the support and produce grapes the following year.

The Kniffen System

Many of us are more practical and less artistic, preferring to grow our grapes simply on a wire fence the way most commercial growers do. One of the easiest and best ways to care for grapes is with the Kniffen system. Begin by choosing a good site. Your vines will need as much sun as possible, and as little of the chilling north wind as you can manage.

Each year, thin fruit clusters whenever too many appear. Usually a healthy, vigorous vine will produce from 30 to 60 bunches a year, with an average of 8 to 15 per branch. Don't allow the plant to produce a greater number, because overproduction weakens the vine, and you'll get quantity rather than quality.

Set up the fence. It should consist of two strands of smooth 9- or 10-gauge wire, stapled on posts set solidly in the ground and spaced about 8 feet apart. Space the lower wire about 3 feet above the ground and the second about 2 feet higher (**1**). Brace the posts at the ends so that the wires won't sag as they get loaded with fruit and vines (**2**). Plant each grapevine midway between the posts (**3**). Your chances for growing thrifty specimens will be improved if you plant and water carefully.

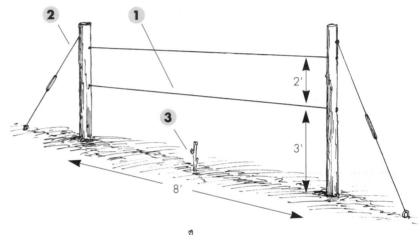

Year one: After the initial cutting back at planting time (see page 149), during the first summer, allow the vine to grow naturally. Remove all side sprouts so that the vine will grow upward toward the wires.

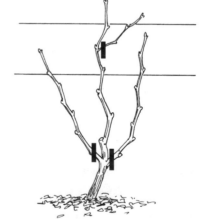

Year two: During the second summer, by pinching and pruning, allow only two vines to grow along the wires in each direction — four in all. If the vines grow well, they should cover the wires by the end of summer. (If they grow more than this, cut back any extra growth and side branches right after the first hard frost.) The tendrils on the grapes should wrap around the wires and hold the vines securely. If any fall off and need to be tied back on, use a material like narrow plastic ribbon (not tape) that won't cut into the grape's tender bark.

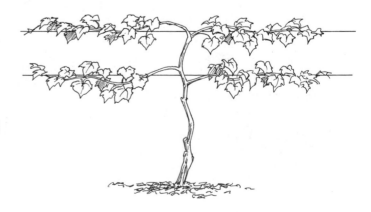

Year three: This is the first bearing year! Allow four more new vines to grow paralleling the first four that grew the previous season. These newcomers are your replacements for the ones that grew the second year. Let these droop on the ground until you have cut off the old vines and are ready to fasten the replacements to the wires.

Meanwhile, the year-old vines should bloom and set grapes all along the wires this summer. Don't allow too many bunches to form, because overbearing will weaken the plant and jeopardize future crops. If you're like I was, you'll be so thrilled with your first crop that you'll hate to part with any. But brace yourself and snip off a few of the clusters of tiny grapes if more than three or four bunches are forming per vine. Throughout the growing season, continue to pinch back any new growth that is headed in the wrong direction. Four new canes are all you'll need.

Year four: In late winter or very early spring of the fourth year, cut off the four canes that bore fruit the previous year, and make sure that you secure the four new canes to the wires. These will replace last year's bearing vines and produce this year's crop. Cut off all extra growth, and during the summer, pinch the new canes occasionally in order to train four more canes that will replace the ones presently bearing. Repeat this process every year.

MASTER GARDENING TIPS

Ways to Grow Grapevines

- ▶ *On an arbor.* This way, you can enjoy the beauty of the vines while watching the ripening grapes hang down from overhead.
- ▶ *On a trellis.* This allows you to espalier the vines against a wall or a building.
- ▶ *Over a fence.* A casual look that softens a fence's lines will provide you with a tasty, easy-to-reach harvest.
- ▶ *The Kniffen system.* This type of fence is meant to be highly practical and is not for show. However,

grapevines grown in this way are easier to care for and most likely to be healthy and productive.

- ▶ *As freestanding plants.* Some gardeners, especially wine growers, like to prune their vines so that they have a single, long, tall trunk, like a cordon. Each year after fruiting, they cut back all the canes almost to this trunk, leaving a few short stubs to bear fruit and from which the new canes appear.

Pruning an Old Grapevine

If it becomes your duty to take over a grapevine that has been neglected for years, you have a difficult job ahead of you. But it can be done. If the vine is badly overgrown, spread out the work over several years with the idea firmly in mind that you will eventually get the vine back to a single trunk with only four strong, well-spaced branches. Then you can train it into a Kniffen or other manageable system. Have a truck standing by to haul away the prunings, or plan a brisk bonfire in a safe place, because you'll have to get rid of lots of deadwood.

MASTER GARDENING TIP

New Plants from Rooted Vines

Vines that have trailed over the ground for many years often root and form many new plants, which can be salvaged. In early spring, cut them back to about a foot. Then dig them up with a ball of soil and replant them where you please.

Or, cut off all rooted vines at ground level, and don't allow them to grow back. Mow or spread a heavy mulch over the area to prevent any regrowth.

1 When the vine is dormant, choose a main trunk and remove all competing-size stems.

2 Choose two canes on each side (this year's growth) and flag them. These will be the bearing canes for this season.

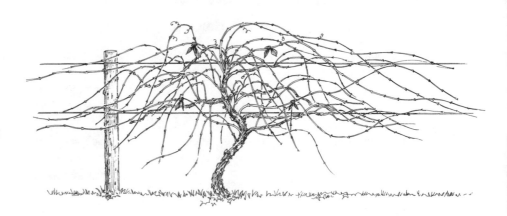

3 Cut back two more canes on each side, leaving two buds on each. These spurs will produce the bearing canes for the following year.

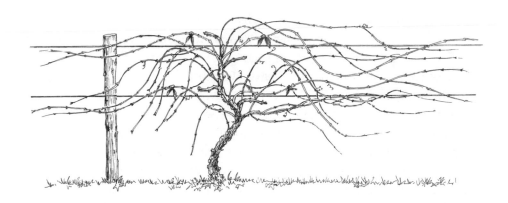

4 Prune out everything except the flagged canes and the spurs.

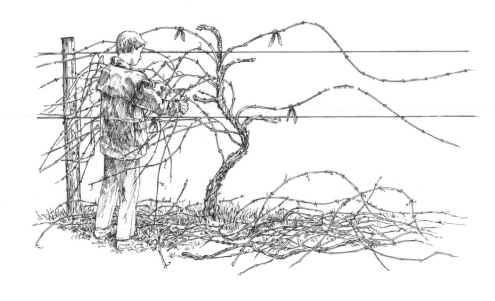

5 Shorten the flagged canes to about 10 fruit buds each for best productivity and tie them loosely to the wires.

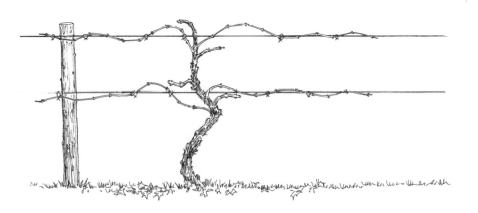

The Bush Fruits

Each year, we discover new ways to use the produce from our currant, elderberry, gooseberry, blueberry, and cranberry bushes, from enjoying them fresh to using them in delicious juices, sauces, conserves, jellies, pies, and other desserts. Last year, we fried elderberry flowers in batter for tasty fritters, and used the highbush cranberries to decorate our Christmas wreaths.

Pruning bush fruits is not nearly as demanding as pruning the tree fruits, brambles, or grapevines. I know of old farmsteads with currant and gooseberry bushes that still produce large crops of excellent fruit after decades of neglect. Comparative newcomers to the garden, they still have many of the good qualities of wild plants. Although they are also highly resistant to disease and insects and, with the exception of blueberries, not at all fussy about soil, each bush can be encouraged to do much better with a little care, including pruning.

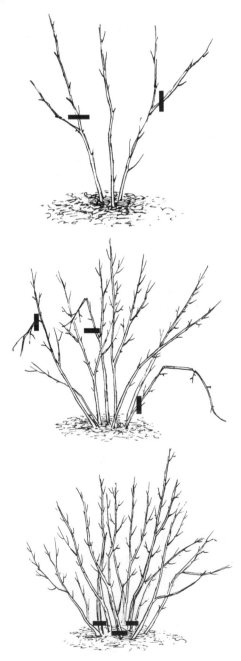

Pruning at planting time. Unless you have bought a potted plant, or one growing with a well-wrapped and undisturbed solid ball of earth, you'll need to prune it when you set it out. Treat a bare-root bush fruit just as you would any low-growing shrub. Cut back each branch about halfway, to a bud or to another branch.

Even though you'll be eager to eat the produce of the bush, encourage it to grow lots of sturdy roots and new branches the first year, instead of wasting its energy producing fruit. In spite of your heavy pruning, it still may have a few blooms. Pinch them off as soon as they appear.

Maintenance pruning. Usually the initial pruning will be all your bush needs for several years. Of course, cut off any twigs or branches that have been broken by weather or birds. Otherwise, just speak to it kindly and let it grow.

Rejuvenation pruning. After your bush has borne several large crops of fruit, you may notice that it looks a bit overgrown and that the fruits are getting smaller. This would be a good time to thin it out. Select a few of the oldest branches and cut them right to the ground, either in late fall or in early spring. If you do this faithfully every few years, the bush should be productive and thrive at least for your lifetime.

Blueberry

Compared to other small fruits, the blueberry *(Vaccinium)* is a slow grower, taking as long as a decade to come into full production. So that you won't delay bearing, prune the bush sparingly during its first years while it is still small. Clip only to shape it and to remove injured or broken limbs.

Blueberries tend to grow in a bushy manner with lots of small twigs, and as the plant gets older, the twigs get thicker and bear less fruit.

1 Cut off the thick, twiggy end growth. Thin out overgrown blueberry plants by cutting two or three of the older main stems right back to the ground (shaded in illustration).

2 Thin out about half of the end twigs from the remaining branches to stimulate the plant to bear more heavily.

MASTER GARDENING TIPS

Regional Blueberry Pruning

Blueberries can be grown almost anywhere the weather is not too extreme. They do require acidic soil (pH of 4.5 to 5), so amend the chosen spot at planting time if necessary. And choose a variety that is known to do well in your climate. There are dozens to choose from, especially in specialty nursery catalogs.

In mild climates. As with many other fruits, blueberries grown in areas where the winter is mild should be pruned heavily. You can do this anytime from when the leaves come off in the fall to the time that growth starts in very early spring.

In cold climates. If you have a short growing season and a cold winter, prune lightly each year, experimenting until you find what amount seems most beneficial to the plant. Fertilize only when it is making poor growth. Overfeeding and overpruning may induce winter injury and severely limit your crop. Many gardeners in the coldest states either do not prune their blueberry plants at all or they thin the twiggy growth at the ends of the branches only occasionally. Just be careful never to prune frozen wood, because your cut won't heal over easily, resulting in additional winter injury to the plant.

There are no definite rules about when and how blueberry pruning is best done in cold climates. Experimentation will show what is effective in your area. Customarily it is done in early spring, so that any wood that was injured during the winter can be removed at the same time. Since late-spring frosts sometimes damage blueberry blossoms, some growers are now pruning their plants in late fall. This delays blooming a few days, and this is often enough to save the crop.

Cranberry, Bog

You probably won't want to tackle the bog cranberry *(Vaccinium macrocarpon)* unless you happen to have a swamp in your backyard, because it is very fussy about climate, soil, and moisture. It needs an abundance of water and acid soil, and it is so particular that there are only a few places in North America where it grows well.

Cranberry thrives in water or very damp soil because the water protects it from spring and fall frosts, and controls insects and weeds. You must be able to regulate the water carefully so that the spot can be flooded or drained whenever necessary. Ordinary watering isn't a satisfactory substitute — commercial growers who have tried to grow cranberries under irrigation rather than in bogs have run into many problems.

Though the initial grading and planting are time consuming and expensive, a well-managed cranberry bog can go on producing practically forever. So if you can get a bog started, you are set for life, but most of us will have to be content with buying our cranberries in bags or cans at the supermarket.

> ## MASTER GARDENING TIP
>
> ### Pruning Bog Cranberries
>
> Pruning is simple. When the plants get overgrown, mow or cut off the tops close to the ground. Then allow them to grow back, thereby creating a whole new plant.

Cranberry, Highbush

I've noticed that new, improved strains of the native American cranberry are appearing in seed catalogs, so this attractive and useful plant may soon be a part of more home fruit gardens. Although few people consider the quality of the fruit as good as that of its cousin the bog cranberry, the berries do make superb jelly after a few hard frosts. They're beloved by the birds, as well.

The native highbush cranberry grows a bit large (12 to 15 feet) for small backyard plantings, but many of the new, improved kinds are smaller and more manageable. If you want cranberries for eating, plant the American *(Viburnum trilobum)* rather than the European cranberry *(V. opulus)*. Although the latter is readily available in nurseries as an ornamental plant, the berries are too bitter for the human palate — and birds don't care for them either.

> ## MASTER GARDENING TIPS
>
> ### Pruning Highbush Cranberries
>
> Highbush cranberries need very little pruning.
>
> ▶ *Thin out some of the old wood* once every several years.
>
> ▶ *Top your bushes* if they start growing too tall.
>
> ▶ *Sometimes bushes bear heavily* every other year, producing only a few berries during the alternate years. If this happens, you can return them to an annual-bearing pattern. During the heavy-producing years, prune off about a third of the blossom clusters as soon as the buds appear.

Currant and Gooseberry

Currants and gooseberries *(Ribes)* are cool-weather plants, grown strictly in northern areas. Although new varieties are being developed for the South, these fine bush fruits grow best where summers are cool and winters are cold. Even the large fruiting hybrids are closely related to their wild cousins and, like them, will grow with little care. Badly neglected plants often continue to produce good crops for decades, although the fruit is small.

Maintenance pruning. For the best yields of the biggest fruit, begin to thin out your bush when it is about three years old. Stems that are older than that bear poorly and should be cut off at ground level or as close to the soil as possible. New, vigorous growth will quickly replace them. To produce its best, a currant or gooseberry bush should have wood that is one to three years old, and practically none that is any older.

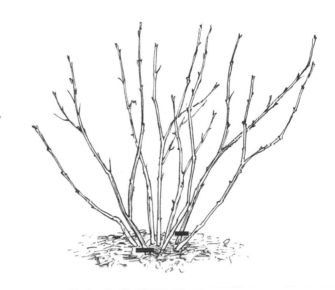

MASTER GARDENING TIP

Rejuvenation Pruning

If you have a neglected bush, give it a new lease on life by cutting it off at ground level and letting a new plant grow back. Doing all this in one year would be hard on even a vigorous plant, so spread out the job over at least a couple of years.

▶ In very early spring, before any green shows, cut off about half of the old stems at ground level, leaving any young, lively ones. That year, you should see a lot of new growth.

▶ The next year, cut the remaining old stems to the ground. These, too, will regrow, and you will have a completely new plant that you'll be proud to show the garden club, and one that you can prune and care for in the usual manner.

Production pruning. With heavier pruning, you can force giant-size gooseberry varieties to produce fruit as large as grapes or small plums. Thin out the berries as soon as they form. Pick off the tiniest berries and leave the remaining ones about an inch apart on the branch. (With the thorny varieties, however, this process may not be an entirely pleasant task, or worth the trouble.) Frankly, the size of currants is not often greatly improved by picking off part of the clusters of blooms.

Gooseberries require only an occasional pruning out of old wood and a heavy annual feeding of manure to keep them producing large crops annually almost forever.

Elderberry

Both wild and garden elderberries *(Sambucus)* are a fine addition to anyone's backyard berry patch. Elderberry is a wonderful fruit, and I'd hate to be without it. However, the plants are tall (to 7 feet) and extremely vigorous growers. Grow them only where you can keep them safely under control by mowing around them regularly. They grow well only in moist areas, and you should never plant them near a vegetable garden, flower bed, or other berries or plants.

Because they are so productive and robust, and since all the improved varieties have only recently emerged from the wild, elderberry plants need minimal pruning to keep them productive.

Maintenance pruning. During the first summer, pinch off the top of the young plants to encourage side branching and earlier bearing (unlike the other bush fruits, early bearing won't hurt an elderberry plant at all). Cut out any wood that gets broken during the winter, and remove old, corky stalks that no longer produce well. Mow or prune off the sucker plants that continually try to grow outside the row. You can prune elderberries anytime, since they are such vigorous growers.

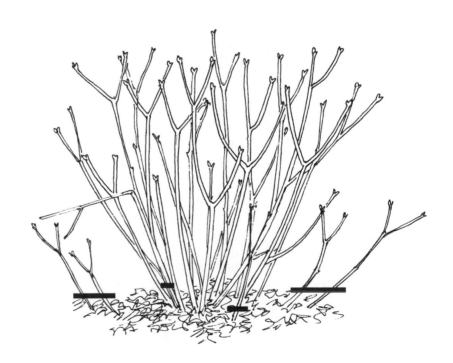

The Bramble Fruits

Raspberry and blackberry plants and their dozens of cousins — including the boysenberry, dewberry, youngberry, and marionberry — are usually referred to as the brambles *(Rubus)*. Unlike the bush fruits, which are really small trees, the brambles are woody biennials. Their canes are woody biennials, that is. The roots are perennial, and under the right conditions, brambles will live for decades, perhaps even for centuries.

Here's how they grow: Each cane sprouts from the roots and grows to its full height in a season. The following year it blooms, produces fruit, and dies that same season. At the same time, other canes are growing that will produce their fruit the following year. And so the patch marches on.

Cutting out the old canes after fruiting is the most important part of bramble-fruit culture. A fellow Yankee neighbor of ours who was quite frugal once told me he "warn't goin' to cut nothin'" out of his patch, because there was always a chance that the dead canes might bear something another year. In about three years, though, he had a jungle of dead canes and almost no fruit — his patch had killed itself by overpopulation. All of us who enjoy wild-berry picking have seen this happen to a wild patch — in a few years, there are no plants left. There is a reason for this: Nature has arranged it so that the brambles are an interim crop, holding their own only until trees can get a foothold. Pruning makes a difference, however. We started a small patch of raspberries in our backyard over 20 years ago, and it is producing good crops today.

MASTER GARDENING TIP

Prune to Control Suckers

The large root systems of red and yellow raspberries and upright-growing blackberries send up lots of suckers, which sometimes appear several feet away from the row. Always cut them off at ground level. Spread a heavy mulch, and mow or cultivate between the rows.

Set the plants 24 to 36 inches apart in a straight row, and if you plant more than one row, keep the rows at least 6 feet apart. While this may seem like wasted space, berry plants are such virile growers that they soon make a wide row. Unless you leave adequate space, you'll have no room to walk between the rows. Also, by spacing them correctly, you won't have to cut out a lot of thorny growth.

Then, after planting, cut back your new berry plants, unless they're potted, to about 2 inches above the ground. I know this sounds severe, but it is the best way to give the roots time to get established before the top outdistances them. Support mature plants with a fence of boards or a smooth wire on each side of the row or, as shown here, by tying clumps of branches to a post.

Maintenance Pruning of Brambles

Burn old canes or get them out of the neighborhood as fast as possible. Never use the canes as a mulch or put them in the compost pile, because they rot slowly and may be harboring harmful insects or disease.

Thin out the new canes to allow better air circulation and reduce the chances of mildew, spur blight, and other diseases. Thinning also results in larger berries. First, cut out all the weak, small, short, and spindly canes. Then thin all the healthy, large canes so that the remaining ones are about 6 inches apart.

Improve productivity by cutting back the flimsy tops of the tall canes in late summer so that they can't bend over. Cut back tall-growing brambles, such as 'Viking' raspberries, 2 feet or more, but short-growing varieties, like 'Newburgh' raspberries, need to have only a few inches snipped off. Canes that have been cut back tend to stand winter winds and snows without breaking, and are better able to hold up the following year's fruit without flopping to the ground.

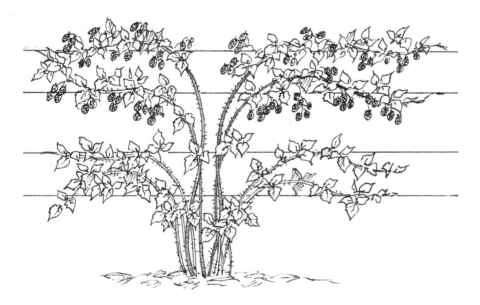

Every summer, without fail, cut out the old canes as soon as they finish bearing. You'll be able to identify them by their appearance: They are tan or brown and tend to be woody, in contrast to the new canes, which are young and green.

MASTER GARDENING TIPS

Diseases and Pests of Brambles

Check your patch often throughout the summer to see that disease and insects haven't launched an assault. Here are the two most common maladies, both easily treatable by timely pruning.

Symptoms: Whole canes wilt and die.
Culprit: Spur blight, a common disease of bramble fruits, is infecting your plants.
Treatment: Prune out and cart away all the dying canes as soon as you notice them.

Symptoms: In early summer, some of the top leaves on the new canes have wilted and the tops are drooping.
Culprit: The cane borer has deposited an egg right between the two circles you will see around the cane.
Treatment: Cut off the top of the cane just below the lower circle and burn it, egg and all. If you don't, the resulting grub will live up to its name by boring down the cane and wrecking it. Then, down near the roots, the grub will develop into a clear-winged moth that will fly about your berry patch some night spreading more eggs and mischief.

Pruning Vine-Type Brambles

Black and most purple raspberries, as well as vine-type blackberries, such as dewberries, boysenberries, and youngberries, should be fastened to wires about 5 feet high supported by posts. Allow three or four strong canes to grow from each plant, and thin out the others. Allow those that grew the previous season to bear fruit, and another set to grow as replacements to produce the following year's crop. Cut out the old canes soon after you harvest the berries. The following year fasten the new canes to the wires.

Pruning "Everbearers"

Several varieties of red and yellow raspberry plants are now being sold in catalogs as "everbearers." They do not produce constantly throughout the summer, as the name implies, but they do bear a crop in midsummer on one-year-old canes (as do most raspberries), plus another, usually smaller, crop in the fall on the new canes that have just finished growing.

If you have only one kind of raspberry and it is an everbearer, you can treat it just as you do the regular bearers. Cut out the old canes just after they finish bearing their summer crop, then harvest a fall crop off the new canes, leaving them to produce again the following summer.

However, many gardeners who have both the regular-bearing and the everbearing varieties prefer to skip the summer crop on the latter to harvest a bigger fall crop. They do this by treating the raspberry canes as annuals, cutting them to the ground right after the fall crop is harvested. Since there are never any one-year-old canes, there is never any summer crop the following year. The fall harvest is not only larger, but earlier as well, since all the plant's energy goes into it. There's only one thing as tasty as a fresh raspberry in season, and that's a fresh raspberry out of season.

Pruning Raspberries and Upright Blackberries

Prune out all the dying canes in late summer after you have picked the berries. Before winter, remove any weak canes and space the larger ones 5 to 6 inches apart. Remove any plants coming up between the rows. Cut back all the canes to about 5 feet in height to make them stiff enough to stand upright over the winter without support. The next spring provide a wire or board fence to support the canes before they are laden with heavy fruit.

MASTER GARDENING TIP

Tip Plants

Purple and black raspberries and trailing blackberries form new plants by a process known as tipping. In late summer their long canes bend over until the ends touch the soil; roots then grow at these tips, and a new plant is born. Keep them under constant control, just as with suckers.

- Old, dying canes that produced fruit this year should be removed by cutting to the ground.
- Small, weak canes should be cut out at ground level to divert the plant's energy into the main stems.
- Remove any plants coming up between the rows.
- Thin strong canes so that they are at least 5 or 6 inches apart.
- Cut back those remaining by a few inches to produce strong, husky canes that can support a heavy crop.

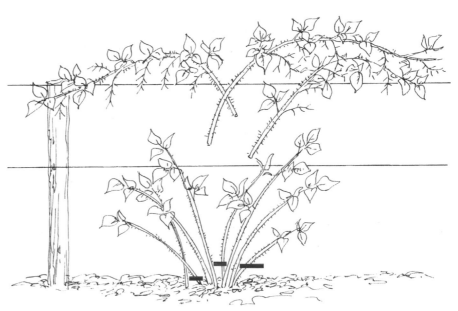

Strawberries

Strawberry plants *(Fragaria)* reproduce by runners. These small, vinelike sprouts come from the main plant, form a whole new plant, and, if unchecked, go on to form another and another. If the plants are set early and growing well, they grow runners and new plants early enough in the season so that the new plants will bear the following summer. On page 163 you will find three different methods for managing your strawberry crop.

On page 163 you will find three different methods for managing your strawberry crop.

HINT FOR SUCCESS

You must be careful to control weeds and grass growth, or the patch's productivity will suffer, especially plants grown in the matted-row style.

1 When your strawberry plants arrive, you'll notice that they have long, stringy roots. The directions you receive will tell you, no doubt, to snip off an inch or two of these root tips. Be sure to do this, even if cutting off valuable roots doesn't make much sense to you — pruning will make it easier for you to spread the roots when setting out your plants, and, even more important, it will stimulate them to grow lots of new little roots. The resulting lush plants will be able to bear heavy crops the following year.

2 Since husky plant growth is what you want most the first season, pick off all the blossoms that try to form during the month after planting. Bearing fruit so soon after it is set out weakens a strawberry plant, and the following year's crop will be diminished.

If you are growing everbearing strawberries, pick off the spring blooms the first year. You can allow them to bear a light crop later in the summer.

The Hill System

If you grow strawberries using this method, and do the necessary mulching or cultivating, your plants will live and produce several years longer than those with runners, getting larger and huskier each year. And you'll avoid having to buy new plants and preparing new soil.

1. Set your strawberry plants 12 to 18 inches apart.
2. Prune off all the runners as they form. Since none of a plant's strength goes into producing new plants, expect a good number of extra-large berries.

The Matted-Row Method

Although the matted-row method is more commonly used and generally more productive than the hill method, you must start new plants each year, since usually the bed bears really well only one time — the year after planting.

1. Set the plants 3 feet apart. Allow each plant to form three or more runners in each direction along the row.
2. The runners will form small plants until, by midsummer, the row is filled with well-spaced plants. As soon as the row is full, prune off all extra runners and the plants that they are forming. It is time consuming, but it's worth the trouble and nets you a large crop of berries.
3. If you prune off all runners from the matted-row plants the second season (so that the beds do not become overgrown), you can sometimes extend the life of your strawberry bed by another year or more.

Compromise Method

Some growers feel this method combines the best of both the hill and the matted-row systems, and it does require fewer initial plants than the hill method.

1. Set the plants 2 feet apart in the row, and allow them to make four runners — two headed in each direction along the row.
2. Allow each runner to make only one plant. Keep cutting off all other plants and runners.

Since the great wild nut forests of early America have been cut for their beautiful lumber, destroyed to make way for civilization, or killed by disease, you'll probably have to grow your own. Most nut trees grow far too large for a small backyard, but some make satisfactory shade trees. The demand for homegrown nuts has spurred a search for better strains, and growers are continuing to develop new varieties of bigger, better-flavored, and easier-to-crack nuts.

Nut Trees

Many thousands of years ago, before men became hunters and herdsmen, nuts were one of the main sources of protein. Nuts had the added advantage of staying fresh for years in their watertight shells. Even after they ceased to be needed as a staple in the diet, they were prized as a dessert.

Most older people in our area remember foraging with their families in the back country each fall, bringing home bags of nuts for winter treats. Now, with the interest in natural foods and vegetarianism, nuts are once again becoming a protein staple in the diets of many people. Each fall, more people are racing the squirrels to the nut trees, and trying to find ways to keep their attics and garages squirrel-proof so that they can store their valued nut caches safely.

Naturally, those nuts that have been grown commercially for centuries, like the walnut, filbert, pecan, and almond, have the most named varieties in cultivation. Most of these are the result of careful scientific crossbreeding of outstanding trees rather than accidents of nature.

The wild native nuts, on the other hand, have been rather neglected, and only in recent years has there been a serious attempt to find superior trees. Growers are crossing these trees with related European and Asiatic varieties. As a result, we are beginning to see improved black walnut, butternut, hickory, and chestnut trees. Beech trees have been developed that produce larger nuts, and oak trees that yield edible acorns. This research has also resulted in trees that are more disease resistant and some that are suited to growing in areas where previously nuts could not be grown.

Planting a Nut Tree

There are several ways to get started. The easiest is to plant the seed (nut) where you want a tree to grow, and thus avoid tricky transplanting and early pruning. In fact, the great American nut forests were probably planted by squirrels who buried the nuts and forgot to dig them up.

Many of the nut trees sold by nurseries are seedlings, but you may also see grafted, named varieties. Although seedling trees may grow as fast as, or faster than, grafted trees, they take a long time to bear — usually from 6 to 12 years. If grafted ones are available and are hardy where you live, they are a much better choice. Not only are the nuts larger and easier to crack, but the trees usually bear earlier and more regularly as well, and produce heavier crops than trees grown from seed.

A distinctive feature of most nut trees is a central taproot that goes straight down. This makes it tricky to dig up and transplant a tree, because the taproot should not be broken or cut off at digging time, nor should it be bent over when planted. Moving any nut tree that is over 6 feet tall is risky, whether from a nursery or from the wild.

Master Gardening Tip

Pinch, Don't Prune

Many nut growers prefer not to prune a small tree at all at planting time. Instead, they pinch off any new sprouts as they form on the side branches. They want to retain all the leaves possible to help feed the young tree, yet prevent new growth that will demand energy that the roots cannot yet supply. Although effective, this method is more time consuming than is pruning off part of the tree, especially since you must pinch frequently during the first few weeks of the growth.

Pruning a Nut Tree at Planting Time

If you buy a nut tree, it will probably be bare-root and wrapped in some packing material. Follow the directions for planting, and don't neglect the pruning. You have a choice of several pruning methods, all of which are designed to accomplish the same thing — to keep the top of the tree from growing faster than the roots' ability to supply it with the necessary nutrients.

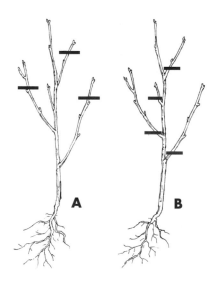

If your tree is lightly branched (**A**), cut back all the branches to the first bud from the end, and cut the top back to the second bud from the top, following the directions in chapter 3. Or, if you prefer (**B**), cut back all the branches to the main stem, leaving the top intact, and plant the tree as a whip.

If your tree has no branches, cut off about a third of the total length of the tree. Cut on a slant to just above the bud, as usual.

Early Training of Nut Trees

Nut trees in a forest tend to grow straight and tall. Their lower limbs gradually die as the trees reach higher for the sun. On the other hand, many varieties of large nut trees living in the open spread out, and their limbs grow huge and in weird shapes. Sometimes the limbs grow straight up, forming a second top, or they may grow straight out. Always do major pruning when the tree is dormant.

MASTER GARDENING TIP

Pruning Small Varieties

If you are growing a smaller nut tree, such as the almond, prune it much as you would a fruit tree (see chapter 9). Easterners prune the filbert into a large bush, however, but on the West Coast they prune it as a small tree.

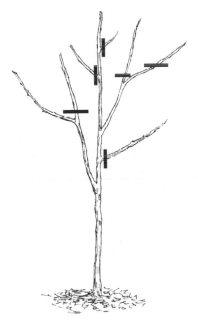

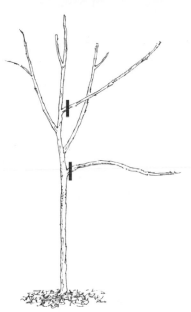

1 If your young nut tree is a large-growing variety, try to train it to grow with a strong central leader (see page 119). Sooner or later, you will have to give up and allow the tree to grow as crotchy and limby as it wants to, but keep after it for as long as you can.

2 Prune off limbs that weaken the tree. Long, heavy, horizontal limbs put a great strain on any tree and will probably eventually split off, so you should remove them early on. Also, take out limbs that grow off at angles, particularly ones that form crotches in a 45-degree angle.

MASTER GARDENING TIPS

Pruning Mature Trees

Prune large-growing nut trees for the same reasons that you would prune a shade tree — to remove dead or injured limbs and to lighten the load on weak crotches. Although home growers don't usually prune to increase nut yields, commercial orchardists boost production by cutting out old wood and thinning out the branches to allow in more light.

If you need to cut off heavy limbs for any reason, do it in stages, as shown on page 30. You may want to seal any large cuts or cavities with tree dressing or paint.

Almond

The almond *(Prunus dulcis)* is a member of the rose family, as are the plum, peach, and other stone-fruit trees, and it closely resembles them in its growth habits. It grows 20 to 25 feet high — somewhat shorter than a standard apple tree. Also, like fruit trees, almonds are pollinated by bees rather than by wind, so you don't need to plant them as close together as you would other nut trees.

Different varieties grow in different shapes — some are low and bushy and others are more upright. Your pruning should conform to your tree's natural growth habit. If you care for it properly, your almond will produce for 50 years or more.

MASTER GARDENING TIPS

Pruning a Young Tree

Train the tree into a good modified-leader system (see page 119). Avoid any unnecessary pruning, as that will stimulate extra leaf growth and delay bearing.

When to Prune

Do all pruning while the tree is dormant.

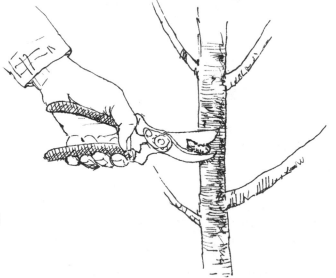

Pruning a bearing tree. Almond trees bear nuts on short, stubby spurs, so as the tree grows older, begin to thin out the bearing spurs by cutting them off flush to the trunk. Open up the branch area to keep the interior of the tree from becoming too dense and dark, just as you would a fruit tree.

Black Walnut and Butternut

These members of the walnut family are valued for both their nuts and their lumber. They look so much alike when they're young that it's difficult to tell them apart. The butternut *(Juglans cinerea)* is hardier than the walnut *(J. nigra)* and grows well throughout the northern United States and southern Canada.

Both butternut and black walnut trees have very strong wood, so the unusual crotches that insist on growing are less hazardous to a tree's health than they would be on many weaker trees.

Pruning a mature tree. As the trees grow taller, prune off a few of the lower branches each fall, always leaving at least twice as much branched area as you have limb-free trunk.

MASTER GARDENING TIPS

Pruning a Young Tree

Train it to grow with a strong central leader for its first few years. The terminal bud is easily damaged by weather, and if this happens, two or three sprouts will grow. Don't let the tree grow into a bush — keep pinching and snipping it into one main trunk for as long as possible.

Don't wait until the tree is fully grown to start cutting off the bottom limbs. Large wounds don't heal over well, and the trunk will be permanently scarred.

If you are growing the tree for its nuts: Site it 30 to 40 feet from other trees. If you are growing your trees for lumber: Space them about 15 feet apart. It's especially important to grow them with a strong central leader so that you'll have a log or two that are straight and free of large limbs.

When to Prune

Do all pruning in early fall, after the nuts have dropped off the tree.

Disease Alert

Both butternuts and black walnuts are subject to Juglans dieback *(Melanconis juglandis),* a disease that apparently came into the country with Oriental nut trees. Afflicted trees have a shortened life span and an unhealthy appearance. Most wild trees are now infected.

Little can be done except to cut off limbs that look sick. Vigorous, healthy trees seldom show symptoms, so keep your trees in excellent condition. Fertilize regularly, and give them plenty of water during dry spells.

Chestnut

If you remember the classic early American poem by Longfellow, you know that the chestnut *(Castanea)* has a naturally spreading habit: "Under the spreading chestnut tree/The village smithy stands...." In the woods, however, these trees grow tall and straight, and produce beautiful lumber. Unfortunately, both forests and smithies lost most of their trees to the great chestnut blight that swept the country in the early 1900s. The few trees that survived the disaster have been propagated and crossed with imported, blight-resistant types, so now there are several varieties of chestnut trees available from nurseries. None is entirely blight-proof, but many are quite resistant.

If you don't have enough space or simply prefer a smaller chestnut, consider the Japanese chestnut *(Castanea crenata),* which seldom reaches more than 30 feet tall, and can be grown as either a small tree or a large bush. Pruning will keep both the Japanese and the widely planted Chinese chestnut *(C. mollissima)* low growing. The Chinese is probably the most blight resistant of those that are commonly grown, and it also produces the best-flavored nuts.

MASTER GARDENING TIPS

Pruning a Mature Tree

Chestnut wood is very brittle, so prune back long branches to prevent breakage.

When to Prune

Prune when the tree is dormant.

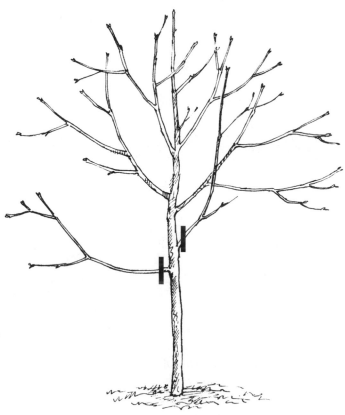

Pruning a young tree. Guide the tree to a strong central leader with a balanced branch formation. Prevent bad crotches that will break easily later on, and remove any branches growing too close to the ground.

Filbert

Filberts *(Corylus)* range from the small native American hazelnut to improved and named varieties of the European filbert, the only member of the species cultivated to any extent. Because the tree stays small, it suits the home garden better than most other nut trees.

The filbert is one of the few nut trees that lack a deep-growing taproot, so it is much easier to transplant. Because it has a fibrous root system, you can also root-prune it, if necessary.

Filberts are usually grown as shrubs or large bushes, except in the West, where they are pruned into a tree form with a single main stem. You can grow them from seeds or via layers. To layer, bend over a low branch and cover the middle section with soil so that it can root. Because filberts are easily propagated in this way, they are seldom grafted.

MASTER GARDENING TIPS

Pruning a Young Tree

If you have a grafted tree, be especially careful to prune away all the suckers growing around the bottom of the main stem so that they won't crowd out the good part of the tree. Prune most of the suckers growing from the roots of nongrafted trees too, to keep the tree from getting too bushy.

When to Prune

Prune your filbert while it is dormant, in late fall or early spring.

Mature filberts need to be pruned mostly to keep them in shape and to let more light into the tree. Cut out some of the old branches while they are dormant, and new ones will replace them.

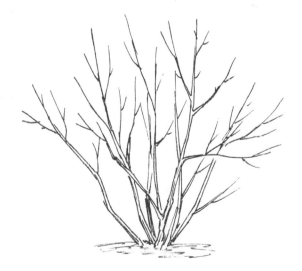

If you are growing your filbert in a clump, keep it pruned to only five or six main stems so that the bush won't become too wide and unmanageable.

Hickory

Although premium meats are often smoked using its bark, the hickory (*Carya*) is practically unknown in most of this country, and its nuts are seldom found in stores. However, hickory wood has long been valued for its strength, and is widely used for tool handles, baseball bats, and skis.

There are several strains of this rugged tree, ranging from the practically inedible bitternut, which is hardy even in Ontario, to the pecan, grown mostly in the South and California. The hickory family is native only to the central part of North America, and includes the shagbark, the water hickory, the mockernut, the pignut, and the shellbark, as well as the pecan and the bitternut. Natural hybrids have originated and others have been developed by breeders. Some are chiefly ornamental, and some produce high-quality nuts and nuts that are easier to crack.

To anchor a tree of this size, Nature has equipped the hickory with a long taproot that develops early in life, so planting or moving even a small tree is not easy. When starting a new tree, unless you want to try one of the hybrids, plant it where you want it to grow so that you won't have to move it.

MASTER GARDENING TIPS

Pruning a Young Tree

Basal-prune your trees as they grow, so that by the time they are 15 feet tall, none of the lower limbs will be closer than 6 to 8 feet from the ground. If you are growing your trees for lumber, you should, of course, prune higher as the tree continues to grow.

Pruning a Mature Tree

Pruning mature hickories is not usually necessary or practical because of their great height (up to 100 feet). They tend to grow upright, and have a naturally strong central leader.

When to Prune

Prune in early fall, after the nuts drop off.

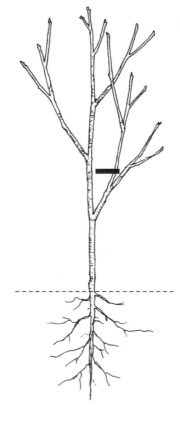

Like many other nut trees, hickories have a major, deep-growing taproot. Never prune this root, and take special care that it is not damaged during planting. Prune to a central leader, and remove crossed branches.

Pecan

Pecans *(Carya illinoinensis),* one of the best-known edible hickories, are grown mostly in the southern and southwestern areas of the United States. Although they are primarily a commercial nut, they are also grown extensively on farms and in backyard gardens.

Some of the newer varieties of pecans have growth habits different from their native relatives. They're smaller and less upright, making them more suitable for the home garden.

Pecans have long, deep taproots, and they need the same care you'd give any of the hickories when you're planting the small trees. Never cut or bend the taproot during the moving process.

MASTER GARDENING TIPS

Pruning a Young Tree

Give it some snipping during the growing season for its first years so that it will grow with a strong central leader.

When to Prune

Trim to shape the tree during the growing season. Do major pruning, such as the removal of lower or damaged limbs, when the tree is dormant.

Prune away a few bottom limbs each year, until it has 6 to 8 feet of branch-free lower trunk. This is probably all the pruning a backyard tree will ever need.

Walnut

The Persian walnut *(Juglans regia)* is the true name of the English walnut. We call it the English walnut because it arrived in the Colonies on English ships. Actually, the cool climate of the British Isles is not at all suitable for the culture of the Persian walnut, since it needs continuous warmth to grow well. Since the introduction of the Carpathian strain of Persian walnut from Poland, these trees grow in home gardens all over the country, and they are no longer restricted to the more temperate West Coast. Careful breeding and seed selection are slowly extending the growing region even into the northern states and southern Canada.

Note: Most walnuts in commercial groves — and even some of those growing in backyard gardens — are grafted, often onto black walnut seedlings. It's easy to see a difference in the bark below and above the graft on these trees.

MASTER GARDENING TIPS

How to Prune

When you buy a tree, ask about its growth and bearing habits and prune accordingly.

When to Prune

Do all pruning in early fall, after the nuts are harvested, since walnuts tend to bleed badly when pruned in the spring.

This young walnut tree has good branch structure, but competing suckers at the base should be clipped off.

Pruning a Young Walnut Tree

Because its wood is rather brittle, stake a newly planted tree to prevent it from breaking off at the graft. Remove any suckers growing from the base (below the graft); they're not Persian walnut, plus they look unattractive and sap energy from the tree.

Some of the walnut hybrids bear such heavy crops of nuts that you should prune them to grow with a strong central leader for their first years.

It's important to basal-prune walnuts. Remove all branches to about 8 feet above the ground as soon as the tree is tall enough to permit this safely.

A Special Note about Winter Care

The bark of a young walnut tree sunscalds so easily that you'd be wise to whitewash the trunk of your newly planted tree or to cover it with tree wrap for its first few years.

Pruning a Mature Tree

Mature walnuts need occasional pruning to let more light into the interior of the tree. Cut out some of the older, unproductive wood so that it will be replaced by new, young branches. It may also be necessary to shorten the limbs on some varieties, since they bear so heavily that the branches sag, and eventually they develop a droopy habit of growth.

In later years, allow your walnut tree, especially if it is one of the heavy-bearing hybrids, to develop with a modified-leader system. Some varieties — 'Mayette', for instance — tend to be of such spreading growth that an open-center method of pruning is best (see page 119). Although the commercial growers who plant walnuts in large orchards prune them so that they can harvest the nuts with a mechanical shaker, most homeowners shake the tree themselves, so the shape isn't as important.

Wisteria is an attractive flowering vine, but it can also be pruned into an equally beautiful shrub.

Vines and Groundcovers

Every gardener's idea of heaven is a place filled with lush fruit trees, brimming with exquisite flowers, and, in the midst of it all, a vine-covered cottage. Although this is a fine daydream, the danger lies in believing that such beauty and perfection will come about without careful planning and some hard work. Vines do not grow quickly, to just the right height, and then stop growing and look nice ever after. And, in spite of our fantasies, no groundcover exists that will spread over a lawn within a few weeks, stay just the right height, and stop growing at the edge of flower beds, vegetable garden, and the neighbor's putting green.

Both vines and groundcovers are useful additions to home landscaping, however, and you can keep most of them looking good and under control with minimal care. The care and pruning of each is similar, and some plants can be used for both purposes; vining ivies, woodbine, and honeysuckle, for instance, also make useful groundcovers.

Of plants with trailing growth habits, some, such as sweet peas and morning glory, are annuals grown from seed each year; others, like wisteria and bittersweet, are perennials. A few vines have roots that are perennial and tops that are annual; many tender vines, such as star jasmine, grow this way in the North but are entirely perennial in the South. Some, such as grape, may develop large trunks when very old; others, like ivy, have thin, wiry stems and can trail over brick walls. With this variety, there is at least one suitable for every need in every climate.

Some small, woody bushes, such as creeping junipers, and herbaceous plants, like thyme, make good groundcovers. They spread by various methods. A number have vigorous root systems that sprout new plants as they spread — goutweed, for example. Myrtle sends out running vines that root and form new plants, while others, like tickseed and crown vetch, scatter seeds that sprout easily.

In This Chapter

- Pruning a Woody Vine
- Pruning a Wisteria
- Pruning Clematis
- Climbing Roses
- Rejuvenating an Overgrown Vine
- Working a Remodeling or Painting Job around a Vine
- Twining Vines
- Clinging Vines
- Annual Vines
- Pruning Groundcovers

Pruning a Woody Vine

Potted vines need no pruning when you plant them, but if you have a bare-root, woody vine — that is, one with a hard woody stem — you should cut the top back by about half, to a bud, on planting day. This will prevent top growth from beginning until new roots get established and start to supply enough energy to support that growth. The vine will become a much more vigorous specimen. Of course, carefully follow all the other proper planting procedures regarding location, watering, fertilizer, and soil.

MASTER GARDENING TIP

When to Prune a Vine

Lightly prune during the growing season. Prune severely only when a vine is dormant, even those vines that make the rankest growth and are able to withstand the hardest cutback.

Early Training

Some early pinching and snipping will add considerably to the general appearance of most vines. Form a mental image of the way you want yours to look in its prime, and prune accordingly.

To get your vine off to a good start, you should know how it grows and especially how it climbs. For more details about specific vines, see the lists on pages 185 and 186.

- **Ramblers.** Some so-called vines, like the climbing and rambler roses (chapter 4), produce long canes that should be tied or interlaced with a trellis for support.

- **Twiners.** Many vines, such as honeysuckle and morning glory, twine around a post or wire, winding their way upward.

- **Clingers.** A few vines are clinging, and they hold on in several different ways. Some attach themselves by springlike tendrils. Grapes and clematis grow in this fashion. Vines with tendrils need something to wrap around, and are not too adept at climbing stone and brick walls. The ivy family is better at that. Boston ivy hangs on with small sucker disks that become attached firmly to hard surfaces. Climbing hydrangea and English ivy can also cling to smooth surfaces, but instead of the sucker disks, they grip with many small rootlets.

Vines that cling to smooth surfaces grow well with little training, support, or other care, on brick and stone structures in climates where they are perennial. They are not a good choice for wooden buildings, because they hold moisture, are likely to rot the wood, and will make painting projects difficult.

MASTER GARDENING TIPS

Pruning a Mature Vine

Trim during the growing season. After the vine has reached the height and width you want, most of your pruning will consist of snipping back any growth that goes beyond those limits.

Promptly remove dead and damaged wood. Occasionally thin out some old wood to keep the vine from choking itself. Also, prune out any part of the vine that has been hurt by winter damage or eaten by insects, or that shows signs of disease. Don't neglect this chore, or eventually you will be faced with a major, tedious job.

Pruning a Wisteria

1 **Set up a support.** You can use a wooden or plastic trellis purchased at the garden center or from a catalog. But for wisteria and other heavier vines, wires are stronger, and you can install brackets to hold them. No matter what you plan to train the vine on, always space it 4 to 6 inches away from the wall to allow for good air circulation.

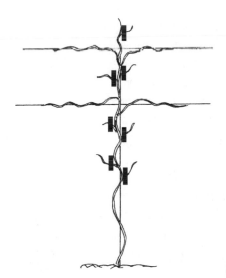

2 **Establish a framework.** While the vine is growing to the desired height, take time to train side branches (to reduce crowding, allow about 1½ feet between them). Tie them at intervals to the wires. Once the main leader reaches the height you want, chop off the top or train it to one side.

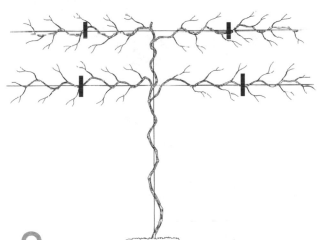

3 **Prune back side shoots.** Keep your plant in bounds and encourage bushy growth by cutting back horizontal-growing stems by about half their length. Do this in summer while the wisteria is actively growing. Main branches can also be shortened by about half, but it's better to do this more substantial pruning in late winter.

4 **Prune to encourage flowering.** Once the vine is trained to the height and shape you wish, confine all major pruning to winter or early spring before growth starts. Cut back all shoots to four or five buds, and remove any suckers that appear at the plant's base. Don't fertilize, as this leads to lush foliage growth at the expense of flowers. (If your wisteria still doesn't bloom after years of this regimen, consider root pruning — see page 35.)

Pruning Clematis

The beautiful clematis is not as widely grown as it should be, possibly because it is fussy about soil, sun, and temperature. Yet it's easy to grow when it's planted in "sweet" soil (pH 7), and has a deep mulch of lawn clippings or similar material over its roots to keep them cool. Also, plant the vine where the hot afternoon sun won't shine on the roots and lower stems. Clematis seems to do best if planted on the east or northeast side of the house, where it gets only morning sun.

Training a Clematis

Pruning is rarely necessary at planting time, since you usually plant a vine that is potted. Let clematis grow thick and bloom heavily all the way up a trellis or post. Start pruning when the plant is still young, in the second or third season. In early spring, when it is about a foot or so tall, pinch off the top buds to encourage them to branch and thus make a bushier plant. A week or two later, again pinch the terminal buds of the new side shoots. Continue this practice until the vine has filled the trellis or covered the post. After that, clematis vines are likely to need only an occasional thinning of old, unsightly, and thick vines.

MASTER GARDENING TIPS

Clematis in Cold Climates

▶ Remove the vines from the trellis, lay them on the ground, and cover them for winter, pruning to get them off the trellis. Work carefully to salvage as much of the vine as possible. In the spring, reattach, pruning off winter injury.

▶ Choose a variety that blooms on the current season's growth, because even if it is covered, a hard winter may kill the vine to the ground.

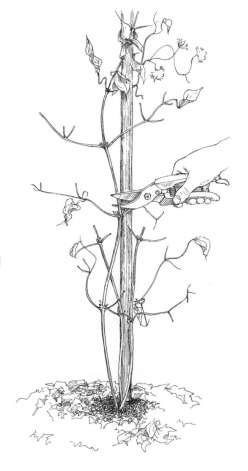

If you ever have to move a fragile clematis vine, pruning will make the job easier and more likely to be successful. In early spring, cut the vines to within a foot or two of the ground. Dig all around the plant roots, and move the entire rootball — soil and all — disturbing the roots as little as possible. On an older plant, the rootball may be nearly the size of a bushel basket. If you manage to save most of the roots, and if the vine has been cut back, survival is practically assured.

Getting a Vine to Bloom

Sometimes a vine doesn't flower or it flowers only sparsely — a disappointing or frustrating situation for the eager gardener. Always make sure to plant it where it will receive sufficient sunlight, and to provide proper care in the form of regular watering and fertilizing. If the plant is still shy, judicious pruning may help.

Know your vine's blossoming habit; this will make a difference in how you prune. Most bloom on wood that grew the previous year (i.e., "year-old wood"). For these:

- **Never cut back severely.**
- **Occasionally thin out the old wood** to let in more light, but avoid any heavy cutback of last year's growth.
- **If an otherwise healthy plant refuses to bloom,** consider root pruning (see page 35).

Exception: Some kinds of clematis bloom on wood that grows the same year. Prune these back to about 1 to 1½ feet in early spring, as they start their second year.

MASTER GARDENING TIP

Blooming Habits of Clematis

The named varieties of hybrid clematis bloom in two different ways. Some bloom on wood grown the previous year, and some on wood grown the same year.

On year-old wood	On current year's growth
'Belle of Woking'	'Comtesse de Bouchard'
'Duchess of Edinburgh'	'Gipsy Queen'
'Nelly Moser'	'Jackmanii'
'President'	'Lord Neville'
	'Mme. Edouard André'
	'Ramona'
	'Ville de Lyon'

Climbing Roses

Climbers look better if you allow a few tall, narrow branches to reach the top of a trellis, where they can grow thickly and cascade downward while blooming heavily. To encourage this kind of growth, remove most of the weak canes so that the plant's strength goes into the few that remain. Cut them in early spring when the plant is dormant. For more detailed information on pruning climbing roses, see chapter 4. Clip off fading flowers to encourage repeat blooming.

1 Climbing roses need good ventilation when grown against a wall. Keep the trellis at least 3 inches from the wall.

2 Tie the stems to the trellis with strips of cloth as it grows. Avoid unnecessary pruning until the rose covers the trellis.

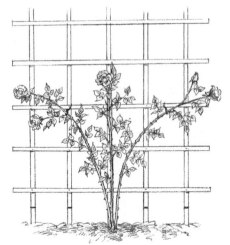

3 Steer some of the new canes to grow outward to cover the trellis early.

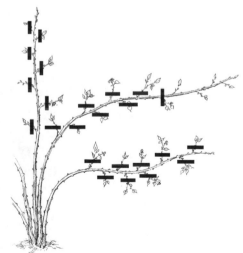

4 Continue to snip off branches that are growing too thick. Every three years cut out a few of the older canes and allow others to replace them.

Rejuvenating an Overgrown Vine

Radical surgery is justified when a vine has gone completely out of control, grown beyond its bounds, and no longer looks healthy and attractive — and the prospect of going in and removing all the deadwood is overwhelming.

MASTER GARDENING TIP

When to Rejuvenate

The best time is very early in the spring while the vine is still dormant, so regrowth can start soon after.

1 Cut back the whole plant, but leave a few young stalks (year-old spurs are best), if there are any, growing near the main stem. Most vines are extremely resilient and will bounce back from this surgery.

2 When the vine begins to send up new shoots, clip most of them off, leaving only three or four of the most vigorous. These will grow rapidly, and soon you will have a full-size, healthy new vine.

Working a Remodeling or Painting Job around a Vine

Sometimes a vine is in the way of a remodeling or painting job. If you want to save the plant, plan your project for early spring or late fall, when the pruning will be least harmful. If you must do the job in midsummer, keep the cutting to the barest minimum to prevent a lot of late-summer regrowth.

1 Unless the vine is very stiff and brittle, cut off just enough to loosen it from its support, and lay it down carefully on the ground.

2 Protect the vine while you work, and don't pile any materials on it. Put a corral of boards or bricks around it, or lay a tarp loosely over it — anything that prevents you from trampling it.

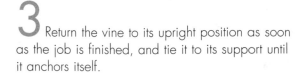

3 Return the vine to its upright position as soon as the job is finished, and tie it to its support until it anchors itself.

Twining Vines

The twining vines can wind their way up wires, trellises, or waterspouts. They are not good choices for planting to cover walls or brick buildings, but they make ideal screens on porches and fences. Some vines twine from left to right, that is, counterclockwise as you look down at them — bittersweet and Chinese wisteria, for example. Others, such as honeysuckle and Japanese wisteria, twine from right to left (clockwise). Prune all woody vines when they are dormant.

Plant	Characteristics	Maintenance
Bittersweet *(Celastrus scandens)*	Although only female plants produce berries, both males and females are needed for pollination.	Keep suckers cut off. Prune only to keep suckers under control.
Dutchman's-pipe *(Aristolochia durior)*	Grows slowly when first planted. Large, heavy leaves are too coarse for some locations, but are ideal in others.	Prune to keep under control and to remove dangling stems. Cut off old wood and signs of winter injury.
Five-leaf akebia *(Akebia quinata)*	Of Oriental origin, nice when planted where there is enough room for it to grow.	Control by cutting back each winter. Every 10 or 12 years, cut to the ground in early spring and it will renew itself.
Honeysuckle *(Lonicera)*	Ideal in the right location, covering old fences, stumps, and eyesores quickly; can become weedy if left unchecked.	Prune heavily during the summer to keep from growing wild. Thin out the vines and remove suckers after blooming.
Japanese wisteria *(Wisteria floribunda)*	A well-known, attractive, and useful vine, with many cultivars — some delightfully fragrant. Hardy enough to grow as far north as USDA Zone 4. Many varieties of wisteria are grafted, and suckers will crowd out the good plant.	Prune heavily in early spring and, if necessary, in summer. Do not allow suckers to grow from the base. Cut nongrafted suckers back nearly to the ground to renew. Grow vine as an attractive large bush by cutting and pinching back all the vinelike tendrils as they grow. Support with stakes, at least for the first 10 years.
Kadsura *(Kadsura japonica)*	An evergreen suitable only for the warmer regions. Produces red berries; nice reddish fall color.	Provide ordinary training and pruning to control.
Kiwi *(Actinidia)*	The bower (*A. arguta*) is hardier and more widely planted than the Chinese variety (*A. chinensis* or *A. deliciosa*), but it's less attractive.	Prune heavily in early spring. Leave some old wood on the plant, as it flowers on wood that is at least a year old. Thin out and cut back during summer for best appearance. For fruit production, cut back stems while plant is dormant, leaving 8 to 10 buds.
Magnolia vine *(Schisandra propinqua)*	For red berries, plant both male and female plants.	Prune only lightly.
Silver lace vine *(Polygonum aubertii)*	One of the fastest-growing vines: It will cover a large trellis in a single season. Blooms in late summer, but thick foliage is lovelier than flowers.	Prune, if necessary, while it is dormant.
Star jasmine *(Trachelospermum jasminoides)*	Fragrant vine has white flowers. New growth is an attractive bronze. In mild climates, it is evergreen over the winter.	Seldom needs pruning.

Clinging Vines

Some clinging vines grow with small tendrils that cling on wire, trellises, or other plants (bignonia, clematis, passiflora, grape). Others (trumpet creeper, English ivy, climbing hydrangea, Boston ivy) have small sucker disks or rootlets, known as holdfasts, that clamp onto brick, stone, or concrete. Some have vigorous tendrils and can support great weights. Others require occasional pruning, or the weight of the vine will become too much for the tendrils to hold. Snip away large masses of dangling green, in any case, for a better appearance.

Plant	Characteristics	Maintenance
Blood trumpet (*Distictis buccinatoria*)	Warm-weather vine. Blooms year-round in its native Mexico. A fast grower with excellent screening qualities, it clings tightly by disk tendrils.	Prune like an ivy.
Boston ivy (*Parthenocissus tricuspidata*); **Virginia creeper** (*P. quinquefolia*)	Boston ivy is hardier than the English ivy. Virginia creeper, or woodbine, is not as clinging, but is hardier. A vigorous-growing vine or groundcover, it is useful for covering banks, unsightly areas, or even to shinny up the trunks of large trees.	Prune anytime.
Cat's-claw creeper (*Macfadyena unguis-cati*)	A clinging vine suitable for Zone 8 and warmer. Has large 3-inch, yellow blooms and evergreen leaves.	Pruning necessary to keep from growing too fast and becoming thin at the base. Trim just after plant has finished blooming to encourage a bushy growth habit.
Clematis (*Clematis* spp.)	These vines are not difficult to grow or care for.	For pruning, see pages 180–181.
Climbing hydrangea (*Hydrangea anomala* ssp. *petiolaris*)	One of the best-clinging vines, it clings to brick with small holdfasts. It looks good even in winter.	Prune in early spring to control and remove loose, hanging parts.
Cross vine (*Bignonia capreolata*)	An evergreen that climbs by means of tendrils. Excellent for screening.	Control by pruning in early spring removing weak shoots.
Euonymus (*Euonymus fortunei*)	Many named varieties suitable for either vines or groundcover. Cling by tiny roots to rocks and even tree trunks, rooting easily wherever the vine touches the ground.	Prune to keep within bounds during spring and early summer.
Grape (*Vitis*)	Both wild grapes and many named varieties of garden grapes.	As ornamentals, prune only to keep under control. For fruit, follow directions in chapter 10.
Ivy (*Hedera*)	Ivies cover brick and stone buildings, as well as concrete foundations. Varieties vary widely in hardiness, appearance, and fruiting habits. All make good groundcovers as well as climbing vines.	Prune to control. Cut off dangling or torn pieces, and any stems that are creeping over doors and windows. Withstand ruthless pruning at any time of the year.
Passionflower (*Passiflora*)	Where hardy, passionflower grows quickly. Unusual flowers are a spectacular sight.	To ensure the best show, plant in full sun and prune annually to keep an open habit.
Trumpet creeper (*Campsis radicans*)	A husky grower, this woody vine uses holdfasts to cling to stone or brick.	Prune to keep from becoming too heavy. Cut off fading flowers, and prune back dangling and trailing branches.

Annual Vines

Annual vines (those that you can grow from seed to their full height in one season) have certain advantages: They're out of the way during the winter, they give you quick results, and many are especially attractive, with colorful blooms or fruit. They usually need little or no pruning, although some pinching of the terminal buds helps keep them thick, and most need a bit of training to start them on their way up their supports.

Some, such as wild cucumbers, usually self-sow; that is, the plants grow back each year on their own. Various climbing beans can be used as annual vines, such as scarlet runner bean (which also produces edible seed), and 'Kentucky Wonder' (which can be eaten green or dried).

Most annual vines are the twining type. A few, like gourds, produce interesting or colorful fruit.

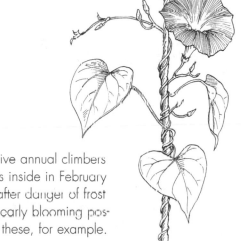

If your growing season is short, give annual climbers a head start by planting the seeds inside in February or March. Set them outside only after danger of frost is over. This procedure will make early blooming possible for morning glories, such as these, for example.

COMMON ANNUAL VINES

Balloon vine *(Cardiospermum halicacabum)*

Balsam apple *(Momordica balsamina)*

Cup and saucer vine *(Cobaea scandens)*

Gourds *(Lagenaria siceraria)*

Japanese hops *(Humulus japonicus)*

Morning glory *(Ipomoea tricolor)*

Nasturtium *(Tropaeolum majus)*

Scarlet runner bean *(Phaseolus coccineus)*

Sweet pea *(Lathyrus odoratus)*

Wild or mock cucumber *(Echinocystis lobata)*

MASTER GARDENING TIPS

Annual and Perennial Vines Serve Many Purposes

Vines as blinds. Some people grow vines to disguise a rainspout, television mast, telephone pole, or other unsightly object. Twining vines, such as bittersweet, fleece vine, and hops, are ideal for this purpose because they are vigorous growers. Just remember to keep the vine well groomed, and prune it to keep it within bounds. Otherwise, the cover itself can become unattractive, defeating the purpose of improving the site's appearance.

Vines as hedges. In areas where a hedge would take up too much valuable space, vines make a good substitute. Install a woven-wire fence with well-spaced and well-braced posts, and plant tight-growing vines along its length. In a few years, you'll have an effective barrier.

Shear occasionally to keep the plants confined to the fence.

Vines for food and drink. Vines that produce food are sometimes favored over purely ornamental vines. Grapes are an obvious choice, but you may also enjoy dewberries, climbing strawberries, climbing cucumbers, pole and flowering beans, kiwis, and hops. You must prune more precisely when your vines are growing food. Most food plants need plenty of sun, so never allow the vines to become thick and overgrown. Because grapes and berries produce best only on year-old wood, you should cut away all wood older than that every year if food is your primary interest (see chapter 10).

Pruning Groundcovers

Groundcovers usually need very little care, which is one of the main reasons we plant them — to avoid mowing steep or unsightly places. Occasionally, though, it's necessary to remove competing weed and brush growth or to cut out dead or damaged parts, so they are not entirely self-sufficient. Rock garden plants, for instance, are grown for their beauty and cannot compete with weeds. Other plants, chosen because they are rank growers, compete well against weeds and soon thickly cover an area. Shear plants that grow along paths, terraces, steps, and borders frequently to keep them within bounds.

MASTER GARDENING TIPS

Controlling Groundcovers

▶ Pinch back modest plantings or use grass shears, an edger, or your lawn mower as needed. Install metal or plastic edgings, bricks, or stone to save time.

▶ Chop back large masses of woody groundcovers such as bittersweet and Virginia creeper when they get badly overgrown. The plant will renew itself in short order.

Plant	Characteristics
Aaron's beard (*Hypericum calycinum*)	A perennial with colorful yellow flowers that grows well in rockeries where weeds are not too threatening. Also known as creeping Saint-John's-wort.
Bearberry (*Arctostaphylos uva-ursi*)	An evergreen plant that turns bronze in the fall. It grows well in poor soil, as long as it has full sun. It is a well-behaved groundcover.
Bugleweed (*Ajuga reptans*)	A good groundcover for sunny places. Can stand light foot traffic. Some varieties have foliage that is splashed with pink or cream.
Climbing hydrangea (*Hydrangea anomala* spp. *petiolaris*)	A magnificent vine, also used as a groundcover. When well established, heavy leaves shade out weed competition. Prune to keep attractive and under control.
Cotoneaster (*Cotoneaster* spp.)	A woody plant with colorful blossoms and fruit. Creeping kinds good for banks. May need hand weeding. Prune deadwood and broken and winter-injured limbs.
Creeping phlox (*Phlox subulata*)	Good on banks or in rock gardens where you can keep weeds and grass away from it. It flowers in white and shades of pink and lavender.
Crown vetch (*Coronilla varia*)	A vigorous plant, good on large banks, away from lawns and gardens. It spreads quite rapidly.
Cypress spurge (*Euphorbia cyparissias*)	A fast-growing groundcover that needs pruning to keep it under control. It may become a weed unless you restrain it.
English ivy (*Hedera helix*)	The ivies are good groundcovers wherever they are hardy. Once established, they grow quickly. Prune off parts that are growing too high and irregularly.
Epimedium (*Epimedium grandiflorum*)	An excellent low-maintenance groundcover for shady spots. It's very competitive and thick growing.
Five-leaf akebia (*Akebia quinata*)	A rank grower that needs tight control if it is to remain attractive and not smother shrubs and even trees.
Fleece flower (*Polygonum* spp.)	Several species of this groundcover are available, but *P. reynoutria* is one of the best.
Goutweed, bishop's weed (*Aegopodium podagraria*)	A good groundcover for difficult places. It can become a vicious weed if planted where it can escape into lawns or flower beds.

Plant	Characteristics
Hen-and-chickens (*Sempervivum tectorum*)	A poor groundcover except in rockeries and other spots that you can weed by hand. It's a colorful plant, but you must keep the fading blooms cut off.
Honeysuckle (*Lonicera*)	A fine groundcover, especially when large areas need to be covered at small expense. It's very competitive and must be pruned to be kept under control.
Ivy geranium (*Pelargonium peltatum*)	Grown as a groundcover only in the warmest parts of the United States. It is colorful and suitable for rock gardens and hillsides, and along paths.
Japanese pachysandra (*Pachysandra terminalis*)	One of the best groundcovers where it's happy. It is attractive, grows rapidly, is well behaved, and you can keep it under control by mowing around it.
Juniper (*Juniperus*)	Woody evergreen plant, with many low-growing, spreading varieties. Form new plants by layering. Competes poorly with weeds. Dead branches susceptible to disease and winter injury; clip often.
Lily of the valley (*Convallaria majalis*)	An old favorite, best in shady places with somewhat acid soil. Its lovely flowers are fragrant. The plant is quite competitive with grass and weeds.
Lowbush blueberry (*Vaccinium angustifolium*)	Good on dry banks with acid soil. It needs little care and will live for years. Cut out deadwood when necessary.
Memorial rose (*Rosa wichuraiana*)	Does well on steep banks. Its long stems root to start new plants easily. Prune only if necessary.
Myrtle, common periwinkle (*Vinca minor*)	A good groundcover for shady areas. Keep it away from flower beds, lawns, and gardens, because it is difficult to control. The most common type bears lovely blue flowers.
Plantain lily (*Hosta*)	A large-leaved perennial, suitable for plantings in shady areas. It's very competitive, but spreads slowly. Prune out the flower stalks at their bases after they fade.
Purple winter creeper (*Euonymus fortunei* 'Colorata')	Useful either as upright vines or groundcovers. 'Colorata' is especially good as a groundcover and has handsome fall color, too. Prune to keep it within bounds.
Scotch heather (*Calluna vulgaris*)	Provides color on terraces and in rockeries. Keep it in groups of the same color for an attractive bed. Prune to remove deadwood and spent flowers.
Sedum (*Sedum spurium*)	A good groundcover for poor soil. Research the variety, because some are better than others for certain applications, and certain types can become quite weedy.
Snow-in-summer (*Cerastium tomentosum*)	A plant with gray foliage and white flowers. Because it's not too competitive, it does best in small areas. Plant it in a rock garden, on a terrace, or as an edging for a path.
Spring heath (*Erica carnea*)	Colorful, heatherlike plants ideal for rockeries; some need heavy pruning of winter injury. Provide sun, a sheltered spot in the North, and well-drained, not too rich acid soil.
Strawberry (*Fragaria*)	Good rockery plants. Can be an effective groundcover where weed and grass competition is not too great.
Sweet woodruff (*Galium odoratum*)	At a height of up to 1 foot, a bit tall for a groundcover. Sweet woodruff creates a tight mat with pretty flowers. It's easy to grow in sun or light shade.
Thyme (*Thymus*)	An excellent rock garden plant that works well among flagstones in terraces and garden paths. It's fragrant and can stand light foot traffic.
Veronica (*Veronica filiformis*)	Although this creeping weed is the scourge of lawns and golf courses, it is fine in its place. Beware of introducing it where it might later haunt you.
Violet (*Viola pedata*)	Grows well on banks, especially under deciduous trees, blooms heavily, and spreads by seed. You can walk on it, and even mow by setting your mower high. Needs little care.
Virginia creeper, woodbine (*Parthenocissus quinquefolia*)	A good groundcover for northern areas, covering unsightly strips, banks, and rocky areas. It needs pruning to keep it under control.
Wild bleeding-heart (*Dicentra eximia*)	Creeping roots spread this everblooming perennial. It is good for rockeries and borders, although it doesn't compete well with weeds. Cut it back to keep it in control.

Pruning techniques like pinching back, disbudding, and deadheading will improve the looks and life of your perennial herbs and flowers.

Garden Plants and Houseplants

The competition among gardeners in my hometown was keen while I was growing up, and each resident along our one main street was anxious to have the best flower garden in town. As an apprentice to several of them, I had a wonderful opportunity to see how they managed their grounds. After a time, it became easy for me to separate the real gardeners from the non-gardeners.

The real gardeners not only planted carefully, fertilized religiously, and watered often, but they were also always snipping away at something. The nongardeners usually neglected any kind of pruning. Their flowers went to seed, and every few years their gardens became overgrown. Finally, when the rank-growing perennials had crowded out the more delicate plants, the garden had to be made over — a job I detested.

Although garden flowers don't need pruning in the same way that evergreens and fruit trees do, some of them benefit greatly from an occasional cutback.

In This Chapter

- Reasons to Prune Perennials
- Perennial Herb Plants
- Perennial Food Plants
- Pruning Houseplants
- Prune to Rejuvenate
- Hanging Baskets
- Pruning for Winter Storage
- Root Pruning

Reasons to Prune Perennials

Certain pruning techniques, such as pinching back, disbudding, and deadheading, will improve the looks and life of your perennial bed. You will also need to cut back plants to get them ready for winter and to keep vigorous plants under control.

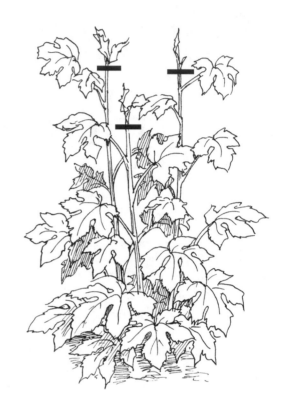

Prune to encourage bushy plants: Pinching back.
Certain plants grow one or two tall stems with only a few flowers on each — unless you pinch them back several times. Pinching gives you a bushy, symmetrical plant that will bear a lot of blossoms. (Of course, this isn't done if you wish to grow a tall plant with only a few giant-size flowers.)

Mums and dahlias: When the plants are about 3 inches tall, pinch off the growing end of the stems. Continue to pinch them off several times during the early part of the growing season. In milder climates, all pinching should be done before July 15. In northern areas with short growing seasons, however, move the deadline back to June 21. The plants will bloom early in the fall, and there will be many more flowers than if you hadn't intervened.

Delphiniums and hollyhocks: These and other tall-growing perennials can also be pinched early in the season. The plants respond by branching out, often saving you the trouble of staking. The drawback is that you may find the plant less attractive than one allowed to grow to its full height.

A

B

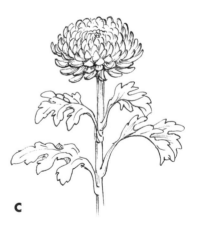

C

Prune to increase the bloom size: Disbudding. By disbudding — cutting off or pinching off most of the small, weak buds on certain plants — you can grow the remaining blooms with longer stems, and they'll be larger, too. You can force peonies, roses, chrysanthemums, asters, zinnias, and dahlias to produce giant-size blooms in this manner. When disbudding mums, take off all but two buds (**A**). Later, remove the smaller of the two (**B**) to produce **C**.

Prune to remove old blooms: Deadheading. Although it seems like an obvious thing for a neat gardener to do, not everybody is careful about picking off spent blossoms ("deadheading"). Biennials and annuals, as well as perennials, benefit from having blooms removed from the plant as soon as they fade. This pruning greatly improves the plant's appearance, and encourages more blooming. If you neglect to deadhead, the plant will form seeds quickly, and when plants go to seed, they tend to stop blooming.

Frequent deadheading will keep pansies, petunias, asters, marigolds, fuchsias, and many other flowers in bloom until frost. Delphiniums often bloom a second time the same summer if you cut them back immediately after blooming (plus, they are likely to live much longer)

There are some exceptions to deadheading. Some biennials and short-lived perennials keep on going year after year only by reseeding themselves. Unless you plan to set out new plants each year, allow a few of the best blooms of Canterbury bells, foxgloves, and sweet Williams to go to seed, so that they will continue to persist in your garden.

Prune to get plants ready for winter. You may have noticed that the well-kept gardens in your neighborhood are always "put to bed" for the winter. Wait until the plants have begun to lose their green color to cut off their tops. Food produced in the leaves must move back into the roots first, or the plants will be considerably weakened. You can recycle the tops in the compost pile. Then, after a hard frost, for the sake of neatness and to aid disease control, remove annuals and cut back perennials to a height of 2 or 3 inches. Finally, fertilize them and mulch them for the winter.

Prune to keep the plants growing in attractive clumps. Plants sometimes need to be disciplined, and you must prevent the ranker varieties from crowding out those that are more desirable. Sometimes all you have to do is simply pull up the encroaching new sprouts. Other times, however, you'll have to divide perennial clumps to keep them in their place. Divide most plants in early spring, soon after they've come up, so that the plants won't wilt. Often you can find new homes for the divisions, so your friends will benefit, as will your garden.

Prune to prevent plants from reverting. Some flowers produce seeds that grow into plants that are not like the parent; instead, they resemble their wild ancestors. A large percentage of phlox seedlings, for instance, are likely to be the wild magenta color, so your planting will quickly deteriorate if you allow the young, vigorous, poorly colored seedlings to crowd out the colorful, attractive, named varieties. Removing flower heads immediately after they have faded prevents this from happening to phlox and lupines, for example.

Perennial Herb Plants

Many perennial herb plants, like the mints and thymes, need frequent cutbacks throughout the growing season to prevent them from taking over the garden. Use the trimmings in the kitchen. It's best to keep vigorous-growing herbs away from the vegetable garden, in a place where you can mow around their bed to keep them under control if need be.

Most of the woody herbs, such as lavender, sage, rosemary, and bay laurel, need little pruning other than shaping and removing old or injured parts. The tall-growing ones, such as rosemary, benefit from an occasional cutting back, especially when they are grown as houseplants. Save the trimmings for drying or for starting new plants.

Herb	Maintenance
Bay laurel (*Laurus nobilis*)	Pick and use or dry the leaves year-round. In areas with frost, grow in a large pot, and bring indoors for the winter. Prune and shape anytime during its growing period. If you want to grow it as a tree, keep the lower side branches cut off.
Lavender (*Lavandula* spp.)	Prune only to shape and remove unattractive branches. Cut flowers just before opening for best aromatic properties. Harvest leaves anytime. Prune back heavily in fall, and mulch for winter protection in the North.
Rosemary (*Rosmarinus officinalis*)	Grow in pots and move indoors for winter except in mild climates. Prune anytime to get cuttings. Rosemary can be grown into an attractive bonsai plant in only a few years.
Sage (*Salvia officinalis*)	Prune to shape anytime. Cut young tender leaves in mid-summer to use or dry. Prune off woody growth in late spring. The plants are hardy but need replacing every four or five years.
Tarragon (*Artemisia dracunculus*)	Cut young sprouts to use or dry in early summer before the lower leaves start to turn yellow. Leave 2 or 3 inches of stem. In the North, cover with wood chips or evergreen boughs in late fall to overwinter.

Perennial Food Plants

Gardeners are sometimes puzzled about how to handle food plants that die down each fall and come back the next year. The following techniques will enable you always to have a healthy, abundant harvest.

MASTER GARDENING TIPS

Jerusalem Artichokes and Horseradish

Spring cutting. These plants should have their roots harvested in adequate amounts in early spring (or, if you prefer, late fall) every year so that you can keep the plants from spreading all over the place.

Fall cutting. Cut off their tops at season's end after they have died back.

Asparagus

Spring cutting. When you harvest asparagus spears in the spring, cut them with a sharp knife just under ground level. This keeps the plants producing throughout the season. Later, you can snip small amounts of the fernlike foliage for an occasional bouquet filler. Don't overdo, though, because the plants need considerable greenery to supply adequate nourishment to the roots.

Fall cutting. Cut the stalks to the ground with clippers as soon as they turn yellow. Take the tops to the compost pile, or use them as a mulch on your berries or fruit trees. If you skip this chore, little red asparagus berries will mature and scatter seed all over, starting new plants that will soon crowd the established ones into unproductivity.

Rhubarb

Spring cutting. You should not try to harvest rhubarb by cutting off the stalks — it isn't good for the plant. Instead, twist each stalk and pull it up gently from the roots so that you don't leave a stub.

Fall cutting. Pull off any dead leaves that still show in late summer or for cosmetic purposes. Otherwise, leave as mulch.

Occasional maintenance. Divide healthy rhubarb plants every seven or eight years to keep them from getting too ingrown. Take a sharp spade and slice off parts of the huge root, and either transplant these or give them away.

Pruning Houseplants

Because of the wide variety of houseplants, it would be impossible to list here the precise pruning directions for each. The general directions that follow apply to most plants.

HINT FOR SUCCESS

Just as with woody outdoor plants, cut or pinch houseplants back to a bud or live branch when pruning so that you don't leave a stub that will die and rot. Do likewise if you are snipping off slips or cuttings to propagate new plants.

Pinch to encourage bushiness (1). Pruning is almost always necessary for shaping houseplants. If a plant becomes scraggly, pinching will stop its leggy growth and encourage some side branches to form. Although blossoming will be delayed a bit, the result is a much better-shaped plant. Many window box plants, as well as those that are potted, rarely look their best because they never get the pinching they need. Coleus, petunias, geraniums, and begonias are just a few of the plants that benefit greatly from regular pinching.

Take off fading blooms (2). Potted plants, window box plants, and those in hanging baskets benefit from having their old blossoms removed just as much as garden flowers do. Removing the old flowers not only is important to a plant's appearance, but most plants will also stop blooming if you let their blossoms to go to seed.

Prune to maintain a houseplant's health (3). Cut off any leaves and stems that are diseased or discolored, when they appear. Watch for damage and prune off any part of the plant that is accidentally broken.

Rotate plants grown on a sunny windowsill once a week, so they will not grow one sided.

Prune to Rejuvenate

Frequent pinching and light pruning will usually eliminate the need for any heavy intervention. But certain plants appreciate an occasional drastic trim. Always cut back to a live branch or bud, leaving no stubs that could possibly infect the plant.

A drastically pruned plant may look for a time like a fugitive from the compost pile. Give it a chance to begin growing before doing any fertilizing. Pinch the new growth regularly. Rest assured it will grow into a nicer shape during the following seasons, and the blooms will be considerably better and more abundant.

Reasons to Rejuvenate

- **A new, healthy top can replace** an aging, less energetic one.
- **A plant that has grown out of proportion** can be reshaped. Houseplants left outside for the summer often go a little wild and need to be tamed when they return indoors. So do poinsettias, azaleas, and other woody favorites.

When to Rejuvenate

The best time to cut back an aging or tired houseplant severely is right after the plant has finished blooming. Cut back overgrown specimens while they are resting, usually in late winter, just before their growing season begins (then, when they start to grow, new shoots will quickly cover the cut areas).

MASTER GARDENING TIPS

Plants to Rejuvenate

The more vigorous growing, or naturally branching, a plant is, the more you can cut it back without fear of damage. Christmas cactus, geranium, and ivy are a few that recover very quickly.

Plants Not to Rejuvenate

Drastic pruning might prove fatal to slower-growing plants. Cutting back hard won't revive a rubber plant, jade plant, or certain cacti.

Plants That Are Better Replaced Than Rejuvenated

Some short-lived houseplants should be replaced every few years. An example is the artillery plant. If you know your plant's life expectancy, you'll be better able to prune it.

HINT FOR SUCCESS

When using tools, guard against letting them spread disease among your plants. If you are cutting a plant that you suspect of harboring a disease, sterilize the tool in alcohol, boiling water, or diluted bleach before using it on another plant. Many diseases, such as botrytis on geraniums, have been spread far and wide by someone who has taken cuttings with a knife that was carrying infection.

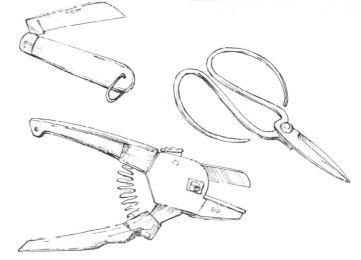

Tools for houseplant pruning. For plant parts that are too tough for pinching by hand you'll need:

- A sharp knife
- Small pruning shears or clippers

Hanging Baskets

Cascading petunias, ivy geraniums, hanging begonias and fuchsias, and other trailing plants in baskets or sitting on pedestals need frequent pruning to keep them in shape. The accomplished gardener realizes that regular shearings are as important to a hanging plant as moisture, the right pot size, fertilizer, and light conditions.

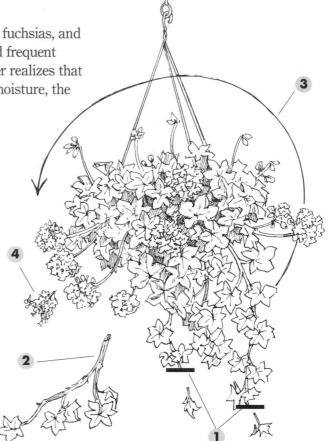

(1) Pinch off the ends of runners that are getting too long.
(2) Snip off parts that are getting too woody.
(3) Turn the plant occasionally so it doesn't grow lopsided.
(4) Keep faded flowers picked off so the plant will bloom for the longest possible time.

Pruning for Winter Storage

You may enjoy growing large numbers of begonias, geraniums, chrysanthemums, fuchsias, and similar plants in window boxes or on a terrace during the summer. When fall comes, if you don't want to throw them away but have no room indoors to use them as houseplants, it is possible to store them in a cool basement or the root cellar for the winter.

1. Leave the plants in their pots, but before you take them into their basement home, allow the soil to get moderately dry.
2. Prune back the tops to a mere 2 or 3 inches.
3. Place them in a winter storage room, such as the garage, cellar, enclosed porch, or unheated room in your home. It should be cool (but not freezing), and not too damp.
4. Check them at least once a month and, when necessary, water lightly so that they don't ever dry out completely. Don't overwater, though, since this may cause the plants to rot or mold.
5. In spring, when danger of frost has passed, bring the plants outside again, exposing them gradually to the sun and wind. Prune off any sickly branches, and in a short time they should be thriving again. Best of all, your salvaged plants will have cost you nothing but a little extra care.

Root Pruning

Many plants cannot be top-pruned successfully, often because they do not heal over properly when cut. Yet you don't want them to attain their full size if you have limited growing space. Cutting back the roots occasionally will enable you to control their size for many years.

Houseplants That Can Be Root-Pruned

- **Succulents** — aloe, echeveria, sempervivum, cactus, sedum, gasteria, and agave.

- **Ferns** (but not epiphytic or "air" ferns)

- **Many tropical plants** such as palms and dracaena

MASTER GARDENING TIP

When to Root-Prune a Houseplant

Early spring is the best time, because cut ends heal over well, and new growth begins more quickly then.

1. Make sure that your plant's soil is just a little damp: Wet soil is messy, and dry soil is likely to fall off the roots.

2. Pop the plant out of its container.

3. Using a long, sharp kitchen knife, chop off the small roots on the outside just as if you were starting to sharpen a pencil with a jackknife. (Don't use clippers — they tend to crush the root ends.) Take off about an inch of roots and soil all around the root ball, being careful not to cut into the thick, fleshy roots.

4. Repot the plant in good soil, then water it.

5. Keep the plant in a sheltered spot for a few days, out of the sun and drafts, while it recovers from surgery. If it has lost a lot of roots, those that remain may not be able to supply enough moisture to the top. Some plant experts therefore feel that it's a good idea to cover the entire plant with a large, transparent plastic bag to retain the moisture while it is recovering.

6. As soon as you see a few new shoots beginning to grow, you'll know that your plant has made it. Take it out of the "recovery room" and begin to treat it as before.

It is difficult to imagine a more advanced form of pruning than that required by bonsai, the Japanese art of dwarfing shrubs and trees. Bonsai demands precise thinning, pinching, clipping, and root-pruning skills.

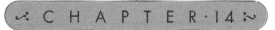

CHAPTER·14

Bonsai

I t takes patience and skill to make a tree that is only a few years old and several inches high look like a miniature version of a gnarled, 100-year-old specimen growing on a windy, rocky hillside. Because of this, in fact, many "finished" bonsai plants sell for hundreds of dollars apiece, although you can buy started ones for a much lower price.

Buying a finished bonsai will save you a lot of time and work, of course, but growing your own can be fun and a most satisfying hobby. Like any form of gardening, however, you never completely finish it. Still, the patience and attention it demands can lead you to a great feeling of achievement. In fact, bonsai plants often become the center of attention in a household. We know people who cannot take a vacation without constant concern for the welfare of their bonsai.

Indeed, a bonsai plant is really more pet than plant and, just like a puppy, cat, or hamster, it must have your attention daily. Unless you're sure you can meet its needs, you'd be better off with a philodendron.

Although the art of growing large trees in miniature form in outdoor gardens has been cultivated for centuries in Japan and elsewhere, growing tiny bonsai in pots is a more recent practice. Many of the techniques now used for training these specimens have been developed within the past century. The art has spawned many different techniques, and a short chapter on the subject is sure to upset any of you who are experts. The guidelines here are simply an introduction for the beginning grower. A serious fancier should read some books devoted entirely to this complex and fascinating subject.

In This Chapter

- Choosing Your Specimen
- Containers
- Equipment
- Soil Mixture
- Planting
- Pruning at Planting Time
- Early Training
- Maintenance Pruning
- Care of Your Bonsai
- Root Pruning and Repotting

Choosing Your Specimen

Although having a skilled bonsai gardener as a mentor would give any-one a tremendous advantage, the best insurance for good results is to start with a good plant. In theory, any variety of tree can be grown successfully as a bonsai, though some (weeping willows and mountain ash, for instance) are more difficult to train than others. Traditionally, bonsai plants are grown from Japanese or other Oriental species of trees. Although an Oriental specimen is ideal if the weather conditions are right, this kind of plant may not be the best choice for northern garden-ers. Luckily, there are plenty of other plants, many of them native and easy to come by, that are well suited for dwarfing.

- **Choose a variety** that is naturally dwarf and slow growing. The height of a mature bonsai should range from a few inches to about 3 feet. Use either a deciduous or an evergreen tree, but choose one with small leaves or short needles, as these plants will look better proportioned (although the dwarfing process accomplishes this to some degree).

- **Pick a plant** that is likely to grow well in poor, rocky soil. Denizens of rich or moist soil not only require higher maintenance, but they also tend to grow faster and lusher, making training more work.

- **Look for a tree** that is already a bit misshapen, distorted, or stunted. Bonsai enthusiasts will search through nursery rows for hours looking for a weirdly shaped transplant or seedling. One-sided growth and a thick trunk at the base are particularly desirable.

> ### MASTER GARDENING TIP
>
> #### Working with Regular-Size Trees
>
> If you don't have the opportunity to search rows of nursery trees or make visits to a mountain range, you can still grow a bonsai that is exclusively yours. It just may take a little longer. Simply start with a small tree that is 8 to 15 inches tall, because trees larger than that often prove too difficult to work with. Since some plants are sure to grow into a better shape than others, start several so that you can choose the best ones for bonsai training.

MASTER GARDENING TIPS

Deciduous Choices

Apple, azalea, beech, birch, boxwood, camellia, cherry, daphne, elm, flowering cherry, flowering quince, ginkgo, hawthorn, maple (especially Amur and Japanese maple), plum, wisteria

Evergreen Choices

Arborvitae, cedar, cotoneaster, cypress, hemlock, Japanese holly, juniper, dwarf-growing pine (especially mugho and bristlecone), pyracantha, spruce, yew

Containers

The container is as important as the plant in bonsai culture, and should be chosen just as carefully.

- **Choose a shallow pot or dish,** an inch or more deep. You don't want space for a large root system, because the roots need to be confined to help keep the plant small.

- **Simple, unglazed pots are preferable.** The Japanese seldom use ornate containers, because they believe that the plant itself should be the center of attention.

- **Pick a shape that complements the plant's habit:** square, round, or oval.

- **Above all, the container must have perfect drainage.** Although there are a lot of attractive pots on the market, many do not have the necessary large holes in them. A bonsai plant cannot tolerate sitting in water for even a short time. You can place small pieces of wire screen over the holes to prevent the soil from falling out.

Equipment

If you're serious about bonsai culture, it is advisable to invest in special tools for the exacting work of pruning small limbs and delicate roots. Many garden stores and mail-order houses offer individual tools as well as kits, at prices ranging from a few dollars to very expensive, for assortments that look like a brain surgeon's instrument tray. Start with a simple, but strong, set of basic tools.

- **Small but sturdy pruning clippers,** for the necessary precise, close-in trimming

- **Eighteen- to 20-gauge copper or aluminum wire,** for training

- **A short wooden chopstick or dowel** (¼ to ½ inch in diameter), for packing the soil when transplanting

- **A pair of large tweezers,** for delicate pruning work

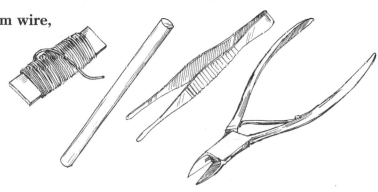

Soil Mixture

An excellent soil mixture is important to the well-being of any potted plant, and vital for bonsai plants, because the soil is shallow and the roots cannot go searching for soil that they prefer. Although the experts vary the texture of their soils, many beginning bonsai growers use the following soil mixture (measures are by volume, not by weight):

1 part good, dry potting soil
1 part sharp sand
1 part peat moss, composted bark, or well-rotted leaf mold
1 tablespoon dried cow, sheep, or poultry manure per quart of mixture
1 tablespoon lime (unless you are working with acid-loving plants such as azalea, hemlock, or pine)

- **Mix the ingredients thoroughly;** you'll be using small amounts and each pot must have a balanced mixture.

- **Sift through a screen** to strain out stones, weeds, worms, plant roots, and big lumps.

- **When potting, dampen the soil first.** Squeeze out excess water and press it gently into place in the container.

HINT FOR SUCCESS

Avoid heavy soil. It inhibits the fine hair-root growth that is important for proper feeding of the plant, and creates a drainage problem that could cause disease, poor growth, or even drowning.

MASTER GARDENING TIPS

Obtaining a Bonsai Specimen from the Wild

Selecting a Specimen

Some gardeners put on their hiking shoes and climb to high elevations near the timberline to search for a plant that has been dwarfed by years of exposure to harsh wind and weather. Before you do this, though, get permission from the landowner. If the mountain is on federal or state land, you may be prohibited from the project altogether. When in doubt, check with your nearest forest service office.

▶ The best plant you can choose often hides in a small pocket of soil among rocky crevices. This growing medium most closely resembles the small disk of soil in which it will reside once you get it home.

▶ Realize that you can't just pull up a tree, stuff it in a bag, and take it home expecting it to survive. Although the specimen may be only a few inches high, it may have already lived on its mountaintop for decades and not take kindly to being uprooted and transferred to your back porch. So try to spread the moving process over a year or more:

Planting Procedure

1. Even though the soil is limited, your targeted plant may have a fairly large root system. Early in the spring, without digging up the plant, take a sharp knife and carefully prune off a major part of the roots. Cut straight down in the soil around the plant.

2. The following spring, after the tree has grown a few new feeder roots close to its main stem and has become adjusted to its more compact root structure, you can safely dig it up and move it. Remove it with as large a rootball as possible.

3. Wrap the rootball in a damp cloth, place the plant in a plastic bag, and set it gently in your backpack or carry it out with care. Replant it at home as soon as you possibly can.

Planting

It's best to plant in early spring, when your candidate can best stand the shock of being root-pruned. Wounds heal more quickly, and new root growth will begin soon.

1 Remove most of the soil from the rootball so that you can better see where to prune. Shake or pry it off, but be careful not to cause any unnecessary damage. As you work, don't allow the roots to dry out. Dip them in water occasionally.

2 To fit the rootball into the container, you may have to cut off a lot of the root system. Leave as many fibrous hair roots as possible, because they are most essential to the plant's survival. Cut the fleshy taproots instead, taking out some entirely and shortening the others until the rootball fills about half of the pot.

3 Cover the bottom of the pot with the sifted planting mix (page 204). Remember to cover the drainage hole(s) with a piece of screen first.

4 Carefully spread out the roots and gently place the planting mixture among them, tamping it with a dowel to eliminate air pockets.

5 Continue to fill the pot with planting mixture, but leave a 3/8-inch space at the top so that future waterings won't overflow the pot.

Pruning at Planting Time

When you have finished planting, it's time to do some initial pruning. Before you start, decide on the way you want your plant to grow. Good bonsai designers have a mental picture of the finished tree when they start training, just as a good artist envisions the finished painting before the first stroke. If you are not familiar with the range of possibilities, it's a good idea to study photographs of bonsai or attend a flower show to get a feeling for the ways professionals do it.

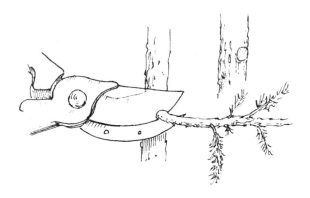

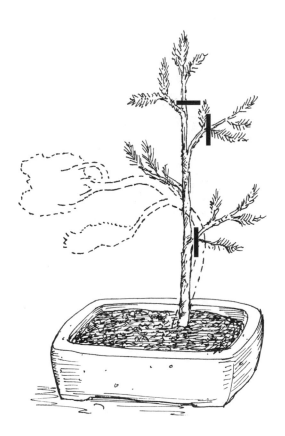

1 Thin out part of the branches. Fewer branches help to make the plant look old. Make all cuts close to the trunk. If large cuts are necessary, concave them into the trunk slightly so that the depressed wound will heal over more quickly.

2 Cut back the remaining limbs according to your bonsai plan. Water the plant heavily, and cover it entirely — pot and all — with a clear plastic bag. Set it in a cool place where it will get plenty of light but no direct sun, and leave it there for two or three weeks while it recuperates. Then move it into the sunlight.

Early Training

Some bonsai fanciers like to begin their training soon after planting, while others prefer to wait several months or even a year to let the tree get well established in the pot first.

Train evergreens in the fall or winter during their dormant season, and deciduous trees in early summer when the sap is flowing and they are flexible. If you shape them in the spring before they begin to grow, the tender, dormant buds are likely to be damaged; wait until the buds begin to grow so that you can wire around them without doing harm.

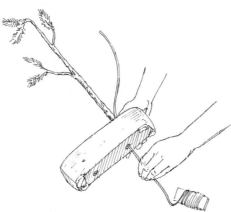

1 Anchor the wire in the pot. Stick it through the holes in the bottom.

2 Wrap the wire around the tree, spiraling it upward at a 45-degree twist.

3 Gently bend the tree to the desired shape (**A**). The wire will hold it. Bent-down branches create an aging look, but avoid distorting the plant too much as you shape it. A century ago, the more grotesque the bonsai, the more prized it was, but today most growers prefer to create more natural-looking specimens. As you work, slip bits of paper under the wire to protect delicate bark (**B**).

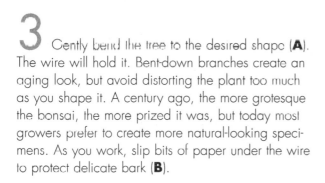

A   **B**

4 After the plant has gotten accustomed to growing in its new shape, you may remove the wires. On deciduous trees, this can usually be done three or four months after wiring. Leave the wires on evergreens much longer, sometimes as long as a year. Don't leave them on any longer than is necessary, however, or the tree may begin to grow around them, permanently disfiguring the trunk.

MASTER GARDENING TIPS

What Will I Need?

▶ **Wire.** Use 8- or 9-gauge wire for trees with fairly heavy trunks. Use a lighter wire, of either 18 or 20 gauge, for trees with smaller trunks and for shaping the branches and tops of larger trees.

▶ **Paper.** Little pieces can be used to cushion especially tender bark.

Maintenance Pruning

As the bonsai plant starts to grow, visit it often to make sure it is growing according to plan.

- **Pinch off sprouts** growing in the wrong places.

- **Trim back branches** that are growing too long.

front

back

Choose one side of your bonsai as the front, and make this the old-looking, thinned-out side.

Allow the backside to have a slightly denser growth, to give body to the plant and to produce additional leaf surface for healthy growth.

Allow one limb near the bottom of the plant to grow freely, while you train the rest of the plant. It will act as a decoy, if you will, using most of the plant's energy and making the shaping of the remainder of the tree easier. After the training is complete, carefully clip off that limb and seal or paint the resulting wound.

Care of Your Bonsai

Whether you buy a bonsai plant or develop a specimen entirely by yourself, you should be aware that even after the training period is over, bonsai need far more care than would another type of plant. Perhaps you can convince a neighbor to join you in the hobby so you'll have a backup when you go on vacation.

Watering

- **Bonsai often require daily watering** (and perhaps more frequent doses if they are exposed to hot, dry air), thanks to their small containers and the tiny amount of soil available to them. Mist, if desired.

- **Always water sparingly.** Overwatering can ruin a bonsai in short order.

- **Check the drainage holes frequently** to see that root growth or hardening soil has not sealed them shut.

Fertilizing

- **Feed only occasionally, and lightly.** Fast growth may be desirable in your corn patch, but it is definitely not your goal in a bonsai.

- **Add fertilizer to the water** rather than directly on the soil surface.

- **Use an organic fertilizer** such as fish emulsion or a tiny amount of dried cow manure.

Pest Patrol

- **Be vigilant.** Check for incriminating damage frequently so you can act promptly.

- **Should pests appear, try to correctly identify them.** If you need help, consult another indoor gardener or a reference book.

- **If you need to spray, always follow label directions to the letter.** The wrong spray or overzealous spraying can ruin all the effort you've put into your bonsai plant.

MASTER GARDENING TIPS

Achieving a Weathered-Looking Trunk

A fleshy, old, weathered trunk is a feature of many bonsai. One way to develop this is to plant your potential bonsai in a deep container for a year or so. Bury the fibrous roots in good soil in the bottom of the pot. Meanwhile, grow the upper part of the roots and the lower section of the trunk in shredded sphagnum moss. Keep both soil and moss moist. After a year has passed, pull away the moss and examine the stem. If it is developing the right appearance, gradually begin to remove the moss. This root will now be a part of the trunk, and by weathering will soon have an aged look. (You can also use this method to grow bonsai with long, rootlike stems that trail over rocks.)

Achieving a Woodland Look

A skirt of moss around the base of your bonsai tree can also help give it a more established or woodland look. Use a short-growing moss species. It's better not to apply a mulch. This makes it difficult to see when the plant needs water, and it also provides a place for harmful insects to breed.

Root Pruning and Repotting

Every few years your bonsai will become rootbound. Ordinarily, deciduous trees should be repotted every year or two, and evergreens need repotting every four or five years.

1 Gently tip the tree out of its container and inspect the roots. If the bottom of the soil ball is a thick, tight mass of root, it's time to repot. Wash most of the soil off the roots by swishing them gently in a tub of water. Clip off about a third of the roots growing at the outside of the rootball.

2 Reach in and cut out part of the large, fleshy roots, making sure first that they are not attached to large masses of fibrous roots. Replant the tree in the same pot in the same method as for the original planting, using a fresh batch of soil mixture (see page 204). Water the tree thoroughly, and cover it with a clear plastic bag. Keep it in a cool place out of direct sun for two or three weeks, just as before.

MASTER GARDENING TIPS

Seasonal Care

Keep in mind that just because your bonsai is alive and growing in a pot, it isn't an ordinary houseplant. It can and should receive different care in different seasons.

Spring and early summer: You may grow it in a sunny window.

Summer to fall: Most plants grown as bonsai are trees that are found outside in a temperate climate, and do best on a sunny, open, yet protected porch, patio, or deck. You can take yours inside the house for short periods, but by mid- or late summer, depending upon where you live, it should go outside to get ready for its dormant season.

Winter: Most bonsai need a cool spot to spend the winter. (Avoid the temptation to interrupt its dormancy by taking the plant into a warm room for Christmas!) Choose the winter quarters with care. Since the roots must always be able to reach moisture, the plant must not freeze hard for extended periods. Some growers bury the pots in moist peat moss in an outdoor cold frame, where the plants will be cool but won't freeze. Others store them in a cool greenhouse or even in a garage that does not get too cold. In milder climates, bonsai can be left outdoors all winter, but still must never be allowed to dry out, so remember to water them occasionally.

Index

Further Reading

The Big Book of Gardening Secrets, by Charles W. G. Smith. Filled with professional advice for growing the best vegetables, herbs, fruits, and flowers. Teaches beginning and more experienced gardeners how to extend their growing season, grow and use dozens of herbs, care for indoor and outdoor container gardens, cultivate bountiful berry patches and fruit orchards, and grow healthy annuals, perennials, bulbs, and even roses in any climate. 352 pages. Paperback. ISBN 1-58017-000-5.

Bonsai Survival Manual, by Colin Lewis. This full-color manual takes the mystery out of bonsai with its straightforward, step-by-step, illustrated instructions for buying, siting, maintaining, and troubleshooting. Appropriate for both beginners and bonsai enthusiasts with at-a-glance profiles on 50 popular varieties. 160 pages. Paperback. ISBN 0-88266-853-6.

Landscaping Makes Cents, by Frederick C. Campbell and Richard L. Dubé. This guide to landscape design explains how to determine a budget, create a landscape plan, choose a contractor, and achieve substantial financial return on a limited budget. Includes tips for the beginning landscaper and handy checklists and charts to ensure the successful completion of any project. 176 pages. Paperback. ISBN 0-88266-948-6.

The Lawn & Garden Owner's Manual, by Lewis and Nancy Hill. This ultimate landscape maintenance guide tells property owners what to do and when to do it throughout the year. 192 pages. Paperback. ISBN 1-58017-214-8.

Quick and Easy Topiary and Green Sculpture, by Jenny Handy. Includes information on the best plants to use for topiary. Each option is evaluated for its approximate growth rate, minimum temperature requirement, and watering and feeding needs. 128 full-color pages. Paperback. ISBN 0-88266-920-6.

Secrets to Great Soil, by Elizabeth P. Stell. Another volume in Storey's Gardening Skills Illustrated series. The ultimate guide to creating fertile, productive soil — anywhere. Explains the properties and value of good garden soil; instructs how to improve soil health with amendments and fertilizer; and includes tips on customizing soil for a variety of vegetables, flowers, fruits, trees, shrubs, and lawns. 224 pages. Hardcover; ISBN 1-58017-009-9. Paperback; ISBN 1-58017-008-0.

Seed Sowing and Saving, by Carole B. Turner. Part of Storey's Gardening Skills Illustrated series. A step-by-step illustrated guide to sowing techniques, the maintenance of seedlings, and seed collecting and storing. Instruction is given for harvesting and saving seeds from more than 100 common vegetables, annuals, perennials, herbs, and wildflowers. 224 pages. Hardcover; ISBN 1-58017-002-1. Paperback; ISBN 1-58017-001-3.

These books and other Storey books are available
at your bookstore, farm store, garden center, or directly from
Storey Books, 210 MASS MoCA Way, North Adams, MA 01247,
or by calling 1-800-441-5700.
Visit our Web site at www.storey.com.